PREFACE

Child abuse is not a new problem. Children have probably been abused since time immemorial, but it is only in comparatively recent times that society has been prepared to acknowledge the extent of the problem and to develop a legal and practical framework in response. The initial impetus for writing this book came from my work as an ancillary probation officer and later as a police constable with the South Wales Constabulary in the 1970s. At this time cases of child abuse seemed comparatively rare and there existed no coherent strategy for planned intervention. In those cases of abuse which did come to the attention of the authorities, the contrasting ideologies adopted by the various professions involved were plainly evident. Great advances have been made over the past 20 years in all aspects of the handling of cases of child abuse and inter-agency co-operation. This book examines society's changing attitudes towards abuse in its various forms and provides a comprehensive account of the framework developed for intervention.

My grateful thanks to Dr Michael Knight, who was able to draw on the extensive practical and professional experience in writing Chapter 5 on the role of the doctor in diagnosing abuse, and to Viv Harpwood, the series editor, for her help and advice. I must also express my gratitude to my family – to my husband, Peter and daughters, Rachel and Kate for their patience, understanding and support. Finally, thanks to my mother and late father for ensuring that my childhood was so very different from the many I have read about while writing this book.

Cathy Cobley
February 1995

CHILD ABUSE & THE LAW

Cathy Cobley, LLB, LLM
Lecturer in Law
Cardiff Law School

Cavendish
Publishing
Limited

First published in Great Britain 1995 by Cavendish Publishing
Limited, The Glass House, Wharton Street, London, WC1X 9PX.
Telephone: 0171-278 8000   Facsimile: 0171-278 8080

British Library Cataloguing in Publication Data

Cobley, C
Child Abuse & the Law
I. Title II. Series
344.1043276

ISBN 1-85941-011-1

Printed and bound in Great Britain

CONTENTS

CONTENTS

CONTENTS

CONTENTS

CHAPTER 1

CHILD ABUSE – WHAT'S THE PROBLEM?

'A social problem is a condition which is defined by a considerable number of persons as a deviation from some social norm which they cherish. Every social problem thus consists of an objective condition and a subjective definition. The objective condition is a verifiable situation which can be checked as to existence and magnitude (proportions) by impartial and trained observers. The subjective definition is the awareness of certain individuals that the condition is a threat to certain cherished values.'[1]

THE PROBLEM OF DEFINITION

Child abuse as a socially defined phenomena

The term 'child abuse' is one which has become a part of every day vocabulary in the UK. A wealth of literature is now available on the subject. Media coverage of cases of child abuse ensures that the subject is never far from the public eye. Newspaper headlines consistently inform the public of 'Another case of child abuse', 'Home Alone – hungry children found alone in cold, dark flat'. Radio and television documentary programmes examine the phenomenon of child abuse and popular women's magazines warn of the dangers of child abuse and recount readers' stories of how they were abused as children. Both professionals and lay people are now being increasingly drawn into the debate over child abuse – how to identify the problem, when and how to intervene once a problem has been identified, how to deal with the abuse, how best to help the victim – the debate continues.

Indeed, the term child abuse is now so familiar and widely used it may be thought unnecessary to define it. Whenever the term is used, there is an implicit understanding that it has the same meaning for all. If questioned about its meaning, there is a tendency to respond by relating different kinds of abuse. The initial image is often one of a baby or young child covered in bruises or cigarette burns – the proverbial 'battered child'. More thought may lead to the ragged, unkempt child – the 'neglected child', or the child deprived of love and affection – the 'emotionally abused child'. In more recent times, a picture of an incest victim may spring to mind, a girl cowering as her father or step father walks into her bedroom – the 'sexually abused child'. All these examples are brought under the umbrella of the term 'child abuse' – surely everybody knows what child abuse is. Yet a closer inspection reveals that

---

1   Parton, N (1985) The Politics of Child Abuse Basingstoke, MacMillan pp 5–6.

there is no one, unique definition of child abuse. Not only do members of the public use different definitions from those used by the professionals involved in the management of such cases, but different professions themselves may adopt more than one definition. Indeed, even members of the same profession do not always agree on how to define child abuse.

Definition can be of critical importance in this area, as with other social concerns. Differing definitions of the problem can lead to confusion. If there is no agreement as to what constitutes the abuse of a child, it becomes very difficult to make effective decisions in any one particular case. Furthermore, any research that is carried out on the nature, extent and effect of child abuse will produce conflicting results if a uniform definition is not adopted by all concerned. Therefore, defining child abuse at the outset may seem crucial. However, any attempt precisely to define the term is fraught with difficulties. Any definition is, in effect, a classification and the defining process involves the setting of boundaries for specifying what does and what does not belong in the classification. The clarity of definition depends on the criteria for demarcating the concept being defined. In essence, the definition of child abuse, in its various forms, depends on the fundamental issues of what is acceptable child rearing in our society – particularly in relation to neglect and emotional abuse.

Who is a child?

The age of the victim is obviously a necessary consideration when defining child abuse. The non-specific term 'child' will suffice when the victim is young, but as the victim approaches the later teenage years it becomes necessary to decide when a child becomes an adult. It is generally accepted that children below the age of 16 years are vulnerable and require the protection afforded to abused children, although it is now agreed that children gradually acquire a certain amount of autonomy as they approach that age (see Chapter 6). It is also accepted that adulthood is reached by the age of 18 years. The years between 16 and 18 are problematic. For many purposes teenagers in this age group are considered adults, although legally they are minors and may still be vulnerable and in need of protection. For the purposes of the Children Act 1989 a child is defined as a person under the age of 18, yet the criminal law only affords specific protection to children under the age of 16.

What constitutes abuse?

The term 'abuse' does not refer to one specific type of act, but covers a wide spectrum of behaviour. At one end of the spectrum, there can be little argument that acts such as severe physical beatings and rape are clearly abusive. Yet proceeding through the spectrum it becomes increasingly difficult to differentiate between acceptable behaviour and behaviour which may be deemed abusive of a child. For example, where is the line to be drawn between acceptable corporal punishment used to discipline a child and assault? What standards should be set, below which a child is said to be neglected or emotionally abused? How should appropriate displays of affection be differentiated from behaviour which amounts to the sexual abuse of a child?

If a broad definition of child abuse is adopted this will dramatically increase the number of children who are classified as abused. This, in turn, may lead to difficulties in identifying the effects of the more serious forms of abuse on the victim and, in practice, may overwhelm the state apparatus established to respond to cases of child abuse. If the term is narrowly defined, this will have the effect of limiting the number of potential victims. Those favouring protection of family privacy argue that such a narrow definition should be adopted to ensure that state intervention is kept to a minimum. Yet a narrow definition may leave children unprotected and at risk of further, perhaps more serious, abuse.

A review of the literature reveals a wide variety of definitions of the term 'child abuse' – as Gilmour[2] points out the fact that there are many only shows that none are adequate. Gilmour suggests the following as a general definition:

> 'child abuse occurs when any avoidable act, or avoidable failure to act, adversely affects the physical, mental or emotional well-being of a child.'

Such a broad definition has the benefit of being simple and easily understood, yet adopting such a definition surely means that the vast majority of children in our society are at least neglected or emotionally abused at some point during their childhood – society must think carefully about the practical and psychological implications of this before labelling so many children as 'abused'.

More specific definitions of the various forms of abuse can be found in the guide to arrangements for inter-agency co-operation for the protection of children from abuse issued by the Department of Health ('Working Together') which provides guidance for registration on the child protection register and for statistical purposes[3]:

- Neglect

  The persistent or severe neglect of a child, or the failure to protect a child from exposure to any kind of danger, including cold or starvation, or extreme failure to carry out important aspects of care, resulting in the significant impairment of the child's health or development, including non-organic failure to thrive.

---

2   Gilmour, A (1988) *Innocent Victims: The Question of Child Abuse* London, Joseph.

3   Department of Health (1991) 'Working Together under the Children Act 1989' London, HMSO para 6.40.

- Physical injury:

  Actual or likely physical injury to a child, or failure to prevent physical injury (or suffering) to a child including deliberate poisoning, suffocation and Munchausen's syndrome by proxy.

- Sexual abuse

  Actual or likely sexual exploitation of a child or adolescent. The child may be dependent and/or developmentally immature.

- Emotional abuse

  Actual or likely severe adverse effect on the emotional and behavioural development of a child caused by persistent or severe emotional ill-treatment or rejection. All abuse involves some emotional ill-treatment. This category should be used where it is the main or sole form of abuse.

The requirements that there be *'persistent* or *severe* neglect ... or *extreme* failure to carry out important aspects of care' and that there be a *'severe* adverse effect ... caused by *persistent* or *severe* emotional ill-treatment or rejection' at least restrict the ambit of neglect and emotional abuse to a more acceptable level than Gilmour's definition. Yet even such detailed guidance does not delineate precisely what amounts to child abuse and does little to determine the boundary between acceptable parenting and the more minor forms of abuse. Perhaps this is inevitable, given the wide spectrum of behaviour that may constitute abuse, and attention should instead be focused on identifying when action needs to be taken. In determining the point at which state intervention is justified, the Children Act of 1989 introduces the concept of 'significant harm' (see Chapter 3). The term 'harm' is defined to mean 'ill-treatment or the impairment of health and development'. Ill-treatment includes non-physical ill-treatment and sexual abuse and will amount to harm whether or not it impairs the child's health or development.[4] But the Children Act fails to define ill-treatment precisely. Furthermore, ill-treatment alone is not sufficient for these purposes – the harm must also be significant. The Act has nothing to say on when harm will be significant, but its dictionary definition means considerable, noteworthy or important. Therefore, the categories of abuse adopted by 'Working Together' do not tie in precisely with the definition of significant harm, which leads to the conclusion that a child may be abused without suffering significant harm.

Child abuse as a legally defined phenomena – the criminal law[5]

'It's criminal – there ought to be a law against it!' This may well be a typical response on discovering a case of child abuse. Of course, in many cases, child abuse is criminal and there is a law against it and one would

---

4   Section 31(9) Children Act 1989.

5   See generally Smith & Hogan (1992) *Criminal Law* 7th ed London, Butterworths.

expect the criminal law to provide specific definitions of the prohibited behaviour. However, there is no single criminal offence of abusing a child and legal definitions of criminal offences that may be committed when a child is abused are of limited assistance in defining a social problem. (A summary of the definitions of the main offences associated with child abuse is contained in the appendix.)

Physical abuse and neglect

The law relating to offences against the person applies equally to children as it does to adults, subject to the right of a parent (or someone who is deemed to be in *loco parentis*) to discipline and punish a child. Such discipline must be moderate and reasonable, considered in the light of all the circumstances.[6] Therefore, in cases of physical abuse, dependent upon the degree of harm caused, abusers may incur liability for assault or battery, aggravated assault or, in extreme cases, murder or manslaughter, but the definitions of these crimes, relating, as they do, to all victims, are of little help in defining child abuse.

Of rather more assistance is the specific offence of cruelty to persons under 16 contained in s 1(1) of the Children and Young Persons Act 1933 (as amended). Any person over the age of 16 years who has responsibility for any child or young person under that age who wilfully assaults, ill-treats, neglects, abandons, or exposes him, or causes or procures him to be assaulted, ill-treated, neglected, abandoned, or exposed, in a manner likely to cause him unnecessary suffering or injury to health (including injury to, or loss of, sight, or hearing, or limb, or organ of the body, and any mental derangement), commits a criminal offence. (This is subject to the right of any parent or other person having lawful control or charge of a child or young person, to administer punishment to him.) But again, what amounts to 'neglecting a child ... in a manner likely to cause unnecessary suffering or injury to health'? Further guidance is given in section 1(2) of the Children and Young Persons Act which provides that [the accused] shall be deemed to have neglected the child in a manner likely to cause injury to the child's health if he has failed to provide adequate food, clothing, medical aid or lodging for the child; or if, having been unable otherwise to provide such food, clothing, medical aid or lodging, he has failed to take steps to procure it to be provided under the enactments applicable. This provision is clearly intended to provide a criminal sanction against those who abuse a child in their care and, as such, goes some way towards providing a definition of child abuse in cases of physical abuse or neglect. But the provision would not appear to include emotional abuse. Lord Diplock has said:

'To "neglect" a child is to omit to act, to fail to provide adequately for its needs; and, in the context of section 1 of the Children and Young Persons Act 1933, its

---

6   *R v Hopley* [1860] 2 F & F 202.

physical needs rather than its spiritual, educational, moral or emotional needs. These are dealt with by other legislation.'[7]

Apparently, Lord Diplock saw emotional abuse as the province of the civil, not the criminal law.

Sexual abuse

Sexual abuse is one area where the criminal law is specific as to the behaviour it prohibits. Again, there is no single offence of sexually abusing a child. The criminal law of England and Wales includes several hundred different sexual offences, the majority of which date from the reign of Queen Victoria or later. The law is now almost entirely embodied in statute, principally the Sexual Offences Act of 1956 which was designed to codify and consolidate the law as it then stood. As with physical abuse, all sexual offences relate to children in the same way as they relate to adults. But in addition, specific offences have been created which relate solely to children and a review of these offences provides clear guidance on the sexual behaviour with children prohibited by the criminal law.

The law has regulated sexual activity with children from early times and one of the methods used has been to impose a statutory age of consent – the primary reason being to protect the individual child, but there are also concurring moral motives which aim to prevent certain forms of behaviour deemed to be socially undesirable. The age of consent for heterosexual behaviour is now 16 years – any sexual activity with a child below that age is a criminal offence, regardless of whether or not the child actually consents. For example, it is an offence to have unlawful sexual intercourse with a girl under the age of 16. If the girl is 13 years or older, the maximum penalty is two years imprisonment, but if the girl is under 13 years, the maximum penalty is life imprisonment.[8] If the girl does not, in fact, consent, the appropriate charge would be one of rape.[9] It is also an offence to indecently assault a boy or girl under the age of 16 and it is specifically provided that a boy or a girl under that age cannot, in law, consent to the assault.[10] Furthermore, it is an offence to commit an act of gross indecency with, or towards, a child under the age of 14 years, or to incite a child under that age to participate in such an act.[11] This offence obviously includes an indecent assault, but is much wider in that it covers any act of gross indecency with the child.[12] In cases of intrafamilial sexual abuse, the offence of incest may well be applicable. The law of incest prohibits sexual intercourse between parent and child, grandfather and

---

7   *R v Sheppard* [1981] AC 394 at 404.

8   Sections 5 and 6 Sexual Offences Act 1956.

9   Section 1 Sexual Offences Act 1956.

10   Sections 14 and 15 Sexual Offences Act 1956.

11   Section 1 Indecency with Children Act 1960.

12   *R v Speck* [1977] 2 All ER 859.

granddaughter, and brother and sister.[13] The relationships are restricted to blood relations, and incest is therefore inapplicable to cases of abuse involving step parents or more distant relatives. (Such abuse will, of course, fall within the definition of other sexual offences previously mentioned.)

Sexual abuse is, therefore, the one area where specific definitions are to be found. But this does not, in itself, assist in delineating the boundaries of sexual abuse. In certain respects the definitions are too wide. For example, what of the age of the abuser? The criminal offences referred to specify the age of the victim, but not the age of the perpetrator. Thus two 15 year olds engaging in any form of sexual activity are committing indecent assaults on each other, but few would argue such behaviour constituted child abuse, which is generally viewed as concerning an adult abuser and child victim. Indeed, one of the most generally accepted social definitions of sexual abuse is 'the exploitation of a child for the sexual gratification of an adult'.[14] Secondly, where should the line be drawn in defining sexual abuse? Whilst there may be general agreement that any sexual contact between an adult and a child is abusive of the child, there is no such agreement with regard to other forms of criminal behaviour such as indecent exposure[15] or taking indecent photographs of children.[16] If such behaviour is included in the scope of child abuse, the number of children classified as abused increases, which in turn has implications for those responding to cases of child abuse.

Thus, whereas within the framework of the criminal law, sexual abuse may be defined more specifically as a criminal act, such a definition may be of limited value within a social framework. The criminal law offers no solution to the problem of defining emotional abuse.

Child abuse and the law of tort[17]

'The law of tort is primarily concerned with providing a remedy to persons who have been harmed by the conduct of others.'[18] This statement would logically lead to the conclusion that the law of tort is directly concerned with the abuse of children. The reality is rather different. Civil actions brought by, or on behalf of, children are rare for a number of reasons. Unlike criminal prosecutions, which are initiated by the state, in many cases there will be no-one willing to bring a civil action on behalf of the child at the time of the abuse. It is the decision of the child whether or not to bring an action on attaining majority, but although the limitation period does not start to run until the age of majority has been attained, this still presents problems unless action is taken quickly (see Chapter 8). Although child abuse clearly falls

---

13   Sections 10 and 11 Sexual Offences Act 1956.

14   Mrazek, PB & Kempe, CH (eds) (1981) *Sexually Abused Children and their Families*. Oxford, Pergamon p 55.

15   Section 4 Vagrancy Act 1824.

16   Section 1 Protection of Children Act 1978.

17   See generally Harpwood, V (1993) *Lecture Notes on Tort* London, Cavendish Publishing.

18   Jones, M (1993) *Textbook of Torts* London, Blackstone Press.

within the remit of the law of tort, it gives limited assistance to the problem of definition.

Trespass to the person

Assault and battery, in addition to being criminal offences, also constitute trespass to the person, subject to a parent's right to administer reasonable chastisement to a child. False imprisonment, which is again a crime and trespass to the person, is 'the unlawful imposition of constraint on another's freedom of movement from a particular place'.[19] Yet again, parents and those having lawful control of a child must be able to restrain the child's freedom of movement to a certain extent. The Court of Appeal[20] has commented that a parent would very seldom be liable for false imprisonment in relation to his or her own child because the sort of restrictions imposed on children are usually well within the realms of reasonable parental discipline and are therefore not unlawful. However, the detention may be for such a period or circumstance as to take it out of the realms of reasonable parental discipline. Although the court in this case was concerned with the criminal offence of false imprisonment, similar reasoning must undoubtedly apply to the tort. Whereas sending a child to their bedroom for a limited period may be acceptable, locking a child into a room for a long period of time could well constitute both child abuse and false imprisonment.

Negligence

The liability of a child abuser for negligence is rather more problematic. Mere 'neglect' of a child will not suffice. It must be established that that abuser owed the child a duty of care, that the duty had been breached and that the child suffered harm or damage as a result. There is a notable lack of authority in this area as very few cases have been brought.[21] In determining the existence of a duty of care, the Court of Appeal[22] has said that the appropriate test is whether there was a reasonable foreseeability of the child suffering injury in the situation under consideration – which implies, not unreasonably, that parents and those having care of a child will owe the child a duty of care in numerous every day situations, as well as exceptional 'dangerous' circumstances. However, the duty will only be breached if the conduct of the parent or carer is not that of a careful parent in all the circumstances – an objective test. Once again, the injury must be foreseeable as a result of the breach. But, as any parent will know, children are not always predictable in their behaviour and, in any event, children must be given sufficient space to

---

19 *Collins v Wilcock* [1984] 3 All ER 374.

20 *R v Rahman* [1985] Crim LR 596.

21 See Wright, J (1994) 'Negligent parenting – can my child sue?'[1994] *Journal of Child Law* Vol 6 No 3 p 104.

22 *Surtees v Kingston-upon-Thames BC* [1991] 2 FLR 559.

become independent and learn to anticipate danger for themselves. The problem is deciding where to draw the line. It seems that the courts are cautious of setting an 'impossibly high' standard and are, understandably, reluctant to find parents in breach of the duty except in clear-cut cases of negligence. The damage suffered by the child must result from the breach of duty. The damage will usually be classified as personal injury, which includes physical injury and mental distress, although the law of tort also compensates property damage and financial loss where appropriate. Wright argues:

> 'Accepting that two of the principle functions of the tort of negligence are to provide deterrence against careless behaviour and to effect a fair distribution of loss, it is questionable whether actions by children against their parents further either of these aims.'[23]

Whilst this may be so in cases where the family unit remains intact, there may be merit in encouraging children to take action against familial abusers where the relationships within the family have been permanently destroyed by the abuse or where the abuser is outside their immediate family.

The practical application of the law of tort to cases of child abuse is surprisingly limited and therefore adds little to the search for a definition of child abuse. The primary concern of society is to protect any child deemed to be in need of protection and, if possible, to prosecute the abuser. Comparatively little attention seems to have been focused on compensating the victim of abuse (see Chapter 8).

THE PROBLEM OF RECOGNITION

Child abuse is now recognised as a significant social problem. Over the last few decades there has been increasing public and professional awareness of the problem and society has responded by establishing a legal framework for dealing with cases of child abuse. Yet, like most other social problems, child abuse is not new. Children have undoubtedly been abused for many years, yet it is only in comparatively recent times that we, as a society, have been prepared to recognise the fact.

It has been suggested that a community comes to recognise the existence of the abuse of children in a sequence of developing stages:

- Stage 1:   widespread denial that either physical or sexual abuse exists to a significant extent.

- Stage 2:   the battered child is recognised. The community begins to find ways of coping more effectively with physical abuse through early recognition and intervention.

---

23   Wright, J supra p 108.

- Stage 3: physical abuse is better handled. More attention is focused on child neglect and more subtle forms of abuse.

- Stage 4: the community recognises emotional abuse as a social problem.

- Stage 5: the community pays attention to the serious plight of the sexually abused child.

- Stage 6: the guarantee that each child is truly wanted and provided with loving care, decent shelter and food, and first class preventive and curative care.[24]

These stages are useful in that they illustrate how society has gradually come to recognise the various forms of child abuse over a period of years. However, it would be misleading to treat the stages as distinct steps in the process of recognition. Perceptions of child abuse vary not only across time, but also between professions and society as a whole. The divisions between each stage are blurred and at any one time different professions may well be at different stages, with public awareness often following a long way behind. Despite this, it is possible to chart the process of recognition throughout the past 150 years and to identify, in general terms, the first five stages.

The late 19th and early 20th centuries

Initial recognition of the abused and neglected child has traditionally been attributed to events in the US, although, in fact, attention had first been drawn to the problem in France in the mid-19th century.[25] The Society for the Prevention of Cruelty to Children (SPCC) was first founded in America in 1871. Five years earlier, the American Society for the Prevention of Cruelty to Animals (ASPCA) had been formed and it was to this Society that appeals were made to intervene when the case of a little girl who was beaten daily by her stepmother came to light. The existing law offered the child no protection until the guilt of the mother had been established and it was only through the efforts of the ASPCA, who succeeded in persuading a court to interpret the word 'animal' to include a child, that the girl was saved. Recognition that the law accorded more protection to animals than it did to children led to the foundation of the SPCC. Within five years 10 more such societies were formed, and more gradually followed.

News of the American experience reached the UK and the first such society was founded in Britain in 1882. Other societies followed and eventually merged to form the National Society for the Prevention of Cruelty to Children (NSPCC) which was granted its Royal Charter in 1894. The NSPCC, together with the

---

24 Ciba Foundation (1984) *Child Sexual Abuse within the Family* London, Tavistock 1984.

25 Tardieu, A (1860) 'Étude Medico-legal sur les services et mauvais traintements exerces sur des enfants' in *Annales d'hygiene publique de medicine legale* 13, pp 361-398.

National Vigilance Association, were successful in highlighting the problem of child abuse and the lack of an adequate legal response. In 1889, Parliament enacted the Prevention of Cruelty Act. For the first time child cruelty and neglect were made statutory criminal offences and the Act gave the police and the courts the power to intervene in cases where ill-treatment was suspected and to remove children from their parents where necessary. Further legislation followed, including the Punishment of Incest Act 1908 which, for the first time, made incest a criminal, as opposed to an ecclesiastical, offence. At the same time, in 1908 the Children Act of that year established juvenile courts as a separate forum with jurisdiction over both abused and neglected children and delinquent juveniles.

However, the subject of child abuse tended to be shrouded in secrecy for many years. Concern was voiced periodically throughout the early part of the 20th century. There was a parliamentary advisory committee on sexual abuse in 1925 and in 1950 guide lines dealing with children ill-treated in their own homes were issued by the Department of Health, the Home Office and the Department of Education.[26] But child abuse was, at this time, not generally regarded as a significant social problem. Both the general public and professionals seemed to have great difficulty in accepting the possibility that adults maltreated or sexually abused children. When presented with a child with injuries, doctors often failed to connect the injuries with child abuse, either because the possibility did not occur to them, or because they were not psychologically prepared to believe that adults, and in particular parents, could commit such atrocities on a child. No criticism can be attributed to doctors for this – they were merely reflecting existing social norms. Even if doctors did recognise the possibility of abuse, they were provided with no formal guidance on the action to be taken, which is in stark contrast to the position today (see Chapter 5). In the absence of a planned strategy of state intervention, doctors were left unsure of their responsibilities and, fearing that reporting the case would involve them in time consuming judicial proceedings that may adversely affect their career, sometimes justified their failure to intervene by taking refuge behind a screen of medical secrecy.

The 1960s – the 'battered baby' syndrome

Similar problems had been experienced in America throughout the first half of this century. Once again, it seems that the American experience was influential in highlighting the problem of child abuse in this country for a second time in the 1960s. In 1962, in an article in the Journal of the American Medical Association, Dr Henry Kempe, an American paediatrician, and his

---

26   Home Office, Ministry of Health, Ministry of Education (1950) 'Children neglected or ill-treated in their own homes' *Joint Circular*, London.

associates put the unthinkable into words. They asserted that some of the physical injuries of children were not caused by accidents at all, but were in fact the result of physical assaults by adults on children. The 'battered baby' syndrome came into being; the problem was forced out into the open and public opinion began to change. Dr Kempe himself has admitted that he used shock tactics in an effort to increase recognition of the problem of physical abuse. During a lecture to the British Association of Paediatricians in 1970 he said;

'I was so exasperated by my colleagues' lack of attention that I deliberately used the words "battered baby" syndrome because they were provocative enough to arouse anger. Indeed, for 10 years previously I had spoken of child abuse, non-accidental injury or inflicted wounds, but few people paid any attention. I therefore wanted to provoke the emotional reaction and shock which more moderate and scientifically more satisfactory terms had not provoked ...'[27]

Dr Kempe's shock tactics worked in America. By 1967, all American states had enacted child abuse reporting laws which made the reporting of suspected child abuse mandatory for certain professionals (see Chapter 2). Although such a system of mandatory reporting has never been enacted in the UK, public awareness of the problem of child abuse has increased tremendously, partly, it seems, as a result of the American experience. By 1974, following the publication of the Inquiry Report into the death of Maria Colwell,[28] Area Review Committees had been set up on the recommendation of the DHSS as an inter-disciplinary management team to supervise the management of non-accidental injury to children.

The 1970s – emotional abuse

During the 1970s attention began to be focused on the emotionally abused child. All abuse inevitably involves some emotional ill-treatment, but it came to be realised that there were various types of behaviour by an adult which were emotionally harmful to a child, even in the absence of physical or sexual abuse or neglect. For example, humiliation, scapegoating, extreme inconsistency, rejection and unrealistic expectations. Although emotional abuse is difficult to define and the scars are less obvious, it is thought to be probably more common than the combined total of physical and sexual abuse.[29]

---

27 European Committee on Crime Problems (1981) Criminological Aspects of the Ill-treatment of Children in the Family Strasbourg, Council of Europe 1981 p 20.

28 Report of the Committee of Inquiry into the Care and Supervision Provided in Relation to Maria Colwell (1974 HMSO).

29 Oates, K (1982) 'Child Abuse - A Community Concern' London, Butterworths p 3.

The 1980s – sexual abuse

However, at this time, there remained a conspiracy of silence over the existence of child sexual abuse. Society was simply not prepared to entertain the possibility that children were being sexually abused to any great extent. Just as many were reluctant to recognise physical abuse in the UK in the 1960s, many were reluctant to accept the reality of certain aspects of child sexual abuse in the 1980s. One of Britain's leading experts on child sexual abuse is Dr Arnon Bentovim of Great Ormond Street Hospital. Dr Bentovim had been working with families involved in physical child abuse since the early 1970s, yet during the 1970s saw no evidence of sexual abuse – believing that even if a child reported a sexual encounter, then it must surely be fantasy. He admitted that he was jolted out of this comfortable illusion at a London conference in 1979 addressed by Dr Kempe.[30] Listening to Dr Kempe, he realised that, despite having worked with children for some considerable time, he, Dr Bentovim, wasn't seeing cases of sexual abuse at all. This prompted him to enquire closely into referrals, carrying out a questionnaire survey of the professionals who referred cases to him at Great Ormond Street. This in turn sparked new referrals and led to an increasing awareness of child sexual abuse. Such awareness continued to increase during the 1980s, culminating in the crisis in Cleveland in 1987. The resulting inquiry[31] and national media coverage of events in Cleveland ensured that the issue of child sexual abuse was pushed to the fore on a nationwide scale.

The 1990s – satanic and ritual abuse?

Having reached stage 5 in the process of recognition, it now seems that an additional stage should be added – the recognition of organised abuse and, arguably, satanic and ritual abuse. If many found the concept of child sexual abuse a difficult one to comprehend, or even believe, events in the early 1990's suggested what many considered to be a more worrying and sinister development – that of satanic or ritual abuse. The term satanic abuse is said to have originated in America after the publication in 1980 of *Michelle Remembers* by Lawrence Pazder, a psychiatrist, which told the story of a girl who recalled being ritually abused by satanists. Influence by American Christian fundamentalists led to allegations of satanic abuse surfacing in the UK in the late 1980s and early 1990s. In Manchester, 23 children were made wards of court after social workers investigating sexual abuse became convinced that the abuse had taken place within a ritual or ceremonial setting.[32] In Rochdale, 20 children from six families were made wards of court due to alleged involvement in satanic or ritual abuse.[33] In the Orkneys, nine children were removed from their

---

30   Laurance, J (1986) 'Bentovim's Technique' in *New Society* 28 November 1986 p 15.

31   Butler Sloss, E (1988) Report of the Inquiry into Child Abuse in Cleveland 1987 Cmnd 412 London, 1988 HMSO.

32   *Re C and L (Child abuse: evidence)* [1991] FCR 351.

33   *Rochdale Borough Council v A and Others* [1991] 2 FLR 192.

homes after allegations that they had suffered ritual abuse – events that resulted in an inquiry being set up to consider the procedures by police and social workers.[34] Following these cases, the Government commissioned an inquiry into ritual and satanic abuse. Three years later, the report of the inquiry, undertaken by Jean La Fontaine a leading social anthropologist, dismissed satanic abuse as an evangelical myth. The report defines satanism as 'sexual and physical abuse of children as part of rites directed to a magical or religious objective' and concludes that there was no evidence of this in each of the 84 cases reported between 1987 and 1991 which were examined by the inquiry. Ritual abuse of mystical powers to enslave children and keep them quiet was substantiated in three of the cases, but this was found to be secondary to sexual abuse and therefore not satanic. However, in almost all cases the families involved were from deprived economic backgrounds and the report concludes:

> 'A belief in evil cults is convincing because it draws on powerful cultural axioms. People are reluctant to accept that parents, even those classed as social failures, will harm their own children, and even to invite others to do so, but involvement with the devil explains it ... The notion that unknown, powerful leaders control the cult revives an old myth of dangerous strangers. Demonising the marginal poor and linking them to unknown satanists turns intractable cases of abuse into manifestations of evil.'[35]

However, the conclusion of the inquiry has not been unanimously accepted. A survey into organised and ritual sexual abuse undertaken by the University of Manchester identified 62 cases of alleged ritual abuse between 1988 and 1991.[36] Whilst doubts about the existence of ritual abuse remain, the existence of paedophile rings or organised abuse is now accepted. 'Working Together' defines organised abuse as a generic term which covers abuse which may involve a number of abusers, a number of abused children and young people and often encompasses different forms of abuse. It involves, to a greater or lesser extent, an element of organisation. The research by the University of Manchester estimates that there would have been 967 cases of organised abuse between 1988 and 1991. Although many cases of organised abuse remain hidden from the public eye, those cases which are successfully investigated tend to hit the headlines. In June 1994 five members of a paedophile ring were jailed at Swansea Crown Court for between four and 15 years for conspiracy to sexually abuse children.[37] The eight month trial leading to the convictions received extensive media coverage. Had the horrific catalogue of events occurred 20, or even 10, years ago, society's response would probably have been one of denial and disbelief – indicating that we should be thankful for the progress made through the stages of recognition in recent years.

---

34 Report of the Inquiry into the Removal of Children from Orkney in Febuary 1991 (1992 HMSO).

35 *The Times* 3 June 1994.

36 *The Times* 18 June 1994.

37 *The Times* 30 June 1994.

The sanctity of family life

One factor which undoubtedly inhibited the whole issue of child abuse taking hold in earlier years was the value traditionally placed on the privity and sanctity of the home in the UK. From early times there has been a common law presumption that 'the house of everyone is his castle'. Any state intervention in family life was made with extreme caution. Ideas of privacy established in legal decisions tended to preclude intervention in the family. Indeed, Article 8 of the European Convention on Human Rights encapsulates the ideal of family privacy. The courts have proved themselves to be very reluctant to intervene more than is strictly necessary with the private affairs of people – claiming 'It is better that people should be left free'.[38] Such reluctance to intervene was manifestly clear in Victorian times. Lord Shaftesbury, in response to a plea to sponsor legislation which would protect children from parental cruelty, acknowledged that the evils were enormous and indisputable, but thought they were of so private, internal and domestic a character that they were beyond the reach of legislation and would not be entertained in either Houses of Parliament.[39]

In more recent times, there has been an increased willingness for the state to intervene in family life. The changing public response to domestic violence, generally, and in particular by the police response to domestic violence is a classic example of this. Just as in the 1960s the Americans were introduced to the 'battered baby' syndrome, so too in the 1970s the UK was introduced to the concept of battered wives. Traditionally, in English law, a man held proprietary rights over his wife and enjoyed, not only a right, but a duty to 'correct' her. Blackstone's *Commentaries on the laws of England* in 1765 stated that the husband had the right to beat his wife provided the stick he used was no thicker than a man's thumb. As the law stands today all forms of violence between husband and wife are governed by the same criminal law as violence between strangers, although it was only in 1991 that it was decided that a husband could be criminally liable for raping his wife.[40] However, for many years the usual interpretation of the law by the police and the courts was governed by the view that domestic violence was of a different and lesser order than violence between strangers. Yet over the past two decades moves have been made to provide more protection for women from domestic violence, which itself inevitably leads to more state intervention in family life. In 1976, for the first time women were given legal remedies specifically for dealing with domestic violence, enabling them to seek injunctions or exclusion orders against husbands or cohabitees.[41]

---

38   *Re Agar Ellis* 24 Ch D 317 at 355.

39   Wohl, AS (ed) (1978) *The Victorian Family: Structure and Stresses* London, Crown Helm 1978.

40   *R v R* [1991] 2 All ER 257.

41   Domestic Violence and Matrimonial Proceedings Act 1976 and Domestic Proceedings and Magistrates Court Act 1978.

These civil remedies were effective to a certain extent, but the police response to domestic violence remained limited during the early 1980s. Yet, over the last decade, police attitudes have changed dramatically. In 1985, Sir Kenneth Newman the Metropolitan Police Commissioner, for the first time, referred to domestic violence in his annual report as a problem with which the police should be concerned. In 1986 a Metropolitan Police working party, set up to investigate police response to domestic violence, reported a highly critical account of police procedures and working practices, and also police training and efficacy in dealing with domestic violence. Since then police policy throughout England and Wales has changed radically. Most police forces have now established specialised units, staffed by officers trained specifically to deal with issues of domestic violence. Such a change in policy reflects the increased willingness on the part of society to intervene in the privacy and sanctity of family life, which has undoubtedly been one of the factors influential in the recent recognition of child abuse.

However, it should not be thought that intervention in family life in cases of child abuse is now made as a matter of course, without justification. As the Lord Chancellor has commented:

'The integrity and independence of the family is the basic building block of a free and democratic society and the need to defend it should be clearly perceivable in the law. Accordingly, unless there is evidence that a child is being, or is likely to be, positively harmed because of a failure in the family, the state, whether in the guise of a local authority or a court, should not interfere.'[42]

THE EXTENT OF THE PROBLEM

Any attempt to assess the prevalence of child abuse encounters two major difficulties. First, as previously discussed, there is no standardized definition of the subject matter. The term child abuse conceals the different meanings which may be attached to it, and these different meanings inevitably affect the results of any research conducted. Secondly, any figures on the prevalence of the problem must either be gleaned from cases reported to the authorities or be obtained from surveys, which must necessarily be retrospective in nature. There are problems inherent in both methods of obtaining a prevalence rate. In the first instance, it is generally agreed that all crimes are under-reported, and this is particularly noticeable in cases of child abuse. The number of cases of child abuse and neglect has been likened to an iceberg, only the tip being visible while the major part is hidden.[43] The vast majority of cases at the base

---

42 Mackay, Joseph Jackson Memorial Lecture [1989] 139 *New Law Journal* 505 at 508.

43 European Committee on Crime Problems (1981) Criminological Aspects of the Ill-treatment of Children in the Family Strasbourg, Council of Europe 1981 p 50.

of the iceberg are unreported and hidden in darkness and are therefore referred to as the 'dark figure'. The cases that are reported form the apex of the iceberg, or triangle, with those cases brought before the court forming the very tip of the iceberg. Therefore, any study of the prevalence of abuse based on reported cases must necessarily underestimate the problem, as no true account can be taken of the 'dark figure' of unreported cases.

The alternative method of researching the problem is to interview a sample of the population and question past experiences. This method has been used in an attempt to establish the prevalence of sexual abuse, but because the subject matter is a sensitive, personal topic, such questions must be restricted to the adult population only, referring, as a general rule, to the adult's experience during childhood. It is inevitable that a person's perceptions of events in the past will change over a period of time, and many respondents will be unwilling to admit to a comparative stranger that such abuse has occurred.

Despite these problems, child abuse has generated such public and professional interest in recent years that efforts have been made to identify the number of cases of abuse ('incidence' of abuse), and the proportion of the population affected ('prevalence' of abuse).

Child protection registers

Child protection registers were initially established as a record of children who were suspected of being physically abused, but were expanded to include physical neglect, non-organic failure to thrive and emotional abuse in 1981. Sexual abuse was not included as an official category for registration until 1988. 'Working Together' now provides four categories for registration – neglect, physical injury, sexual and emotional abuse. The registers are not records of children who have been abused but of children for whom there are currently unresolved child protection issues and for whom there is an inter-agency protection plan. Thus, the registers cannot be relied upon as a definitive statistical source for establishing the incidence and prevalence of child abuse. However, they do provide some indication of the extent of the problem. Statisitcs issued by the Department of Health and the Welsh Office estimate that in the year ending 31 March 1993, the number of children on child protection registers in England was 32,500, with 1,789 registrations recorded in Wales.[44] The total of over 34,000 children registered in England and Wales gives a clear indication of the extent of concern over children thought to be at risk of abuse. However, the statistics also reveal a somewhat

---

44   Department of Health and Welsh Office (1994) *Children Act Report* 1993 London, HMSO.

surprising trend in recent years. In England, the number of registrations increased from 41,200 in 1989 to 45,300 in 1991, but then fell to 38,500 in 1992 and to 32,500 in 1993. A similar picture emerges in Wales where the numbers increased from 2,062 in 1989 to 2,406 in 1991, but then fell to 2,130 in 1992 and to 1,789 in 1993. The significance of these figures cannot be ignored, but, it seems, cannot be adequately explained. The Children Act 1989 was implemented in October 1991 and it seems that registration levels have fallen from this time against the previously recognised trend. The Department of Health and the Welsh Office Children Act Report 1993 acknowledges this decline, but comments:

> '... registration figures for a single year need to be interpreted with caution. The nationwide figures collected since 1989 have shown that there are considerable differences between authorities both in the rates of registration and the numbers on the register. For many individual authorities, numbers also fluctuate considerably from year to year. These differences are so great that it is difficult to identify any consistent trend over time.' (para 3.13)

It seems that one possible explanation for the decline in registrations is the loss of the category 'grave concern' which, prior to the most recent edition of 'Working Together', was used as a fifth category of registration for:

> 'those children whose situations do not currently fit the [other] categories, but where social and medical assessments indicate that they are at significant risk of abuse. These could include situations where another child in the household has been harmed or the household contains a known abuser.'

The withdrawal of the category appears to have had an impact on the overall numbers of registration. Yet it seems that this category is still substantially – although erroneously – used by some authorities, although the number registered under this category has dropped in recent years. The Department of Health seems content with this explanation. Although it has stated an intention to find out why this category is still used (para 3.15), it has stated no intention to find out if the decrease in registration is soley attributable to this factor. From an optimistic point of view, it can be argued that the decrease in registration reflects the success of the Children Act 1989 in encouraging professionals to work in partnership with parents and carers, providing help and support with the ultimate aim of reducing levels of abuse. However, efforts must be made to substantiate this view – it would be unduly complacent to do otherwise.

Criminal statistics

In 1993, the number of offenders found guilty in England and Wales for all offences was nearly 1.5 million (1,174,300 males and 251,000 females). Of these, 35,500 males and 3,400 females were convicted of indictable offences involving violence against the person and 4,300 males and 100 females were convicted of indictable sexual offences. However, criminal statistics are of limited use in determining the extent of child abuse. Very few cases of child abuse are ever the subject of prosecution and even fewer result in a conviction. For example, the NSPCC estimated that, during the period 1983-1987, prosecutions were planned in only 9% of the physical abuse cases and 28% of the sexual abuse cases that had come to light.[45] Although recent reforms are aimed partly at increasing the prospect of a conviction in all such cases, the criminal statistics will nevertheless reflect only a very small percentage of the number of actual cases of child abuse. Furthermore, criminal statistics are categorised by offence and offender – not by victim. Therefore, unless the offence is one in which the age of the victim is an integral part, the statistics will give no indication of this.

In cases of physical abuse and neglect, the only reliable statistics are those relating to cautions and convictions for cruelty to, or neglect of, a child. In 1983, 130 defendants were cautioned or found guilty of such an offence. By 1993, the figure had increased to 391. It is interesting to note the use of police cautions as an alternative to prosecution. Where the offender admits his guilt, there is sufficient evidence for a conviction and the offender consents, if it does not seem in the public interest to instigate criminal proceedings, a formal caution may be given by the police. In 1993 47% of the total figure were cautioned for cruelty to, or neglect of, children.

In cases of sexual abuse the statistics report the total number of offences of rape, incest and indecent assault without specifying whether the victims were adults or children. Unlawful sexual intercourse with a girl under 16, unlawful sexual intercourse with a girl under 13 and gross indecency with a child are the only recorded sex crimes which necessarily involve children. In 1983 149 offenders were cautioned or convicted of unlawful sexual intercourse with a girl under 13 and 1,673 were cautioned or convicted of unlawful sexual intercourse with a girl under 16. In 1993 the number of convictions for unlawful sexual intercourse with a girl under 13 remained fairly constant at 143, but the number for unlawful sexual intercourse with a girl under 16 dropped to 723 – perhaps reflecting the growing tolerance of sexual relations between adolescents approaching the age of consent. In the same year 47% of the offenders were cautioned for unlawful sexual intercourse with a girl under 13, but 76% of the offenders were cautioned for unlawful sexual intercourse with a girl under 16. Statistics of cautions and convictions for gross indecency with a child show a steady increase from 255 in 1983 to 304 in 1993, with 33% of offenders being cautioned in 1993.

---

45   Home Office (1989) *Report of the Advisory Group on Video Evidence* London, HMSO.

Further indications of the extent of sexual abuse – the use of surveys

In 1981, Mrazek, Lynch and Bentovim attempted to establish the incidence and prevalence of cases of child sexual abuse in the UK by carrying out a postal survey of 1,599 GPs, paediatricians, child psychiatrists and police surgeons.[46] Based on the responses, the researchers suggested an annual incidence of 1,500 cases, or 1 in 6,000 children. This is now viewed as a very conservative estimate. The estimated prevalence of 0.3% of the population over childhood has subsequently been shown to be much too low, perhaps because of insufficient account being taken of the 'dark figure' of unreported cases. Further research was carried out in the UK during the period 1982-1984 by Nash and West.[47] Two sample groups of young women were questioned on their early childhood experiences. The percentage of women who experienced some degree of sexual contact with an adult was high in both samples, 42% and 54%, – an average rate of 48%. However, the research definition of sexual abuse was very wide, including verbal suggestions, obscene telephone calls and 'flashers'. This would suggest that the figure of 48% is, perhaps, too high to reflect the true prevalence of the problem. A first attempt to establish a national prevalence rate was made by Dr Baker and Dr Duncan who reported their findings in 1986.[48] The authors collaborated with Market and Opinion Research International (MORI) to produce a nationally representative sample of the population. Those interviewed were aged 15 years and over. The definition of child sexual abuse was given as:

> 'A child (anyone under 16 years) is sexually abused when another person, who is sexually mature, involves the child in activity which the other person expects to lead to their sexual arousal. This might involve intercourse, touching, exposure of the sexual organs, showing pornographic material or talking about sexual things in an erotic way.'

The response rate was high – 87%. Of the 2,019 respondents, 206 (10%) reported sexual abuse as defined. (Interestingly, in 63% of the cases reported there was only a single abusive experience, compared with only 19% of such cases in the Nash and West survey.) The demographic data provided by the research carried out by Baker and Duncan shows that there is no increased risk associated with specific social class categories or area of residence.

The results of these surveys are inconsistent, with estimated prevalence varying between 0.3% and 48%. More extensive research has been carried out in the US. With the exception of the Nash and West survey, American research has consistently suggested higher rates of abuse than that reported in

---

46   Mrazek, PB & Kempe, CH (eds) (1981) *Sexually Abused Children and their Families* Oxford, Pergamon p 35.

47   West, DJ (1985) *Sexual Victimisation* Aldershot, Gower.

48   La Fontaine, J (1988) *Child Sexual Abuse* ESRC Research Briefing p 2.

the UK. For example, Russell[49] found a prevalence rate of 38% amongst a random sample of 930 women aged 18 years and over in San Francisco. This survey did not use quite such a comprehensive definition as that used by Nash and West, and therefore the two results are not incompatible. If the age and sex of the respondent are taken into account, the results of the Nash and West survey and those of the Baker and Duncan survey become less incompatible. Nash and West interviewed only women, aged between 20 and 39 years of age, whereas Baker and Duncan interviewed a sample of both males and females with only a lower age limit of 15 years. It was found by Baker and Duncan that 15-24 year olds reported more abuse than their elders, and that females reported more sexual abuse than males (12% of females reported abuse compared to 8% of males). The survey by Nash and West was carried out on a sample of younger females – a sample within which more abuse is expected. This fact could go some way towards accounting for the discrepancies in the results between the two surveys. In addition, the fact that younger adults are more likely to have been abused may lead to speculation that there has been an increase in child sexual abuse over the years. However, this could well be due to the increased openness with which society regards sexual matters and the recent public awareness and acknowledgement of child sexual abuse.

CONCLUSION

It seems that a 10% prevalence of child sexual abuse in the UK is a somewhat conservative estimate. Using this figure of 10%, Baker and Duncan estimate that over 4.5 million adults (15 years and over) in this country will have been sexually abused as children, and a potential 1,117,000 children will be sexually abused before they are 15 years of age; an estimated 143,000 of these will be abused within the family. When these figures are added to the number of children who are physically or emotionally abused, or neglected, the potential scale of the problem of child abuse becomes clear. As our society acknowledges the problem, the law has responded by providing a framework for intervention, investigation of suspected abuse, the protection of the child and the prosecution of the abuser. Returning to the stages of recognition of abuse, our society certainly seems to have reached stage 5. With the advent of the Children Act 1989, within which there are provisions for children in need and for the support and help of families, it may be hoped we are close to approaching the utopia of stage 6 – the guarantee that each child is truly wanted and provided with loving care, decent shelter and food, and first class

49   Baker, AW & Duncan, SP (1985) 'Child Sexual Abuse: A study of prevelance in Great Britain' in *Child Abuse and Neglect* vol 9 p 457 at p 462.

preventive and curative care. How close we actually are can only be assessed after consideration of the legal framework developed in response to the problem. The details of the framework are addressed in the following chapters.

CHAPTER 2

THE TIP OF THE ICEBERG – DISCLOSURE OF ABUSE

THE FIRST TO KNOW – 'REPORTING' CHILD ABUSE

The concept of 'reporting' is generally seen as bringing child abuse to the attention of one or more of the agencies with statutory duties and/or powers to investigate or intervene. It is, however, accepted that many cases of child abuse never come to the attention of the authorities. Reference has already been made in the previous chapter to the iceberg of child abuse and the 'dark figure' – those cases of child abuse that are unreported and therefore hidden in darkness. Within the body of the iceberg, knowledge of abuse may exist at different levels:

Level I: cases are unknown to any persons other than the victim and the abuser.

Level II: cases may be known to close relatives or neighbours who do not report them.

Level III: cases may be unknown to the authorities, but may be known to, or suspected by, other persons, for example, teachers or doctors who are concerned with the child in a professional capacity.

Level IV: cases will be known to the authorities – those agencies with responsibility and/or power to intervene (the police, social services or the NSPCC).

Most cases of abuse begin in the depths of the iceberg at level I. The journey through the iceberg to level IV may well be far from easy. 'Working Together' states:

> 'The starting point of the process is that any person who has knowledge of, or a suspicion that a child is suffering significant harm, or is at risk of significant harm, should refer their concern to one or more of the agencies with statutory duties and/or powers to investigate or intervene – the social services department, the police or the NSPCC.' (para 5.11.1)

The UK has no mandatory child abuse reporting laws. Any person who has knowledge or suspicion that a child is being abused or is at risk of abuse, whether concerned with the child in a professional capacity or otherwise, is under no specific legal duty to report the matter to the authorities (although certain professionals may well be in breach of a professional code of conduct in such circumstances). Indeed, in most circumstances, the law does not impose upon citizens of this country an enforceable legal duty of volunteering any information to the police or other authority. There are, of course, exceptions to this general rule, but none that relate directly to the abuse of children. For example, if a doctor treats a patient suffering from a notifiable disease such as cholera, smallpox or typhus, he must send to the designated officer of the local authority a certificate giving details of the patient and of the disease from which he is suffering.[1] A doctor who terminates a pregnancy is required to give notice within seven days to the Chief Medical Officer.[2] Under the Road Traffic Act 1988 any person, if so requested by the police, has a duty to give information which might lead to the identification of a person who has committed an offence under the Act. The Prevention of Terrorism (Temporary Provisions) Act 1989 provides that it is an offence to fail to give information which may be of material assistance in preventing the commission of certain acts of violence for political ends. At one time it was a criminal offence to conceal knowledge of a 'felony' (a serious criminal offence). But in 1967 this common law offence was repealed and a statutory offence was created of accepting, or agreeing to accept, a consideration for not disclosing information which might be of material assistance in securing a prosecution, knowing or believing that an arrestable offence has been committed.[3] Therefore, as a general rule, if a person knows that a child is being abused, as long as they do not accept anything for not disclosing information and do nothing to impede the abuser's apprehension or prosecution,[4] they are under no specific legal obligation to take active steps to report the matter to the authorities – even if the child continues to suffer harm. The law has always drawn a distinction between the infliction of harm through some positive action and merely allowing harm to occur by failing to prevent it. Like the priest and the Levite, members of the public can safely 'pass by on the other side'. It is hoped that their conscience would demand otherwise, but they will incur no legal liability for failing to act. However, the same cannot be said of parents, or indeed anyone with custody, charge or care of an abused child. Specific criminal liability may arise under section 1 of the Children and Young Persons Act 1933 if such a person knows of the abuse and in failing to report it would 'expose the child to unnecessary suffering' (see Chapter 1). Furthermore, the courts have established that there are a number of relationships which give rise to an affirmative duty to prevent harm and both criminal and tortious liability may be incurred by failing to report the abuse if the child continues to suffer harm as a result. The relationships certainly include parent and child,[5] but extend well beyond this to include

---

1   Public Health (Control of Disease) Act 1984 and Public Health (Infectious Diseases) Regulations 1968 (SI 1968 No 1366).

2   Abortion Act 1967, section 2 and Abortion Regulations SI 1968 No 390 (as amended).

3   Section 5(1) Criminal Law Act 1967.

4   Section 4(1) Criminal Law Act 1967.

5   *Camarthenshire County Council v Lewis* [1955] AC 549, *Gibbons and Proctor* [1918] 13 Cr App R 134.

relationships where one person has voluntarily undertaken to care for another.[6] Thus, for example, anyone who has undertaken to care for a child will be under a positive duty to act to prevent the child suffering harm. The enforcement of such a duty is obviously problematic and the few cases that have been brought before the courts for failing to act involve serious consequences for the victim – usually death.[7] In the vast majority of cases the only duty to report suspected abuse is a moral duty. So, how do cases of abuse work their way through the iceberg and reach level IV?

LEVEL I – VICTIMS AND ABUSERS

Hidden in the depths of the iceberg, cases of abuse at level I are known only to the victim and abuser. Cases which remain at this level tend to involve abuse which leaves no obvious visible signs – primarily emotional and sexual abuse. The abuse may remain hidden at this level for several reasons. In some cases, the age of the child itself will be enough to ensure the abuse remains a secret. Very young children do not have the linguistic ability to tell anyone what is happening and, if there are no outward signs of abuse and the abuser is not 'caught in the act', the abuser has little to fear.

As children grow older, they develop the linguistic skills necessary to tell of the abuse, but, particularly in cases of long term sexual abuse, the child may not realise that anything is wrong. This belief may be reinforced by the abuser: 'this is daddy's way of showing he loves you' or 'all daddies do this to their little girls'. As children grow older, it becomes harder to sustain such a belief. When children begin to mix socially with their peer groups, it is inevitable that the realisation will eventually dawn that the abuse is not 'normal' behaviour and that other children are not treated in the same way. The abuser may try to delay this realisation as long as possible by keeping the child socially isolated, but the older the child, the harder this becomes. Threats are then frequently brought into play by the abuser: 'if you tell anyone, I'll kill you' or '... I'll kill your mother'. Such threats can be tremendously effective in keeping the abuse secret. An extreme example occurred several years ago in Holland when over 70 children between the ages of three and six were abducted by five men and two women dressed in clowns' costumes and masks. They were sexually abused and in some cases burnt with cigarettes, and the incident was recorded on video film. The children were returned home after being threatened that, if they told anyone, their mothers would be killed. The threats were so effective that it was only when one mother found burns on her daughter's body and consulted a doctor that the evidence of the abuse emerged.[8] In cases of intrafamilial abuse, the

---

6   *Nicholls* [1874] 13 Cox CC 75.

7   *Stone and Dobinson* [1977] 1 QB 354.

8   Search, G (1988) *The Last Taboo: Sexual Abuse of Children* London, Penguin.

relationship between the abuser and child is often of crucial significance. The victim may well have strong emotional feelings towards the abuser. Although they hate the abuse, they still love the person who abuses them – the 'good daddy/monster daddy' syndrome. The victim may also feel an overwhelming need to protect the non–abusing parent and threats may focus on the consequences of revealing the abuse: 'if you tell anyone, they'll send you away' or 'if you tell anyone, they'll send daddy away'. The family is often the only security the victim knows and fear of breaking up the family by disclosing the abuse ensures that the abuse remains hidden and therefore remains known only to the abuser and victim.[9]

LEVEL II – RELATIVES, FRIENDS AND NEIGHBOURS

The first 'outsider' to suspect the existence of abuse may well be a close relative, friend or neighbour. The suspicion may be aroused by outward signs of abuse – either physical or behavioural. There is an understandable tendency in cases of long-term sexual abuse to think 'surely the mother must know', but it is argued that this is not so. Richard Johnson, Director on Incest Crisis Line, estimates that around 70% of the mothers with whom he has come into contact genuinely did not have the slightest idea about what was going on.[10] Even if there are no outward signs of abuse to arouse suspicion, the victim may confide in a trusted adult – a non-abusing parent, friend or neighbour. Faced with such knowledge or suspicion, a decision has to be made about what action, if any, should be taken. One of the most important factors influencing such a decision will be the person's relationship with the victim and alleged abuser. In cases where a parent suspects the child is being abused by a partner, their main concern may well be the consequences of reporting the abuse to the authorities. Considerations such as the effect of intervention on family life may well influence the decision whether or not to report the abuse. Any moral duty to report may well be subjugated, either to a desire to protect the abuser, who may figure strongly in their emotions, or to a desire to protect themselves from the consequences of reporting. Clearly, such a parent may incur criminal liability by failing to report if this exposes the child to unnecessary suffering. But even if the parent was under a specific legal duty to report suspected abuse, it is doubtful whether this would result in more abuse being disclosed in view of the strong emotional feelings involved.

Similar considerations may influence friends and relatives of the abused child. If a family friend suspects abuse, once again fear of the consequences of

---

9   See Furniss, T (1991) Chapter 2 – 'Child sexual abuse as a syndrome of secrecy for the child' in *The Multi Professional Handbook of Child Sexual Abuse* London, Routledge

10   Search, G (1988) *The Last Taboo: Sexual Abuse of Children* London, Penguin.

reporting will influence any decision to act. This problem may be alleviated to some extent by encouraging anonymous reporting, either to the police, the social services or a voluntary organisation such as the NSPCC. However, to encourage anonymous reporting may also encourage malicious reports – which can result in precious resources being diverted away from genuine cases and possibly result in unwarranted intervention and distress for the family concerned. The general public may also be unsure to whom they should report the suspected abuse. 'Working Together' states:

> 'The statutory agencies must ensure that people know how to refer to them, and they must facilitate the making of referrals and the prompt and appropriate action in response to expressions of concern. It is important in all these cases that the public and professionals are free to refer to the child protection agencies without fear that this will lead to unco-ordinated and/or premature action. The Area Child Protection Committees should publish advice about whom to contact with details of addresses and telephone numbers.' (para 5.11)

Studies have shown that the choice of agency is influenced by the nature of the abuse:

> '... when abuse occurs at the hands of someone outside the family, such as a stranger or neighbour, families and agencies give priority to catching the offender, punishing them and referring cases to Criminal Justice Agencies. When abuse occurs at the hands of a parent, however, those involved often wish to avoid the prosecution of the offender. In these cases there is much more concern about the well-being of the child, so that child protective, mental health and social services agencies are called into play.'[11]

If the reporting is not anonymous, and as long as the report is made in good faith and the withholding of the information will not prejudice the welfare of the child, the informer should be assured that his or her identity will be confidential and there should be no risk of reprisals. In the case of *D v NSPCC*,[12] the NSPCC received information that the plaintiff was maltreating her child, and promised the informant that his identity would not be revealed. The plaintiff claimed damages for the injury to health caused by the alleged negligence of the NSPCC in investigating the allegations of the informant, which eventually proved groundless. The House of Lords upheld the NSPCC's application to withhold from discovery documents disclosing the identity of the informant by relying on the analogy of established judicial refusal to compel disclosure of sources of police information. As Lord Simon explained:

> 'Sources of police information are not subject to forensic examination. This is because liability to general exposure would cause those sources of information to dry up, so that police protection of the community would be impaired.

---

11   Finkelhor, D (1984) *Child Sexual Abuse: New Theory and Research* New York, Free Press pp 203-204.
12   [1978] AC 171.

Exactly the same argument applies in the instant case if for "police" you read "NSPCC" and for "community" you read "that part of the community which consists of children who may be in peril".'[13]

Obviously, encouraging the reporting of suspected abuse by the general public is no easy task. The numerous child abuse inquiries and the surrounding media publicity may well have done much to increase public awareness of the existence of child abuse, but it has not necessarily had the effect of encouraging members of the public to report suspected abuse. Many appear to have been left with the impression of over-zealous doctors and social workers removing children from their families for long periods of time. Such an impression will do little to encourage reporting. Perhaps the most effective encouragement is to ensure that the consequences of reporting the abuse are seen to be beneficial rather than detrimental to the child.

LEVEL III – PROFESSIONALS ACTING IN THE COURSE OF DUTY

Approaching the tip of the iceberg, child abuse may be known or suspected by those in contact with the child in a professional capacity – typically those in the education service, the probation service, or the health service. Although not subject to a strict legal duty to report suspicions of abuse, such professionals will be guided by their professional associations as to the action they should take. In most cases such guidance actively encourages reporting of suspicions of abuse, to the extent that professionals may find themselves in breach of their professional duty if they fail to report.

The education service

As 'Working Together' acknowledges, although the education service does not constitute an investigation or intervention agency, it has an important role to play at the recognition and referral stage. Teachers and other school staff are thought to be particularly well placed to observe outward signs of abuse, changes in behaviour or failure to develop because of their day-to-day contact with individual children during school terms. Bruises, lacerations and burns may be apparent, particularly when children change their clothes for sporting activities. Possible indicators of neglect and emotional abuse – such as inadequate clothing, poor growth or hunger and excessive dependence or attention seeking may be noticeable. Physical signs of sexual abuse may be seen or substantial behavioural change, which could be indicative of abuse, may be observed. Whilst these signs, and others, are not in themselves proof that abuse has occurred, they may give rise to suspicion of abuse and, as part

---

13   Ibid at 241.

of their pastoral role, teachers should be alert to such signs. Alternatively, a child may choose to volunteer information about abuse to a teacher, who could well be seen as the only trusted adult in the child's life. If the information is offered in confidence, teachers will need tact and sensitivity in responding to the disclosure. They will need to reassure the child, and retain his or her trust, while explaining the need for action, which will necessarily involve other adults being informed.[14] Education welfare officers and educational psychologists also have important roles because of their concern for the welfare and development of children.

Each Local Education Authority (LEA) is responsible for identifying a senior member of staff as having responsibility for co-ordinating policy and action on child abuse in schools and the youth service throughout the area and who acts as the point of contact with the local social services department and other agencies. Each school should then designate a senior member of staff as having responsibility, under the procedures established by the LEA, for co-ordinating action within the school and for liaison with other agencies. In the case of educational establishments not maintained by the LEA, the social services department is responsible for ensuring that the establishments are aware of the local inter-agency procedures and provide advice on appropriate procedures within the establishment. The advent of grant maintained schools thus has implications which have yet to be fully explored. At the present time the number of grant maintained schools is comparatively small and do not therefore impose an impossible burden on over-stretched social services departments. But if the Government continue a policy of encouraging schools to 'opt out' of local authority control, more thought will need to be given to ways of ensuring all schools are suitably advised.

In all cases the designation of a co-ordinating teacher should not be seen as diminishing the role of all teachers in being alert to signs of abuse. Any member of staff who considers they have good cause to suspect abuse should report their suspicions to the co-ordinating teacher, who then follows the procedures laid down by the LEA, which generally involve contacting a named member of the social services department and, where necessary, taking immediate action to protect the child. A record should be kept of all the information available – staff should note carefully what they have observed and when they observed it and any comment made by the child concerned, or by an adult who might be the abuser, should be recorded, preferably *verbatim*, as soon as possible after the comment was made. These procedures, if followed, should ensure that cases of suspected abuse reach level IV – the tip of the iceberg. 'Working Together' recommends that, for establishments maintained by them, LEAs should keep up-to-date lists of designated staff and ensure that these staff receive appropriate training and support. In

---

14   DES (1988) *Working Together for the Protection of Children from Abuse: Procedures within the Education Service* Circular No 4/88.

practice it may well be equally, if not more important, for *all* members of staff to receive appropriate training and support. Awareness of possible signs of abuse and an understanding of the consequences of reporting suspicions by those most closely involved with the child are crucial if the abuse is to reach level IV. Without training and support, suspicions of those in the education service may go unreported through ignorance or fear of the consequences.

The probation service

As part of their professional duties, probation officers are frequently involved with children and their families and may, on occasions, be well placed to identify abused children or those at risk of abuse. Section 7(1) of the Children Act 1989 empowers a court, when considering any question with respect to a child under the Act, to ask either a probation officer or a local authority to report to the court:

> 'on such matters relating to the welfare of that child as are required to be dealt with in the report.'

Such reports are likely to be called for in cases involving the breakdown of family relationships and the welfare officer is generally expected to investigate the circumstance and background of the child concerned and report to the court. This will usually involve visiting the home and talking to the child – thus providing a potentially ideal opportunity to identify children at risk. If suspicions are aroused, the probation officer will be expected to refer his concerns to his senior officer in the first instance, and then make a referral to the social services department and ensure that appropriate action is taken. Probation officers may also have a role to play in identifying children at risk through their responsibilities for the supervision of offenders, including those convicted of offences against children. Arrangements exist to ensure that when convicts of offences against children are discharged from prison, probation services inform the local authority in the area in which the discharged prisoner plans to reside. This allows the social services department to make enquiries and take action if they believe there may be a danger to children residing at the same address – thereby helping to ensure that cases of child abuse reach level IV.

Medical practitioners

Medical practitioners are obviously well placed to diagnose abuse and may well play a crucial part in bringing cases of suspected abuse to the tip of the iceberg. The role of the doctor in diagnosing abuse as part of an inter-disciplinary team and the related problems of confidentiality are considered in more detail in Chapter 5. It is now evident that doctors have a discretion whether or not to disclose information. The paramount consideration must obviously be the child's welfare and in many cases this will require the doctor to pass information on to other agencies. But, this conflicts with the hippocratic ideology of medical treatment which embodies the concept of confidentiality and which is deeply rooted in every medical practitioner's training. Part of the hippocratic oath (in translation) states:

> 'whatever, in connection with my professional practice, not in connection with it, I see or hear, in the life of men, which ought not to be spoken of abroad, I will not divulge, as reckoning that all such should be kept secret.'

The doctor's task is clearly not an enviable one and in many respects the imposition of a legal *requirement* to report suspected abuse (see below) may seem preferable as it removes the element of discretion and thus, arguably, removes the conflict between maintaining patient confidentiality and disclosure. However, although many cases will clearly call for disclosure, situations may arise, particularly in the case of an older child, where maintaining confidentiality actually serves the child's best interests. If the child's welfare is truly to be treated as paramount the element of discretion is essential. As long as medical practitioners are in possession of the full facts of the case, they can surely be trusted to make such judgments. In response to concerns expressed about legal challenges to professional decisions, the recent guidance produced by a joint working party of the Department of Health, British Medical Association and Conference of Medical Royal Colleges[15] concludes that, if a doctor believes that child abuse may have occurred and raises this with the statutory agencies based on sound clinical evaluation and judgment, then he or she could not be blamed for acting in good faith and in the best interests of the child.

Those cases of child abuse which work their way up through the iceberg to reach level IV thereby become known to the authorities with duties and/or powers to investigate and take steps to protect the child. Once this level is reached the concept of inter-agency co-operation should ensure that information is shared between the professions to allow effective action to be taken. This is discussed in more detail in Chapter 4.

MANDATORY REPORTING – THE AMERICAN EXPERIENCE

Provisions of the legislation – an overview

Who must report?

Between 1963 and 1966, all states in America passed some type of statute requiring health care professionals to report suspected abuse and neglect. Initially, only physicians were mandated to report, presumably because it was believed that their roles and diagnostic skills placed them in a unique position to recognise abuse and neglect. The American Medical Association argued that

---

15 Department of Health, British Medical Association and Conference of Medical Royal Colleges (1994) *Child protection: Medical Responsibilities* addendum to 'Working Together Under the Children Act 1989'.

singling physicians out in this way was discriminatory and expressed concern that parents would avoid bringing their children for medical care following an injury for fear of being suspected of abuse and being reported. It was also argued that, since physicians tended to be the last professional group to see an injured child, other professionals, such as teachers, nurses and health visitors would be more effective in initiating early protective intervention and thus should be mandated to report. A review of current reporting legislation in the states shows a considerable expansion of reporting statutes over the past three decades so that, today, most individuals working with children in a professional capacity are now required to report suspected abuse. Five distinct categories of mandated reporters can be identified[16] – medical professionals/institutions, education professionals, legal/law enforcement professionals, helping services professionals and persons in the community. The detailed scope of mandated personnel within each category varies considerably between states and this is particularly noticeable in the medical professionals category.[17] For example, some states adopt a broadly defined category, requiring any medical, dental or mental health professional to report, whereas other states adopt a policy of naming specific practitioners, including such diverse occupations as neuropathic physicians and practitioners who rely solely on spiritual means for healing. The same is true, to a more limited extent, in the other professional categories, with some states variously requiring any person engaged in the practice of education, law enforcement officials and any person paid to care for, or work with, a child in any private or public facility to report; whereas other states specifically require school teachers, principals and counsellors, state fire inspectors and clergymen to report. These first four categories relate to those with suspicions of abuse at level III in the iceberg. The final category relates to non-professionals – those at level II. Nine of the 50 states require any person, who has reason to suspect abuse, to report it and a further three states require any person or institution who has cause to suspect abuse to report it. Only one state – Arizona – places a specific duty to report on parents. No state specifically requires children to report suspected abuse. Whilst this may seem entirely reasonable, given the controversial issues that would arise as to competency and liability, it has been argued that children are perhaps the most promising and resourceful group for noticing the abuse of other children.[18]

Research has shown that increasing the number of professionals required to report leads to an increase in the number of reports made, although it is acknowledged that compliance is far from complete and compliance rates

---

16 Small, M (1992) 'Policy Review of Child Abuse and Neglect Reporting Statutes' in Law and Policy vol 14 Nos 2 & 3 p 129.

17 Ibid Appendix 2.

18 Ibid p 132.

vary considerably between the professions.[19] However, the effect of requiring non-professionals to report does not appear to have been monitored in the same way and little is known about the effect of imposing a legal duty to report on such people.

What must be reported and when?

Having decided who should be a mandated reporter, the next question is what must they report and when must they report it? The problems encountered in defining the term child abuse were referred to in Chapter One. Similar problems are encountered in mandatory reporting legislation. As a minimum, all states define child abuse in terms of non-accidental physical or mental injury; some states also provide distinct definitions of neglect – usually no more specific than failure to provide adequate food, clothing or medical care – and many states specify various sexual abuses ranging from intercourse or contact to allowing, permitting, encouraging or engaging in obscene or pornographic filming, photographing or the depicting of a child for commercial purposes.[20] Those statutes that define child abuse broadly have the advantage of flexibility, but unless they provide adequate guide lines to mandated reporters unfounded reports may result. On the other hand, narrow definitions of abuse may restrict reporting, thereby frustrating the primary aim of reporting legislation – to protect children. In addition, all statutes specify when a report must be filed or the level of suspicion the reporter must have. The standard varies between knowledge, reasonable cause to know or suspect, reasonable cause to suspect, and cause to believe or suspect. Those states which specify reasonable grounds for the suspicion, knowledge or belief are, in effect, incorporating an objective standard into the assessment – based on the perceptions of a hypothetical reasonable practitioner – and would appear to exclude suspicions based on instinct or a 'hunch'. Furthermore, whereas some states require reporting of any situation in which a suspicion of abuse arises, including situations where suspicions are aroused by a report from a third party, other states impose restrictions on the conditions under which reporting is required, for example by specifying that the reporter must observe the suspected victim of abuse before being required to report. The abuse must be reported 'immediately' or 'promptly' once the duty to report arises. The agency mandated to receive the report varies between the police, the family court and child protective services. In most

---

19 Lamond, D (1989) 'The Impact of Mandatory Reporting Legislation on reporting Behaviour' in *Child Abuse and Neglect* vol 13 p 471.

20 Small note 16 supra appendices 3 & 4.

states there is provision that, in cases of emergency, the report should be made to the police, who are available 24 hours a day.

Consequences of reporting

Reporting legislation in almost all states makes provision for the consequences of reporting such cases which are later determined to be unfounded,[21] and also provides sanctions for failure to report.[22] In total 44 states explicitly provide civil and criminal immunity for reporting in good faith. Failure to report when required constitutes a misdemeanour violation in most states with maximum penalties of five or 10 day jail sentences and/or fines of up to US $1,000. Exceptionally, one state – Rhode Island – provides for a jail sentence of up to one year for failure to report. Some states also include tortious liability for harm done to the child by failure to report. Although in the early years of reporting requirements there appeared to be no criminal proceedings brought against professionals for failing to report, in more recent years, presumably as a result of increased public and professional attention to child abuse, the number of criminal proceedings, although still small, appears to be increasing. It has been suggested[23] that criminal prosecutions are rare for three main reasons. First, there are substantial problems of proof. Secondly, there is a feeling that criminal sanctions are inappropriate because there is no criminal culpability and because an otherwise law-abiding citizen should not be prosecuted and finally because the would-be reporter's co-operation is often necessary to prove the case against the parents.

Compliance with the legislation

In the late 1960s, it was estimated that 7,000 cases of child abuse were reported annually in the US. In 1990, 2.5 million reports of child abuse were filed.[24] This vast increase in reporting is no doubt attributable to numerous factors, including increased societal awareness of child abuse. One of the most significant factors is thought to be the initial introduction of mandatory reporting laws and the subsequent expansion in the range of mandated reporters over the years. However, research shows that compliance with the reporting laws is far from complete. In 1986, a national study sponsored by the National Centre for Child Abuse and Neglect found that only about one third of the cases of abuse known to community professionals were officially

---

21 Ibid appendix 6.

22 Ibid appendix 5.

23 Small note 16 supra.

24 Kalichman, S & Brosig, C (1992) 'Mandatory Child Abuse Reporting Laws: Issues and Implications for Policy' in *Law and Policy* vol 14 p 153

reported as required by the law.[25] For sexual abuse cases alone, the estimated reporting rate was consistently higher, perhaps indicating an increased willingness, on behalf of professionals, to report cases of sexual rather than physical abuse. It could be that this is because sexual abuse of children, although clearly a form of child abuse, is treated as a special category due to the public, institutional and judicial reactions of repugnance it creates – thereby making reporting of such cases more likely.

Numerous studies have been undertaken into reporting behaviour amongst mandated professionals.[26] In the early days of mandatory reporting, it was evident that many professionals were unaware of the reporting requirements and it was thought that this was the primary reason for non-compliance. More recent studies have shown a marked increase in the level of knowledge of reporting laws, yet compliance with the laws is far from complete and it is now acknowledged that many other factors influence the decision to report. In 1987 a national survey was carried out into the child abuse reporting behaviour of 1,196 mandated reporters, including family and general practitioners, paediatricians, child psychiatrists, clinical psychologists, social workers, public school principals and child care providers drawn from 15 nationally representative states.[27] The respondents were presented with five vignettes, selected from a set of core vignettes, each of which described a case of possible maltreatment, including neglect, physical abuse and sexual abuse. The core vignettes varied on several factors (eg severity, history of previous abuse, family socioeconomic status), the objective being that each respondent received a unique set of vignettes. Through extensive open-ended pretesting, the researchers concluded that the following five factors influenced any professional's decision as to whether or not to report suspected abuse: the seriousness of the incident, whether the incident should be labelled 'abuse' or 'neglect' (as appropriate), whether the law would require a report to be made and whether the child, and, separately, the rest of the family would benefit from a report being made. The respondents were asked to make judgments on each of these five issues and were then asked to indicate how likely they would be to report the incident if they encountered it.

The responses revealed a mean likelihood of reporting across all respondents of 68 on a 100 point scale on which no-one equated with 'definitely would not report' and 100 equated with 'definitely would report', indicating that respondents fell between 'somewhat' and 'very likely to report'. Analysis showed that all five factors considered were related to reporting intentions. The most influential factor was whether the law required a report to be made. This, combined with judgments as to the seriousness and operational

---

25   Ibid.

26   Zellman, G (1990) 'Report Decision Making Patterns Among Mandated Child Abuse Reporters' in *Child Abuse and Neglect* vol 14 325.

27   Ibid.

definitions of abuse, was the major consistory to reporting decisions. However, the judgments of perceived benefit to the child, and less significantly, to the family, were also significant predictors of likelihood of reporting. The results of the study confirm that the existence of mandatory reporting has achieved, at least in part, its primary objective – to ensure more cases of child abuse and neglect are brought to the tip of the iceberg. Yet it also shows that the existence of a mandatory duty is not the sole factor which influences reporting behaviour – judgments as to the seriousness of the incident, the labelling of the incident as abuse or neglect and the perceived benefits to the child and family of making a report all influence reporting decisions, particularly in cases of possible neglect. Whereas the seriousness and labelling issues can be addressed to a certain extent by incorporating clearer definitions of abuse within the reporting statutes, judgments as to the perceived benefits of reporting will undoubtedly continue to influence reporting decisions. It is only when professionals are fully acquainted with what is required by the law and are confident that making a report is in the best interests of the child and the family that the mandatory duty to report will be truly effective.

Substantiation of reports

The existence of a mandatory duty to report suspected abuse and neglect in the US may have been one of the most significant factors in the huge increase in the number of cases reported in recent years, but evidence exists to suggest that whereas the number of reports has steadily increased, the percentage of those reports that have been substantiated following investigation has decreased.[28] For example in New York State, over 50% of all reports were substantiated in 1974 but in 1984, only slightly over 35% were substantiated. The following year, a research study was carried out on reports received by the state of New York Child Abuse and Maltreatment Register between 1 April 1985 and 31 August 1985. A total of 48% of the physical abuse reports, 39% of the sexual abuse reports and 28% of the neglect reports were substantiated, giving an overall substantiation rate of approximately 30%. The research showed that reports from professional sources were more likely to be substantiated, particularly in cases of neglect where the substantiation rate for reports from professionals was three times greater than that for non-professionals. Further research has confirmed that this is, in fact, a national phenomenon.

The trend for substantiation rates to fall as the rate of reporting increases has potentially serious implications for policy and practice. As the purpose of

---

28   Eckenrode et al (1988) 'Substantiation of Child Abuse and Neglect Reports' in *Journal of Consulting and Clinical Psychology* vol 56 No 1 p 9.

mandatory reporting is to bring more cases to the tip of the iceberg in order for a full investigation to be carried out, the increase in reporting results in many more cases being investigated and more resources being expended. As the percentage of reports that are found to be unsubstantiated grows, resources are inevitably diverted away from the handling of substantiated cases. In practice, increasing pressure is being put on child protective services throughout the states as they struggle to ensure that substantiated cases receive the attention they deserve, while continuing to investigate adequately the increasing numbers of reports being made. This, in turn, has led to the development and implementation of risk assessment models – formalised methods that provide a uniform structure and criteria for determining risk – in an attempt to prioritise resources.

There is also the understandable concern that many families are being subjected to an investigation by the state which intrudes on family autonomy, only for the majority of cases to be unsubstantiated. Whether or not such intrusion into family life is warranted is a difficult question, involving a delicate balancing of the rights of parents and family privacy against the need to protect children in danger of abuse. But if the proportion of unsubstantiated reports continues to grow, there will inevitably come a time when the balance will need to be restored in favour of family privacy.

MANDATORY REPORTING – POSSIBILITIES FOR ENGLAND AND WALES?

The American experience of mandatory reporting has not been without its problems, but yet has undoubtedly succeeded in bringing more cases of child abuse to the tip of the iceberg. Given that this is a primary objective of the system of child care and protection operating in England and Wales, it may be thought that the implementation of such a mandatory duty here would be expected. However, the idea of mandatory reporting in this jurisdiction has not, in general, found favour with those involved and the prospect of legislation enacting such a duty seems remote. Given the remit of the existing law, which, as a general rule, imposes no legal duty on the general public to disclose information, it seems very unlikely that a general duty would be enacted to require reporting of abuse by the general public. As far as professionals are concerned, it appears that those involved in a professional capacity would rather work together bound by mutual trust and professional guidance than by a legal duty. The issue was considered by an inter-departmental working party established as part of a review of child care law in 1985.[29] The working party appears to have restricted its consideration to imposing a legal duty on professional groups only, and cite doctors and teachers as an example. The working party

---

29   DHSS (1985) *Review of Child Care Law: Report to Ministers of an interdepartmental Working Party* London, HMSO.

distinguished the situation in the US, where most doctors are consulted privately and pointed out that there is unlikely to be a financial disincentive to doctors reporting suspected abuse in the UK where most patients do not pay directly for their medical care. The working party concluded that, given the overall structure of health and social services care in England and Wales, there was no demonstrable need for a mandatory reporting law, stressing that those professionals who might be covered by a mandatory reporting law are imbued by their training, tradition and character of their work with a strong emphasis on the 'welfare' of children and their families. Furthermore, they were of the opinion that the enactment of a mandatory duty might be counter-productive and increase the risk to children overall; first by weakening the individual professional's sense of personal responsibility and, secondly, in casting the shadow of near automatic reporting over their work, by raising barriers between clients and their professional advisers and even between professionals in the same case. A further possible consequence was thought to be to set back the advances made over the years in encouraging inter-disciplinary communication and co-operation between all those involved in the health and welfare of families and their children.[30] Given the huge efforts that have been made to encourage such co-operation in recent years, particularly since the working party considered the issue in 1985, it seems that inter-agency co-operation and the extensive professional guidance issued to all involved will be relied upon to ensure that cases of suspected abuse reach the tip of the iceberg. The enactment of a mandatory reporting duty would obviously require additional resources for enforcement. Such resources would be better aimed at ensuring the effectiveness of inter-agency co-operation, educating the general public about child abuse and encouraging the voluntary reporting of suspected abuse. In practice, the action taken once a case has reached the tip of the iceberg will be crucial. This was recognised in the US over 25 years ago when it was said:

'Reporting is, of course, not enough. After a report has been made something has to happen. A multi-disciplinary network of protection needs to be developed in each community to implement the good intention of the law. If child protective services are not available, reporters will no longer report. The promise of case finding legislation such as reporting laws is that when a case is found, something is done about it. The legislators which require reporting but do not provide the means for protective action delude themselves and neglect children.'[31]

---

30 Ibid para 12.4
31 Paulson (1966) quoted in Smith, S (1975) *The Battered Child Syndrome* London, Butterworths p 98.

CHAPTER 3

'IN THE CHILD'S BEST INTERESTS' – THE LEGAL FRAMEWORK OF CHILD PROTECTION

THE PHILOSOPHY UNDERLYING THE CHILDREN ACT 1989

The Children Act 1989, (refered to as the Act hereafter) was implemented on 14 October 1991, and is recognised as being the most comprehensive and radical piece of legislation relating to children. The Act reflects new thinking on the relationship between parents and their children, encourages co-operation and partnership between families and the agencies charged with the duty of safeguarding and promoting the welfare of children and aims to provide an effective legal framework for the protection of children. In so doing, it enshrines five main principles:

- the child's welfare is the paramount consideration;

- children are best cared for by both parents wherever possible;

- the state and the courts should intervene only where it will make improvements for the child;

- delay is not generally in the interest of the child;

- the laws and procedures regarding children should be unified.

The welfare principle

Section 1(1) of the Act lays down the fundamental principle underlying the Act:

> When a court determines any question with respect to:
> (a)   the upbringing of a child; or
> (b)   the administration of a child's property or the application of any income arising from it;
> the child's welfare shall be the court's paramount consideration.

The idea that a court should consider the welfare of the child in making decisions which affect the child is by no means new to the Children Act. In the last century, the Guardianship of Infants Act 1886 directed the court, when deciding custody cases, to have regard to the child's welfare as well as to the conduct and wishes of the parents. The early part of this century saw increasing emphasis being placed on the child's welfare and the Guardianship of Infants Act 1925 provided that in deciding issues concerning the custody or upbringing of a child all courts were to regard the child's welfare as the first and paramount consideration. Later statutory provisions affirmed this principle which now forms the cornerstone of child law. The change in wording from 'first and paramount consideration' to 'paramount consideration' was not intended to lead to a change in the law.

What is the child's welfare and how is it determined?

The Act provides no definition of the term 'welfare'. It is common to refer to the court acting in the child's best interests, but a court cannot intervene simply because it thinks alternative arrangements would give a child a better life. Before any state intervention is justified, preconditions must be satisfied. In the case of an abused child, the court must be satisfied, *inter alia*, that the child is suffering or likely to suffer significant harm (see below) before reaching the stage of considering the child's welfare. Judicial definitions of the meaning of welfare are surprisingly limited, but decisions of the courts make it clear that welfare is to be interpreted in a wide sense. It should not be measured by money or other material factors alone, but should include consideration of the child's emotional stability and moral welfare.

In determining the child's welfare, the Act provides in section 1(3) a check-list of factors to which the court should have particular regard:

(a) the ascertainable wishes and feelings of the child concerned (considered in the light of his age and understanding);

(b) the child's physical, emotional and educational needs;

(c) the likely effect on him of any change in his circumstances;

(d) the child's age, sex, background and any characteristics which the court considers relevant;

(e) any harm which he has suffered or is at risk of suffering;

(f) how capable each of the childs's parents, and any other person in relation to whom the court considers the question to be relevant, is of meeting his needs;

(g) the range of powers available to the court under this Act in the proceedings in question.

The objective of the check-list is not to define the meaning of the child's welfare, but to guide the court's thinking and ensure a greater consistency in decision making.

What is 'paramountcy'?

According to the Oxford English Dictionary, the word 'paramount' means 'above all others in rank, order and jurisdiction, supreme'. Clearly, then, the child's welfare ranks above all other considerations, but does that mean that the responsibilities and wishes and feeling of others, including parents, are to be ignored?

One of the leading cases on the paramountcy principle is *J v C*[1] which concerns the interpretation of similar words in the Guardianship of Minors Act 1971 (repealed), section 1 of which provided that in any question concerning the custody or upbringing of a minor:

'... the court, in deciding that question shall regard the welfare of the minor as the first and paramount consideration.'

The effect of this provision was described by Lord MacDermott:

'Reading these words in their ordinary significance, ... it seems to me that they must mean more than that the child's welfare is to be treated as the top item in a list of items relevant to the matter in question. I think they connote a process whereby, when all the relevant facts, relationships, claims and wishes of the parents, risks, choices and other circumstances are taken into account and weighed, the course to be followed will be that which is most in the interests of the child's welfare as that term has now to be understood. That is the first consideration because it rules upon or determines the course to be followed.'

This, and later cases, make it clear that the child's welfare has become, in practice, the sole consideration, at least in the sense that all the other factors are considered in the light of the child's welfare.

Keeping the family together – provision of services

The second principle underlying the Act is based on the belief that children are generally best looked after within the family with both parents playing a full part and without resorting to legal proceedings. By virtue of Part III of the Act, every local authority has a general duty to safeguard and promote the welfare of children in their area who are in need and, in so far as is consistent with that duty, to promote the upbringing of such children by their families by providing a range and level of services appropriate to those children's needs (section 17(1)). For the purposes of this part of the Act, children shall be taken to be in need if:

(a) they are unlikely to achieve or maintain, or have the opportunity of achieving or maintaining, a reasonable standard of health or development without the provision of services by a local authority under this part;

---

1 [1970] AC 668.

(b) their health or development is likely to be significantly impaired, or further impaired, without the provision of such services; or

(c) they are disabled,

and 'family' in relation to such children, includes any person who has parental responsibility for them and any other person with whom they have been living (section 17(10)).

This definition of children in need obviously includes abused children or those at risk of abuse, but it is far wider than that as it also includes disabled children. In pursuance of their general duty, local authorities have specific duties and powers, including a duty to take reasonable steps, through the provision of services, to prevent children within their area suffering ill-treatment or neglect (Schedule 2 para 4), and to reduce the need to bring proceedings for care and supervision orders with respect to children within their area (Schedule 2 para 7). Once a child has been identified as being in need, local authorities must provide a range and level of services appropriate to meet the need. These services may include day care for pre-school children and appropriate care or supervised activities outside school hours and during school holidays for children of school age (section 18). If it is not possible or appropriate to maintain a child at home, local authorities have a duty to accommodate children in need. Section 20(1) requires every local authority to provide accommodation for every child in need within their area who appears to them to require accommodation as a result of:

(a) there being no person who has parental responsibility for him or her;

(b) his being lost or having been abandoned; or

(c) the person who has been caring for him or her being prevented (whether or not permanently, and for whatever reason) from providing him with suitable accommodation or care.

The provision of such accommodation is seen as a service provided by the local authority which parents accept on a voluntary basis. An 'accommodated' child is not in care and as a general rule may be removed at any time without prior notice.

The principle of non-intervention

Section 1(5) of the Act provides that where a court is considering whether or not to make one or more orders under the Act with respect to a child, it shall not make the order, or any of the orders, unless it considers that doing so would be better for the child than making no order at all. Prior to the 1989 Act, section 1(2) of the Children and Young Persons Act 1969 required that, in order for a care or supervision order to be made under the Act, the child should be in need of care and control and that this need was 'unlikely to be met unless the court made an order'. In practice, it seems that the test was often satisfied by proof that a child's needs would not be met outside care, rather than by positive proof that a care or supervision order would result in the child's needs being met or at least better cared for.[2] In the private law context, custody and access orders were often made as if they were part of a package on divorce, and frequently only served to polarise the attitudes of all involved.

The non-intervention principle contained in section 1(5) now requires the court to be satisfied that any order will make a positive contribution to the welfare of the child, thus helping to avoid unnecessary state intervention and preserve the integrity and independence of the family.

Avoidance of delay

For some time prior to the implementation of the Act, concern had been expressed about delay in cases involving children and its potentially detrimental affect on the child. Children require stability in their lives and, in most cases, prolonged litigation was thought to be damaging to all involved. Section 1(2) of the Act now requires the court, in any proceedings in which any question with respect to a child's upbringing arises, to have regard to the general principle that any delay in determining the question is likely to prejudice the welfare of the child.

In applications for section 8 orders and care and supervision orders under Part IV of the Act (see below), courts are now specifically required to draw up a timetable with a view to determining the question or disposing of the application without delay (sections 11(1) and 32(1)). In public law cases, there is a presumption that a full hearing will take place within 12 weeks. The practical implications of this are discussed further in Chapter 7.

Unified laws and procedures

The final principle underlying the Act was to unify the law relating to children and to provide one set of remedies which would be available to all courts with jurisdiction over children. Prior to the Act, there existed distinct systems of private law (eg custody and access orders made on divorce) and public law (eg applications by local authorities for care and supervision orders) which

---

2   DHSS (1985) Review of Child Care Law: *Report to Ministers of an Inter-departmental Working Party* London, HMSO para 15.24.

operated in different courts at different levels. In addition, there existed the inherent wardship jurisdiction of the High Court, which could be invoked in either private or public law cases, but which tended to be used primarily by local authorities to obtain a care order as an alternative to the statutory schemes provided for the same purpose. The relationship between public and private law remedies was uncertain and there was no underlying general philosophy. The Act remedies this by creating a new three-tiered court comprising the High Court, county court and magistrates' court (family proceedings court), each with concurrent jurisdiction under the Act, enabling cases to be transferred up, down and across the court system subject to certain criteria (see Chapter 7). The vast majority of public law applications are commenced in the family proceedings court.[3]

KEY CONCEPTS UNDER THE CHILDREN ACT 1989

Parental responsibility

What is it?

One of the key concepts introduced by the Act is that of parental responsibility. Over the course of the last century, parents have acquired a number of rights, powers and duties in respect of their children. It was common practice to refer to 'parental rights'; the rights of children, if recognised at all, were generally viewed in a negative way - the right not to be abused or neglected. In line with the increased status being accorded to children in recent years, for the first time the Act refers to the concept of parental responsibility rather than parental rights. The concept is defined by section 3(1) of the Act as:

> '... all the rights, duties, powers, responsibilities and authority which by law a parent of a child has in relation to the child and his property.'

However, 'all the rights, duties etc ...' are not specified in the Act as it was not considered practicable to include a list of factors which would necessarily change at various times in a child's life. In essence, the effect of having parental responsibility is to empower a person to make most decisions in a child's life. If more than one person has parental responsibility of a child, they may act independently of each other (section 2(7)). If a dispute arises concerning the exercise of responsibility, and the parties concerned are unable to resolve the dispute by negotiation, an application may be made to the court for a specific issue order under section 8 of the Act (see below).

---

3   Children (Allocation of Proceedings) Order 1991.

Who has it?

Parental responsibility is automatically conferred on the mother, and on the father if he is married to the mother (section 2(1) and 2(2)). The natural father who is not married to the mother can acquire parental responsibility in a number of ways:

- He may enter into written agreement with the mother of the child in the required form – a parental responsibility agreement – or alternatively, he may apply to the court for an order – a parental responsibility order (section 4)

- He may be granted a residence order under section 8 of the Act, in which case the court is obliged to make a separate parental responsibility order (section 12)

- He may be appointed guardian of the child (section 5)

    Parental responsibility may be acquired by other adults in the child's life through a court order. Any person who is appointed as a guardian has parental responsibility of the child concerned (section 5(6)); any person in whose favour a residence order has been made has responsibility while the order remains in force (section 12(2)); a local authority has responsibility while a care order is in force (section 33(3)(a)); and any person who has been granted an emergency protection order has limited parental responsibility (section 44(4)(c) and (5)). The fact that someone else acquires responsibility in one of these ways does not, in itself, remove the parents' responsibility (section 2(6)), although in some cases its use may be curtailed. For example, if a care order is in force, the local authority has the power to determine the extent to which a parent or guardian may meet his parental responsibility insofar as it is necessary to do so to safeguard or promote the child's welfare (section 33(3)(b)).

The concept of significant harm

Prior to the implementation of the Act, the grounds for state intervention in a child's life were diverse. For example, a child could be taken into the care of the local authority by one of more than 17 routes and the conditions determining whether such compulsory measures could be taken varied according to the route by which each case proceeded. Although the welfare principle ensured that ultimately, the question of whether or not to take compulsory measures should depend on the child's best interests, it was feared that to adopt this alone as a standard could result in:

'a substantial proportion of the child population [being] ... taken into care simply on the basis that they would be better off with foster parents.'[4]

For this reason, it was decided to introduce a uniform threshold criterion, below which state intervention was not justified. The criterion adopted is that of 'significant harm'. Thus the concept of significant harm will be encountered at various stages in a child abuse investigation (see Chapter 4). A duty to investigate will be imposed on a local authority if they have reasonable cause to believe that a child is suffering, or likely to suffer, significant harm (section 47). The conditions which must be satisfied before the courts can make a child assessment order (section 43) or an emergency protection order (section 44), or before a police officer can take a child into police protection (section 46) all involve suspicion or belief of the child suffering significant harm. Similarly, the courts cannot make a care or supervision order (section 31) unless satisfied, *inter alia*, that the child is suffering or likely to suffer significant harm.

Wherever the concept of significant harm is used, harm is defined to mean ill-treatment or the impairment of health or development (sections 31(9) and 105). 'Health' is defined to mean physical or mental health and 'development' is defined to mean physical, intellectual, emotional, social or behavioural development. 'Ill-treatment' is not defined exhaustively, the Act merely stating that it includes sexual abuse and forms of ill-treatment which are not physical. Although not expressly stated, it seems clear that this includes physical abuse and presumably also extends to cover emotional abuse, even if no physical harm results. There is, therefore, potential overlap between ill-treatment and the impairment of health or development.

The harm must be 'significant'. The review of child care law undertaken in 1985 thought it should be necessary to show some *substantial* deficit in the acceptable standard of upbringing for a child and suggested that minor short-comings in health care or minor deficits in physical, psychological or social developments should not give rise to compulsory intervention unless they were having, or likely to have, serious and lasting effects upon the child.[5]

The Act does not define 'significant', but does provide that, where the question of whether harm suffered by a child is significant depends on the child's health or development, his or her health or development shall be compared with that which could reasonably be expected of a similar child (sections 31(10) and 105). How this comparison is to be made is by no means clear, requiring a comparison to be made with a hypothetical 'reasonable' child. It seems that the appropriate standard for any individual child will not

4   DHSS (1985) note 2 supra para 15.10.
5   Ibid para 15.15. Working Together under the Children Act 1989' London, HMSO.

necessarily be the best that could possibly be achieved, but only what is reasonable for that particular child. Clearly some children have specific characteristics which means they cannot be expected to be as healthy or as well-developed as other children; therefore the hypothetical child must be attributed with similar characteristics. But whether or not the same would apply to a child's background, as opposed to physical or intellectual characteristics, is doubtful.

INITIAL INTERVENTION – THE EMERGENCY PROTECTION OF CHILDREN

Once a case of suspected child abuse reaches level IV of the iceberg and becomes known to the agencies with powers and/or duties to intervene, the primary concern will be to protect the child from further abuse. However, in many cases this will not necessarily mean taking immediate action to remove the child from home. As 'Working Together' states:

> 'The removal of children from their home gives rise to public and professional concern, causes great distress if not handled sensitively, and can be damaging both for the child and for the rest of the family. Therefore, **except when a child is in acute physical danger it is essential that the the timing of the removal of children from their homes should be agreed following consultation with all appropriate professionals.** They should weigh up the likely immediate and long term effects of removing the child against the possibility of harm if they leave the child at home, and balance this with the need to secure evidence of criminal offences and, in some cases, to arrest the abuser...' (para 3.8)

Therefore, in many cases, the first stage of the investigation will involve consultation and planned intervention (see Chapter 4). However, there will be cases of extreme urgency where there is a risk to the life of a child or likelihood of serious injury and when immediate protective action is required. Such immediate protection may be achieved in one of three ways – by obtaining an emergency protection order, by taking the child into police protection or by removing the abuser from the home, either on a voluntary or compulsory basis.

Emergency protection orders (section 44)

Emergency protection orders provide immediate, short-term protection where there is a likelihood that a child will suffer significant harm without an order or where access to a child thought to be at risk of suffering such harm is denied. As the name suggests, these orders are for use in emergency situations and are not intended to be used as a routine response when suspicions of child abuse are aroused. Applications for an order are made to a family proceedings court, unless other proceedings in respect of the child concerned have already commenced in the High Court or county court. The application can be made *ex parte* and for these purposes a single justice can discharge the functions of the court.[6] Therefore, orders can be obtained at short notice where necessary outside normal court hours.

Who may apply and on what grounds?

There are three separate grounds for an emergency protection order:

- Significant harm.

  The court may make an order on the application of any person if, but only if, it is satisfied that there is reasonable cause to believe that the child is likely to suffer significant harm if:

  (i) he is not removed to accommodation provided by, or on behalf of, the applicant; or

  (ii) he does not remain in the place in which he is then being accommodated.

  In theory anyone can apply for an order on this ground, but if the child is to be removed from where he is, the applicant must be able to provide accommodation or have it provided for the child on his behalf. Whilst other family members may be quite willing to provide alternative accommodation themselves, the local authority will necessarily become involved by virtue of their duty to investigate under section 47 of the Act, and, in practice, the vast majority of orders are applied for by the local authority or NSPCC.

- Frustrated access – enquiries under section 47.

  The court may make an order on the application of the local authority if it is satisfied that:

  (i) enquiries are being made with respect to the child under section 47(1)(b); and

  (ii) those enquiries are being frustrated by access to the child being unreasonably refused to a person authorised to seek access and that the applicant has reasonable cause to believe that access to the child is required as a matter of urgency.

  A person authorised to seek access means an officer of the authority or a person authorised to make enquiries on the authority's behalf (section 44

---

6   FPCR (MR) 1991 Rule 2.

(2)(b)(i)). Unlike the previous ground, whereby the *court* must be satisfied that there is reasonable cause to believe that the child is likely to suffer significant harm, if enquiries are being made under section 47(1)(b) (whereby the local authority have reasonable cause to suspect that a child who lives, or is found, in their area is suffering, or likely to suffer, significant harm), the *applicant* must have reasonable cause to believe that access to the child is required as a matter of urgency.

• Frustrated access – enquiries by authorised person.

   The court may make an order on the application of an authorised person if it is satisfied that:

(i)   the applicant has reasonable cause to suspect that a child is suffering, or likely to suffer, significant harm;

(ii)   the applicant is making enquiries with respect to the child's welfare; and

(iii) those enquiries are being frustrated by access to the child being unreasonably refused to a person authorised to seek access and the applicant has reasonable cause to believe that access to the child is required as a matter of urgency.

Similar in effect to the previous ground, this allows an authorised person – defined to mean the NSPCC and any of its officers (section 31(9)) – to make the application.

Consequences of the order

An emergency protection order operates as a direction to any person, who is in a position to do so, to comply with any request to produce the child to the applicant (section 44(4)(a)). If it appears to the court making the order that adequate information as to the child's whereabouts is not available to the applicant for the order, but is available to another person, the court may include in the order a provision requiring that other person to disclose, if asked to do so by the applicant, any information that he may have as to the child's whereabouts (section 48(1)). The order may authorise the applicant to enter premises specified by the order and search for the child with respect to whom the order is made (section 48(3)). If the applicant has reasonable cause to believe that there may be another child at risk in the premises to be searched, the court may make an order authorising the applicant to search for that child on the premises concerned (section 48(4)). If the other child is then found on the premises and the applicant is satisfied that the grounds for making an emergency protection order exist with respect to him, the order has effect as if it were an emergency protection order (section 48(5)). Any person who intentionally obstructs the applicant in exercising these powers commits an offence (section 48(7)).

The order also operates to authorise the removal of the child, at any time, to accommodation provided by or on behalf of the applicant (section 44(4)(b)(i)), or the prevention of the child's removal from any hospital, or other place, in which he was being accommodated immediately before the making of the order (section 44(4)(b)(ii)). Therefore, the effect of the order is to allow the applicant to see the child and, if necessary either remove the child from where he or she is – eg an unsatisfactory home, or prevent the child from being moved away from existing accommodation – eg if the child is in hospital or being accommodated by the local authority. It is an offence to intentionally obstruct any person exercising the powers to remove, or prevent the removal of, a child (section 44(15)). In some circumstances there will be concern as to the immediate physical or mental condition of the child. The court may direct that the applicant, in exercising any of these powers, be accompanied by a registered medical practitioner, registered nurse or registered health visitor, if he so chooses (section 45(12)), and the court may also give such directions (if any) as it considers appropriate with respect to the medical or psychiatric or other assessment of the child (section 44(6)(b)).

However, the powers conferred by the order must only be exercised where necessary in order to safeguard the welfare of the child (section 44(5)(a)). Therefore a child produced unharmed, with no likelihood of significant harm occurring, should not be removed from home. If a child is removed or detained and the situation changes so that there is no longer any risk to the child, the applicant must return the child, or allow him to be removed, as the case may be (section 44(10)). If, during the period of the order, it becomes necessary to remove the child again in order to safeguard his or her welfare, this may be done. Obviously, in practice, it would be highly undesirable to remove a child on more than one occasion within such a short period of time.

The applicant is given parental responsibility for the child for the duration of the order (section 44(4)(c)), but may only take such action in meeting parental responsibility as is reasonably required to safeguard or promote the welfare of the child (having regard in particular to the duration of the order) (section 44(5)(b)). The acquisition of parental responsibility is not intended to be for the purpose of making long–term decisions about the child's life.

Duration of the order and contact with the child

An emergency protection order may only be granted initially for a period not exceeding eight days (section 45(1)), although provision is made for orders that would otherwise come to an end on public holidays (including Sundays) to end the following day (section 45(2)). A local authority or the NSPCC may apply to extend the order for up to a further seven days. The court may only extend the order if it has reasonable cause to believe that the child concerned is likely to suffer significant harm if the order is not extended, but an order can only be extended once (section 44(4)-(6)).

There is no right of appeal against the order, but the child, a parent, any person who has parental responsibility or any person with whom he or she was living immediately before the order was made may apply for the order to be discharged (section 45(8)-(10)). However, such an application cannot be made until the order has been in force for 72 hours, which should allow all involved 'breathing space', and allow time for reflection and, where necessary, initial assessment of the child.

During the continuance of the order, the applicant has a duty to allow the child reasonable contact with:

- his or her parents;

- any other person with parental responsibility;

- any person with whom he was living immediately before the order was made;

- any person with the benefit of a contact order under section 8 of the Act;

- any person who is allowed to have contact by virtue of a contact order under section 34 of the Act;

- any person acting on behalf of those persons (such as a doctor or an independent social worker) (section 44(13)).

If the applicant wishes to deny contact with any of these people, direction from the court must be sought (section 44(6)).

Police protection (section 46)

Emergency protection orders, although capable of being obtained at any time and at very short notice, nevertheless require application to be made to a court which necessarily results in some delay. In extreme emergencies, this delay could endanger the child and may even prove fatal. Police officers, however, have power under the Act to take immediate action by removing or detaining a child without a court order where the officer has reasonable cause to believe that a child would otherwise be likely to suffer significant harm (section 46). No specific powers of entry and search are conferred by the Act, but police officers have a general power under section 17(1)(e) of the Police and Criminal Evidence Act 1984 to enter premises without a warrant for the purposes of saving life and limb.

No child may be kept in police protection for more than 72 hours (section 46(6)). The officer taking the child into police protection must inform the local authority of the area in which the child was found of the steps that have been taken and the reason for taking them as soon as is reasonably practicable. If the child has sufficient understanding he must be given the same information, told of further steps which may be taken and his wishes and feelings ascertained (section 46(3)). The officer must also take reasonable steps to notify the child's parents, and other person with parental responsibility and any person with whom the child was living immediately before being taken into police protection of the steps taken in relation to the child, the reasons for taking them and any further steps which may be taken (section 46(4)).

Each police area has a designated officer who is responsible for inquiring into the case (section 46(3)(e)). The child must be released from police protection unless the designated officer considers that there is still reasonable cause for believing that the child would be likely to suffer significant harm if released (section 46(5)). If the child is kept in police protection, the designated officer may apply, on behalf of the appropriate authority, for an emergency protection order to be made, whether or not the authority knows of the application or agrees to it being made (section 46(7) and (8)). Unlike the situation with emergency protection orders, no parental responsibility is acquired by any police officer, but the designated officer has power to do what is reasonable in the circumstances to safeguard or promote the child's welfare (section 46(9)).

Just as contact between the child and specified individuals is provided for when an emergency protection order is made, when a child is taken into police protection the designated officer or the local authority looking after the child are required to allow those specified individuals reasonable contact (section 46(10) and (11)). However, as there will be no opportunity for a court to deny contact, the designated officer or local authority are only required to permit such contact if it is in the child's best interest.

Recovery of missing children

If a child is in care (see below), or is the subject of an emergency protection order or in police protection and it appears to the court that there is reason to believe that the child has been unlawfully taken away or is being unlawfully kept away from the responsible person (ie any person who, for the time being, has care of him or her by virtue of the care order, emergency protection order or section 46), or that the child has run away or is staying away from the responsible person the court may make a recovery order (section 50). The order secures the return of the missing child in the following ways:

- it directs any person who is in a position to do so to produce the child on request to any authorised person;

- it authorises the child's removal by any authorised person;

- it requires any person who has information as to the child's whereabouts to disclose that information to a constable or an officer of the court, if asked to do so;

- it authorises a constable to enter any premises specified in the order and search for the child, using reasonable force if necessary.

An authorised person for these purposes means any person specified by the court, any constable or any person who is authorised by a person who has parental responsibility for the child by virtue of the care order or emergency protection order, after the recovery order is made, to exercise any power under the recovery order (section 50(7)).

Any person who knowingly, and without lawful authority or reasonable excuse, takes a child away from the person responsible for his or her care by virtue of a care order, emergency protection order or police protection, or induces, assists or incites such a child to run away or stay away from the responsible person, commits an offence (section 49)), subject to restrictions concerning certified refuges for children (section 51)).

Removing the abuser

Voluntary removal

It is generally accepted that removing a child from home will inevitably be traumatic for the child. In cases where the suspected abuser is identified, if there is a non-abusing partner capable of caring for the child, the preferred course of action may well be to remove the abuser rather than the child. This may be done by informal pressure. The abuser, if faced with the stark choice of either leaving the family home himself or the child being removed, may well agree to leave voluntarily while the matter is further investigated. Indeed, it has been said:

'For the abuser to leave home following disclosure can be the most caring parental act possible under the circumstances.'[7]

Provision is made in the Act for local authorities to provide assistance with finding alternative accommodation or cash to the abuser who 'proposes to move from the premises' (section 17 and Schedule 2). However, bearing in mind the financial constraints local authorities now find themselves under, it seems doubtful that this provision will be relied on to any great extent in practice and, in any event, requires the co-operation of the alleged abuser which will not always be forthcoming.

Involuntary removal – ouster and exclusion orders

If the alleged abuser is not willing to leave the family home voluntarily, the non-abusing partner may be prepared to initiate domestic violence proceedings and apply to the court for an ouster or exclusion order, the central purpose of which is to regulate the conduct of spouses and cohabitees with regard to each other and with regard to the occupation of the family home.[8] However, such measures are dependent upon the non-abusing partner being prepared to take action. The Law Commission has recently proposed that the police should have the power to apply for such a civil remedy on behalf of the victim in appropriate cases.[9] But even if this recommendation is acted on, it will rarely be satisfactory as a means of child protection in an emergency situation.

During the passage of the Act through Parliament, there was considerable support for the inclusion of a power to oust a suspected abuser from the home instead of having to remove the child. It was proposed that, where a court had made an emergency protection order or an *interim* care order (see below), and it was satisfied that the child's welfare would be satisfactorily safeguarded or promoted if a person who was resident in the child's household were removed from that household, the court may in addition either make an order (exclusion order) requiring that person to vacate the household or accept an undertaking from that person that he or she would vacate the household.[10] However, it was decided to await the recommendations of the Law Commission's study on domestic violence and the occupation of family homes and no such power was included in the Act. The Law Commission has since recommended that the Act be amended to give courts the power to make a short-term emergency ouster order for the protection of children.[11]

---

7   Furniss, T (1991) *The Multi Professional Handbook of Child Sexual Abuse* London, Routledge p 234.

8   Domestic Violence and Matrimonial Proceedings Act or Domestic Proceedings and Magistrates Court Act 1978.

9   Law Commission No 207 (1992) *Report on Domestic Violence and Occupation of the Family Home.*

10   HL debate 27 October 1989.

11   See note 9.

Involuntary removal – the criminal law as a means of child protection[12]

Powers of arrest

Arrest is not primarily thought of as a means of protecting the child victim of abuse. However, a suspected abuser may be arrested under the powers contained in the Police and Criminal Evidence Act 1984 (PACE) if there are reasonable grounds to suspect that a criminal offence has been committed when a child has been abused and reasonable grounds to suspect the identity of the abuser (section 24(6)). The criterion of 'reasonable grounds to suspect' is the legal threshold for the exercise of coercive police powers under the Act. Generally, 'reasonable cause to suspect' requires a lower level of proof than 'reasonable cause to believe'. It has been said:

> 'If ... there are 10 steps from mere suspicion to a state of certainty ... then reasonable suspicion may be as low as step two or three, whilst reasonable belief may be as high as step nine or 10.'[13]

Therefore, whenever it is believed that a child has been abused and there are grounds for a court to make an emergency protection order or for the police to take a child into police protection (see above), then, provided there is reasonable suspicion as to the identity of the abuser, there would appear to be no reason why the abuser could not be arrested – an action which would obviate the need to remove the child from home.

Charging the suspect

The protection for the child by the arrest of the suspected abuser may only be short-term. In general, the arrested person may only be detained without charge for up to 24 hours (section 41 PACE). If, at the end of this period, no charge has been made, the suspect must be released and alternative forms of child protection considered. If, however, the police are satisfied that they have a reasonable prospect of conviction (bearing in mind the standard of proof in court and the available evidence) (see further Chapter 7) they may charge the abuser with a criminal offence. Once charged, the police will usually release the accused on bail. At the present time the police have no power to attach conditions to the bail, other than to require the accused to provide a surety. Section 27 of the Criminal Justice and Public Order Act 1994, which, along with other revised bail provisions in the Act, will be brought into force in

---

12 See Cobley, C (1992) 'Child Abuse, Child Protection and the Criminal Law' in *Journal of Child Law* 4(2) p 78.

13 Bevan, L & Lidstone, K (1985) *A guide to the Police and Criminal Evidence Act 1984*. London, Butterworths p 5.

Spring 1995, will give the police the power to attach conditions to bail where they are necessary to prevent the accused absconding, committing an offence, interfering with witnesses or otherwise obstructing the course of justice. This provision should help ensure the continued protection of the child (see below).

Alternatively, in certain circumstances the suspected abuser may be detained by the police and brought before a magistrates' court, usually within 24 hours of being charged (Section 38 PACE). In cases of child abuse, if there are reasonable grounds to believe (note: *believe* not *suspect*) that the abuser may commit further offences causing the child physical harm (but not moral or psychological harm), the abuser may be detained by the police after charge. In future, the continued detention of the accused will be easier to ensure as section 28 of the Criminal Justice and Public Order Act 1994 will also permit detention after charge if there are reasonable grounds to believe that it is necessary to prevent the accused from committing a further offence. Once the abuser is brought before a magistrates' court, the continued protection of the child can be assured in one of two ways – by a remand in custody or by a remand on bail with conditions attached.

Remands in custody

If a suspect has been detained by the police after charge, when he first appears before a magistrates' court the Bail Act 1976 normally provides him with a statutory right to bail. (Section 25 of the Criminal Justice and Public Order Act 1994 will restrict the statutory right to bail in serious offences where the accused has specified previous convictions.) However, where the suspect is accused of an offence punishable with imprisonment (as the vast majority of child abuse cases are), this statutory right to bail can be denied if the court is satisfied that certain conditions are met (section 4 of the Bail Act 1976). These conditions include there being substantial grounds for believing the suspect would commit further offences whilst on bail, or interfere with witnesses. The court will take various factors into consideration, including the seriousness of the offence, the character, antecedents and community ties of the accused, his or her record in respect of the fulfilment of his or her obligations under previous grants of bail in criminal proceedings (if relevant), the strength of evidence against him or her and any other matters which may be relevant.

In cases of intrafamilial abuse, it is unclear whether the court will take into consideration the presence or absence of the victim at home. Obviously, if the child has already been removed from home there may be less likelihood of the suspect committing further offences or interfering with witnesses – for example by putting pressure on the child to withdraw allegations of abuse. Yet it may well be that the child protection agencies will await the court's decision as to a remand in custody to save the unnecessary removal of the child from home. In such a case, will the court take this into consideration when deciding? Given the presumption in favour of bail, it would seem doubtful, especially as in most cases the protection of the child may be assured by attaching conditions to a bail order.

Remands on bail

The balance of the decision of the court to remand a suspect in custody or on bail may well rest on the ability of the court to impose meaningful conditions of bail. The most common requirement of bail is to provide a surety, but of more practical importance in cases of child abuse is the court's ability to impose any conditions of bail which are designed to prevent the suspect from absconding, committing further offences, interfering with witnesses or otherwise obstructing the course of justice (section 3(6) Bail Act 1976). With such flexibility, the court may impose conditions requiring the abuser to live at a specified address, or not to contact a specified person or go within a certain distance of a specified place. In this way the protection of the child may be continued as the abuser can be prevented from having any contact with the child.

It can be seen how the initial arrest of the alleged abuser may well act as a form of protection for the child. If there is insufficient evidence to charge, the protection may be short-lived (up to 24 hours), but if a charge is made, the protection may continue right up until the trial – and beyond if a conviction is obtained.

PROTECTING CHILDREN – LONG-TERM SOLUTIONS

In many cases of suspected abuse, no immediate protective action will be deemed necessary. An investigation will be conducted in accordance with the Area Child Protection Committee procedures (see Chapter 4), the prime tasks of which are to establish the facts about the circumstances giving rise to the concern, to decide if there are grounds for the concern, to identify sources and levels of risk and to decide protective or other action in relation to the child and any others.[14] At various points during the investigation, certain legal procedures may be invoked (see below).

---

14 Department of Health, (1991) 'Working Together under the Children Act 1989' London, HMSO para 5.14.3.

Child assessment orders (section 43)

The local authority has a duty to investigate when there is reasonable cause to suspect that a child is suffering, or is likely to suffer significant harm (see Chapter 4). In situations where the child is not thought to be in immediate danger, no emergency action will be necessary. Typically, the nature of the harm suspected may be long-term and cumulative rather than acute and severe – the child may be failing to thrive, there may be suspicions as to neglect or sexual abuse which give cause for concern but which do not place the child at serious immediate risk. However, the local authority will need to see the child and will often want the child to be assessed in order to establish if the concern of significant harm is justified. The assessment may take several forms – a medical assessment carried out by a doctor, an assessment of the child's developmental level carried out by a doctor, health visitor or child psychologist, an assessment of the child's general health, including height, weight, vision, hearing and immunisation record carried out by a health visitor or school nurse, a comprehensive assessment conducted by social workers to collect and evaluate information on the child and his or her family on which to base long-term decisions, or a special educational needs assessment in order to make appropriate educational provision for the child. The parents, or those responsible for caring for the child, will often be prepared to co-operate and the court's intervention is usually not required at this stage.

Inevitably, though, there will be occasions when the local authority is denied access to the child and so is unable to carry out an assessment. In such circumstances an application can be made to the court for a child assessment order. If the local authority already has firm evidence that the child is suffering, or is likely to suffer significant harm, an application should be made for an emergency protection order or a care or supervision order. A child assessment order is not intended for use in emergencies. The order has been described as a 'multi-disciplinary assessment in non-emergency situations'[15] and is clearly less interventionist than an emergency protection order. The order is new to the Act and its inclusion is mainly due to the recommendation by the report into the death of Kimberley Carlile.[16] The purpose of the order is to allow an assessment of the child to take place, but to avoid the unnecessary removal of a child from home.

Application and criteria for the order

The decision to apply for a child assessment order will usually be taken at a child protection conference (see Chapter 4). Only a local authority or a person

---

15 HC Debate, 23 October 1989, Vol 158, Col 596.
16 DHSS (1987) 'A Child in Mind: Protection of Children in a Responsible Society'.

who is authorised to apply for a care or supervision order (namely the NSPCC or its officers) may make an application (section 43(1)). Unlike applications for emergency protection orders, which may be made *ex parte*, the applicant for a child assessment order must take such steps as are reasonably practicable to ensure that seven days' notice of the application is given to the child, his or her parents, any other person who has parental responsibility for the child or with whom the child is living or in whose favour a contact order is in force (either under section 8 or under section 34 in respect of a child in care) (section 43(11)).

The court may make an order if it is satisfied that:

(a) the applicant has reasonable cause to suspect that a child is suffering, or is likely to suffer significant harm;

(b) an assessment of the state of the child's health or development, or of the way in which he or she has been treated, is required to enable the applicant to determine whether or not the child is suffering, or is likely to suffer, significant harm; and

(c) it is unlikely that such an assessment will be made, or be satisfactory, in the absence of a child assessment order.

Even if these conditions are satisfied, the court must bear in mind the welfare principle and the concept of 'no order'. Furthermore, if the court is satisfied that there are grounds for making an emergency protection order, and that this would be a more appropriate order to make, the application should be treated as an application for an emergency protection order and a child assessment order should not be made (section 43(3) & (4)). A guardian *ad litem* will usually be appointed to represent the best interests of the child and to advise the court (see Chapter 6).

Effect of the order

A child assessment order imposes a duty on any person who is in a position to do so to produce the child to any person named in the order and to comply with any directions for assessment the order may contain (section 43(6)(a)). It also authorises any person carrying out the assessment, or part of it, to do so in accordance with the terms of the order (section 43(7)). However, if a child has sufficient understanding to make an informed decision, he or she may refuse to submit to a medical or psychiatric examination or any other assessment (section 43(8)). The order must specify the date on which the assessment is to begin and will have an effect for a maximum of seven days from that date unless limited to less (section 43(5)). The child may only be kept away from home if this is specified in the order and if it is necessary to do so for the purpose of the assessment (section 43(9)). The court is unlikely to allow a child to be kept away from home overnight solely for the convenience of those carrying out the order, but on occasions this may be necessary if the child is to be properly assessed. In view of the fact that an order only extends for a maximum of seven days, arrangements for carrying out the assessment will usually be made in advance of the application being made to a court, thus ensuring that once intervention is authorised, delay is kept to a minimum.

Once the assessment is complete, the applicant must decide what further action, if any, is required. If the assessment produces evidence which affirms the initial suspicions as to significant harm, steps should be taken to protect the child, either by application for an emergency protection order, if appropriate, or by the provision of voluntary accommodation or application for a care or supervision order (see below).

Care and supervision orders (section 31)

Applying for the order

Prior to the implementation of the Act, a care order could be made by a variety of different routes, not all of which involved the child's development being impaired. The Act radically reformed the law in this area by providing only one route into care – that contained in section 31 of the Act. Only a local authority or authorised person can apply for a care or supervision order. At the present time only the NSPCC has been so authorised by order of the Secretary of State. The NSPCC must, if reasonably practical to do so, consult with the local authority in whose area the child resides before making an application under section 31 (section 31(6)). In practice, if arrangements for inter-agency co-operation are adhered to, such consultation will be automatic. Before a care or supervision order can be made, the court must be satisfied that the criteria set out in section 31(2) are met. These criteria are:

(a) that the child concerned is suffering, or is likely to suffer, significant harm; and

(b) that the harm, or likelihood of harm, is attributable to:

   (i) the care given to the child, or likely to be given if the order was not made, not being what it would be reasonable to expect a parent to give him; or

   (ii) the child's being beyond parental control.

The concept of 'significant harm' has already been discussed. In deciding whether or not the child *is* suffering' significant harm, the courts initially adopted the same approach as had been adopted under the old law. In *Northampton County Council v S and Others*,[17] Ewbank J said:

'... the words "is suffering" in s 31(2)(a) ... relate to the period immediately before the process of protecting the child concerned is first put into motion ... That means that the court has to consider the position immediately before an emergency protection order, if there was one, or an interim care order, if that was the initiation of protection ...'

However, in the later case of *Re M (a minor) (Care order: significant harm)*,[18] Balcombe LJ, in the Court of Appeal, stated that the relevant time is that at which the court is considering whether to make the relevant order. It therefore followed that if the child was no longer suffering significant harm at the time of the hearing of the application for a care order, the relevant criterion would not be satisfied. On the facts of the case, at the time of the final hearing, the child concerned was settled with foster parents and was not, at that time, suffering significant harm, nor was he likely to suffer such harm if a care order was not made as his mother was dead, his father was serving a sentence of life imprisonment for the mother's murder and an aunt had applied for a residence order in respect of the child. The Court of Appeal therefore ruled that the threshold criteria were not met and that a care order should not have been made. This ruling caused considerable concern amongst practitioners working to protect children. It was pointed out that if one had to look at whether a child, who may have been looked after by the local authority for several months subject to emergency protection and interim care orders, was continuing to suffer significant harm at the date of the full care hearing, it meant that the more a local authority did to protect a child before a full hearing, the less chance it had of proving its case[19] – a situation which is patently illogical and surely cannot be what Parliament intended. Although in many cases the local authority would be able to satisfy the alternative anticipated harm test, this will not necessarily always be so, as the facts of *Re M* itself illustrate. The case was appealed to the House of Lords, where Lord Templeman described the appeal as:

'... an illustration of the tyranny of language and the importance of ascertaining and giving effect to the intentions of Parliament by construing a statute in accordance with the spirit rather than the letter of the Act.'

The House of Lords ruled that the natural construction of the conditions in section 31(2) is that where, at the time the application is to be disposed of, there are arrangements in place for the protection of the child by the local authority on an *interim* basis which protection had been continuously in place

---

17   [1993] 1 FLR 554.
18   [1994] 1 FLR 74 CA, [1994] 3 All ER 298 HL.
19   Smith, V (1994) 'Significant Harm' in *Family Law* [1994] 197.

for some time, the relevant date with respect to which the court must be satisfied is the date at which the local authority initiated the procedure for protection under the Act from which these arrangements followed. This is undoubtedly a logical construction of the statute. As Lord Mackay commented: 'it would be odd if the jurisdiction of the court to make an order depended on how long the court took before it finally disposed of the case'.

Alternatively, the court may be satisfied that the child 'is likely to suffer' significant harm. In recommending the inclusion of such a criterion, it was suggested in the *Review of Child Care Law*[20] that it would place a burden of proof upon local authorities which would be sufficiently difficult for them to discharge and that it would prevent unwarranted intervention. The courts have since made it clear that the phrase 'likely to suffer' is not to be equated with the burden of proof in civil proceedings – 'on the balance of probabilities' (see Chapter 7) – but that an *assessment* of future risk is required. In many cases both the present and anticipated harm criteria will be satisfied, but the inclusion of anticipated harm in the threshold criteria allows, for example, care proceedings to be considered in the case of newborn babies.

Before a care or supervision order can be made, the court must also be satisfied that the harm or likelihood of harm is attributable to poor parenting or the child being beyond parental control. In circumstances where it is suspected that a parent has abused the child, there will usually be little difficulty in proving this causal link, particularly in cases of deliberate physical or sexual abuse. Cases of neglect or emotional abuse may be more difficult. The standard of care required is clearly objective from the parent's point of view – that which it would be reasonable to expect a parent to give. However, the standard of care must also be related to the needs of the child concerned, which incorporates a subjective element into the test. Thus some children, for example those with a disability, may require a higher standard of care than others and a reasonable parent will be expected to provide this higher standard in the circumstances. So, if parents are doing the best they can, but are nevertheless failing to meet the required standard of care, and as a consequence the child is suffering or is likely to suffer significant harm, the threshold criteria will be satisfied and an order may be made. In situations where abuse by a third party is suspected, the causal link will only be satisfied if the parent has failed to do what it would be reasonable to expect a parent to do to prevent the harm.

Even if these criteria are satisfied, an application for a care or supervision order will not necessarily be successful. The court will have to consider the principle of non-intervention (section 1(5)) and is also required to have regard to the range of powers available to it under the Act (section 1(3) & (4)). These include the making of section 8 orders, family assistance orders and education

---

20   DHSS (1985) note 2 *supra* para 15.18.

supervision orders (see below). It must be remembered that the child's welfare is the court's paramount consideration (section 1(1)). Care orders are generally viewed as state intervention in its most draconian form and if alternative orders are available that would ensure the child is protected from abuse and would best serve his or her welfare, such alternative orders should made.

Effect of care order

Section 33 of the Act provides that where a care order is made in respect of a child it shall be the duty of the local authority designated by the order to receive the child into its care and to keep him in their care while the order remains in force. Section 100 of the Act excludes the wardship jurisdiction and the inherent jurisdiction of the High Court in respect of children to be placed in care or who are in care (see below). Therefore, once a care order is made, the court can no longer monitor the administrative arrangements for the child. Responsibility for the care of the child is firmly with the local authority and the responsibilities of the court cease unless a substantive issue comes before the court, for example, an application for a contact order under section 34 (see below). The court has no power to add any direction to the care order. In the case of *Re T (a minor) (Care order: conditions)*[21] the local authority had applied for a care order with a view to placing the child for adoption, an application initially supported by the guardian *ad litem*. The parents had conceded that the threshold criteria under section 31 of the Act were met, but had argued that a supervision order was appropriate. The judge made a supervision order with conditions attached. The local authority appealed. Between the hearing before the judge and the hearing of the appeal the guardian's view changed and she recommended that there should be a care order with the child remaining with his parents. The local authority stated that if the court allowed the appeal and made a care order, the care plan would remain the same and the child would be removed from his parents and placed for adoption. The guardian then, on balance, supported the parents' submissions. It was argued that, if the welfare principle is truly paramount, the court must have the power, when initiating the placement into care, to make an order which reflects the full scope of its perceptions of the child's welfare. This argument was rejected by the Court of Appeal, who dismissed the local authority's appeal. It was held that the only care order which can be made is one which 'places' the child in care. The welfare test is applied when the court 'is considering' whether or not to make a care order. Nourse J pointed out that:

> '... it is the duty of any court hearing an application for a care order carefully to scrutinise the local authority's care plan. If it does not agree with the care plan, it can refuse to make a care order. The cases in which it is appropriate to take such a course will no doubt be rare.'

---

21 *Re T (a minor) (care order: conditions)* [1994] 2 FLR 423.

When an order is made, the local authority acquires parental responsibility, one that is shared with those who already have it in relation to the child and there are limits on the powers of the local authority while it has a care order (section 33(3). For example the local authority may not change a child's religion, consent to his adoption, or appoint a guardian for the child (section 33(6)). The local authority is specifically given the power to determine the extent to which the parent or guardian may meet his or her parental responsibility for the child (section 33(3)(b)), but the local authority may only exercise this power if it is satisfied that it is necessary to do so in order to safeguard or promote the child's welfare (section 33(4)). The parent or guardian of a child remains able to do whatever is reasonable in the circumstances to safeguard and promote the child's welfare.

In the past it was common to refer to a child being 'taken into care' with the emphasis being placed on the physical removal of the child from his parents, who subsequently lost all rights over the child. Although, in many cases, it will be necessary for the child to be removed from home if the courts have seen fit to make a care order, this is not necessarily true of all cases. A child who is the subject of a care order may be accommodated in a residential home, may be placed with foster parents or may be allowed to remain at home with parents. In any event, parents retain parental responsibility for the child. Parents and local authorities are expected to work in partnership to ensure that the child's best interests are served. The local authority has ultimate control, but is expected to consult those with parental responsibility for the child and, wherever possible, reach agreement before taking action. As the Children Act Advisory Committee pointed out:

'The granting of a care order should not of itself impede a local authority from continuing its efforts at working in partnership with the parents. The two processes are not mutually exclusive. Each has a role to play, often simultaneously, in the case management of a child at risk.'[22]

A care order will continue in force until the child reaches the age of 18 (section 91(11)). However, the child, the local authority or any person with parental responsibility for the child may apply to the court for the order to be discharged before that time (section 39(1)). In practice, most applications for discharge are made by local authorities. [23]

Contact with children in care

Prior to the Children Act, contact with children in care was totally at the discretion of the local authority, who had the power to control or deny access to or by a child in care, although parents, guardians and custodians were

---

22   Children Act Advisory Committee Annual Report 1992/93 p 34.
23   Bromley & Lowe (1992) Bromley's *Family Law* 8th ed London, Butterworths p 528.

entitled to challenge a refusal to allow access in court.[24] The Act introduces a presumption of reasonable contact between a child in care and his parents, guardians, those who had a residence order in force at the time the care order was made, and those who had care of the child under a High Court Order (section 34(1)). In addition, the local authority has a duty to promote contact between the child and his parents, relatives, friends and others connected with him (Schedule 3 para 15(1)). These provisions emphasise the desirability of the child maintaining links with his family whilst in care. If a dispute arises and reasonable contact cannot be agreed, the local authority, the child or any person entitled to reasonable contact can apply to the court for a contact order. The court can make whatever order it considers appropriate and conditions may be imposed (section 34(2) & (3)). However, there will inevitably be situations, particularly in cases of child abuse, where continued contact with his or her family may not be thought to be in the child's best interests. If the local authority wishes to deny contact to a parent or any other person entitled to reasonable contact, it must first apply to the court, which may make an order refusing contact (section 34(4)). A similar order can be made on the application of the child. However, in an emergency, the local authority can refuse contact for up to seven days if it is necessary to do so in order to safeguard or promote the child's welfare (section 34(6)).

Supervision orders

A supervision order places the child under the supervision of a local authority or, if the local authority so requests, a probation officer. Unlike a care order, the local authority does not acquire parental responsibility and the court cannot make both a care order and a supervision order. The order lasts for one year, but on an application by the supervisor it may be extended by the court for up to three years from the date it was made (Schedule 3 para 6). The order ends automatically when the child reaches the age of 18 (section 91(13)). While a supervision order is in force, the supervisor has a duty to:

(a) advise, assist and befriend the supervised child;

(b) take such steps as are reasonably necessary to give effect to the order;

(c) consider whether or not to apply for discharge or variation where the order is no longer wholly complied with or may no longer be necessary (Section 35(1)).

Conditions may be imposed in supervision orders requiring those responsible for the child (with that person's consent) and the child himself to comply with directions given by the supervisor. Such directions may specify where the child lives and may require the child to participate in specified activities (Schedule 3).

---

24 Section 12A Child Care Act 1980.

Psychiatric and medical examinations and treatment

The supervisor is not empowered to give a direction as to the child's medical or psychiatric examination or treatment, but the court itself may include such directions in the supervision order. The court may direct that the child submit to a psychiatric examination or submit to any examination from time to time as directed by the supervisor (Schedule 3 para 4(1)). This examination will usually be as a non-resident patient. However, if the court is satisfied on the evidence of a registered medical practitioner that the child may be suffering from a physical or mental condition that requires, or may be susceptible to, treatment and a period as a resident patient is necessary if the examination is to be carried out properly, then the court may direct that the child be required to attend a hospital or mental nursing home as an in-patient (Schedule 3 para 4(3)).

If the court is satisfied on the evidence of a registered general practitioner that the physical condition of the supervised child is such as requires, or may be susceptible to, treatment, the court may include in the order a requirement that the child submit to specified treatment (Schedule 3 para 5(3)). Similar conditions apply to requiring the child to submit to psychiatric treatment, except that the doctor must be approved under section 12 of the Mental Health Act 1983 and the court must be satisfied that the child's condition does not warrant detention under the mental health legislation (Schedule 3 para 5(1)).

Where the medical practitioner, under whose direction the treatment is to be given, is unwilling to continue to treat or direct the treatment or is of the opinion that:

(a) the treatment should be continued beyond the period specified in the order;

(b) the supervised child needs different treatment;

(c) the child is not susceptible to treatment; or

(d) the child does not require further treatment;

the practitioner must make a written report to the supervisor who must then refer the matter to the court which may cancel or vary the requirement (Schedule 3 para 5(7)).

In all cases, the court must be satisfied that satisfactory arrangements have been, or can be, made for the examination or treatment and, in cases where a child has sufficient understanding to make an informed decision, the child must consent before the court can include a requirement of examination or treatment in the supervision order (Schedule 3 paras 4(4) and 5(5)).

Interim orders

There may well be circumstances where the court will not be in a position to make a final care or supervision order, yet steps may need to be taken to ensure the child is suitably protected while proceedings are progressing. In these circumstances, the court has the power to make an interim care or supervision order. It also has the power to make a section 8 order for a limited period (see below). If the court adjourns proceedings on an application for a care or supervision order, or the court gives a direction under section 37 and is satisfied that there are reasonable grounds for believing that the threshold criteria in section 31(2) are satisfied, the court may make an interim care or supervision order (section 38 (1) & (2)). Such orders are limited by the Act for an initial maximum of eight weeks, although extensions of up to four weeks may be granted following an application. However, the court must ensure that the statutory criteria are still met when extending the interim order. The effect of an interim order is essentially the same as a full order, except that the power of the court to include in a final supervision order a requirement for medical or psychiatric examination or treatment does not apply to interim supervision orders. However, the court has specific power, on making an interim care or supervision order, to give such directions as it considers appropriate with regard to the medical or psychiatric examination or other assessment of the child, which the child, if of sufficient understanding to make an informed decision, may refuse (section 38(6)). Such a direction may be to the effect that there is to be no examination or assessment, thus protecting children from being subjected to repeated examinations for forensic or other purposes (section 38(7)).

When making interim orders, the court must have regard to the welfare principle (section 1), the principle of non-intervention (section 1(5)) and the presumption that delay is likely to prejudice the welfare of the child. The Children Act Advisory Committee has expressed the view that interim care orders should, in fact, be used only rarely and are essentially designed to preserve the decision pending a final hearing.

Section 8 orders

In any family proceedings under Parts I, II and IV of the 1989 Act (which includes applications for care and supervision orders (section 8(4)), subject to certain restrictions, the court has power to make any of the following four orders under section 8:

- a residence order – an order settling the arrangements to be made as to with whom a child is to live;

- a contact order – an order requiring the person with whom a child lives, or is to live, to allow the child to visit or stay with the person named in the order, or for that person and the child otherwise to have contact;

- a prohibited steps order – an order that no step, which could be taken by a parent in meeting his parental responsibility for a child, and which is of a kind specified in the order, shall be taken by any person without the consent of the court;

- a specific issue order – an order giving directions for the purpose of determining a specific question which has arisen, or which may arise, in connection with any aspect of parental responsibility for a child.

A section 8 order may contain directions about how the order is to be carried into effect and may also impose conditions which must be complied with by any person in whose favour the order is made, who is a parent of the child concerned, who is not a parent but who has parental responsibility or with whom the child is living (section 11(7)).

Local authorities and section 8 orders

There are restrictions on the ability of the court to make section 8 orders, particularly in the case of local authorities. If a care order has been made in respect of a child, then only a residence order can be made under section 8 (section 9(1)). (If a residence order is made in respect of a child in care, it has the effect of discharging the care order.) Contact with children in care is governed by section 34 (see above) and so a contact order under section 8 is not relevant. Even if no care order has been made, the local authority is not entitled to apply for a residence order or contact order and the court may not make such an order in their favour (section 9(2)). Furthermore, the court cannot make a specific issue order or a prohibited steps order with a view to achieving a result which could be achieved by making a residence or contact order (section 9(5)).

These restrictions limit the potential use of section 8 orders in cases of child abuse and the Court of Appeal has recently made it clear that local authorities are expected to use the 'public law' route to protect children rather than seeking to use section 8 orders. In *Nottingham County Council v P*,[25] a father had sexually abused his eldest daughter, and his two younger daughters were at risk of abuse while he remained in the family home. The local authority sought a prohibited steps order requiring the father neither to reside in the same household as the girls nor to have contact with them unless they wished, and any such contact was to be supervised by the local authority. At first instance it was held that the court had no jurisdiction to make a prohibited steps order because it was, in reality, being sought to achieve a result which could be achieved by making a residence or contact order. However, the judge made a residence order in favour of the mother, with conditions imposed under section 11 that the father be excluded from the home. On appeal, the Court of Appeal ruled that the judge had been right to refuse the local authority's application for a prohibited steps order but wrong to have made the residence order, holding that it was both artificial and inappropriate to make the order on the authority's initiative because the authority could neither enforce it nor prevent the mother from applying for it

---

25 [1993] 1 FCR 180 FD.

to be discharged. The court made it clear that where children are found to be at risk of suffering significant harm, authorities are required to assume responsibility and to intervene in family arrangements to protect the children. They should do this, however, under Part IV of the Act which is specifically designed to accommodate public law applications.[26]

Family assistance orders (section 16)

In any family proceedings (see above) the court has the power to make a family assistance order which requires a local authority or probation officer to advise, assist and (where appropriate) befriend any person named in the order. Those who may be named in the order include the child, any parent (which includes the unmarried father) or guardian, any person with whom the child is living or in whose favour a contact order is in force. Such orders can be made whether or not any other orders are made, but the court must be satisfied that the circumstances of the case are exceptional and that any adult named in the order consents to the order being made. A family assistance order is intended only as a short-term remedy and thus has effect for a maximum of six months. The order will not be appropriate if there are unresolved child protection issues.

Education supervision orders (section 36)

Prior to the implementation of the Act, a care order was available as a sanction for failure to attend school. In certain circumstances, a court may now find that failure to attend school is evidence that the child is suffering or likely to suffer significant harm and may make a care order,[27] but the Act creates a new order specifically devised for such situations. A local education authority may apply for the order, which the court may make if it is satisfied that the child concerned is of compulsory school age and is not being properly educated (section 36(1) & (3)). The order puts the child under the supervision of the local education authority, but this order cannot be put into effect with respect to a child who is in the care of the local authority (section 36(6)). Such an order is unlikely to be of use in cases of child abuse. Although many neglected children have poor attendance at school, an education supervision order affords no protection for the child and it is unlikely that the local education authority would wish to take action independently of the local authority.

---

26 See further Cobley & Lowe (1994) 'Ousting Abusers - Public or Private Law Solution? in *Law Quarterly Review* [1994] 110 p 38.

27 *Re O (a minor) (care order: education: procedure)* [1992] 2 FLR 7.

WARDSHIP AND THE COURT'S INHERENT JURISDICTION

The Act provides extensive statutory jurisdiction over children and, in the vast majority of cases of child abuse, the provisions of the Act will be sufficient to ensure the protection of the child. However, in addition to this statutory jurisdiction, the High Court retains an inherent jurisdiction, which includes wardship, and cases may occur when it will be necessary to invoke this jurisdiction. If a child is made a ward of court, legal control over the child vests in the court and, prior to the implementation of the Act, local authorities made frequent use of wardship as, once made a ward of court, the child could be placed in the care of the local authority. However, the Act makes wardship and local authority care incompatible. Wards of court can no longer be committed into local authority care (section 100(1)) and the clear message is that local authorities should use the statutory provisions to protect abused children. Although it remains possible for a third party to invoke the wardship jurisdiction to protect an abused child, this should rarely be necessary. The local authority will have the means to protect the child through the statutory jurisdiction and concerned relatives of the child can now seek, albeit with leave, section 8 orders in the lower courts.

Despite the decline in the use of wardship, it is now clear that the High Court retains a separate inherent jurisdiction, referred to in section 100 of the Act. The precise scope of this jurisdiction is a matter of some debate,[28] but it certainly includes the use of injunctions and the sanctioning of medical treatment contrary to the child's wishes[29] (see further Chapter 6). The jurisdiction may be invoked by any person, but in practice it is most likely to be used by a local authority. Once a care order has been made, the court is unable to make any section 8 order with respect to the child and thus, if further child protection issues arise, it may be necessary to apply to the High Court to exercise its inherent jurisdiction. However, the local authority requires the leave of the court. Section 100(4) makes it clear that the court will only grant such leave if it is satisfied that the result which the authority wishes to achieve could not be achieved through the making of any other order and there is reasonable cause to believe that if the court's inherent jurisdiction is not exercised with respect to the child he or she is likely to suffer significant harm. No such restriction is placed on applications made by other individuals, although, in practice, it is doubtful whether the jurisdiction could be successfully invoked by third parties for child protection purposes, especially when the child concerned is in the care of the local authority.

---

28 Bromley & lowe (1992) Bromley's *Family Law* 8th ed London, Butterworths p 480.
29 *Re W (a minor) (consent to medical treatment)* [1993] 1 FLR 1.

IS THE LEGAL FRAMEWORK SUFFICIENT TO PROTECT CHILDREN?

The restrictions placed on local authorities' use of wardship and the court's inherent jurisdiction by the 1989 Act have given rise to some concern. In *Nottingham County Council v P* (see above), the local authority declined to apply for a care or supervision order, despite a direction pursuant to section 37 of the Act, and the decision of the Court of Appeal, although technically correct, meant that there were no orders in force which were capable of regulating and safeguarding the position of the children. The local authority responded to the direction, as required by section 37(3) by merely stating 'it did not feel it appropriate' to make an application for a care or supervision order as it did not believe the orders would be effective in the protection of the children. As the court noted, that is clearly not a satisfactory answer, yet the court had no power to take further action, being prevented from using wardship or its inherent jurisdiction by section 100 of the Act. As the President of the court concluded:

> 'The court is deeply concerned at the absence of any power to direct this local authority to take steps to protect the children. In the former wardship jurisdiction it might well have been able to do so. The operation of the Children Act 1989 is entirely dependent upon the full co-operation of all those involved. This includes the courts, local authorities and the social workers, and all who have to deal with children. Unfortunately, as appears from this case, if a local authority doggedly resists taking the steps which are appropriate to the case of children at risk of suffering significant harm it appears that the court is powerless ... The position is one which it is to be hoped will not recur and that lessons will be learnt from this unhappy catalogue of errors.'

The concern is that there is no guarantee that the problem will not recur. The Court of Appeal in *Re T* (above) had no doubt that there are other circumstances in which the court's wish to impose a particular result which it perceives to be in the interests of the child will be frustrated by the restrictions on the court's powers imposed by Part IV and section 100 of the Act.[30] The provisions of the Act are perfectly adequate to protect children when the views of the court and the local authority as to what action should be taken in the child's best interests coincide, but conflict is inevitable when they do not. If the local authority applies for an order, the court can refuse to make the order, even if the relevant criteria are met, having regard to the presumption of no order and what it perceives to be the child's best interests. However, if a local authority are reluctant to make what the court perceives to be a necessary application – whether the reluctance stems from a genuine belief that the application is not in the child's best interests or, more worryingly, because of

---

30 *Re T (a minor) (care order: conditions)* [1994] 2 FLR 423 at 427.

the financial implications involved – the court has no power to take any action to protect the child. Such circumstances are, thankfully, likely to be rare. Yet it strongly suggests that the court itself needs a residual power to control matters – a power that is evidently lacking at present.

CHAPTER 4

'WORKING TOGETHER' – THE PRACTICAL FRAMEWORK OF CHILD PROTECTION

'WORKING TOGETHER' – THE UNDERLYING THEORY

Once an allegation or suspicion of child abuse has been brought to the tip of the iceberg (see Chapter 2) and come to the attention of the authorities, investigations need to be made. The primary responsibility for this is placed on the local authority who are under a statutory duty imposed by section 47 of the Children Act which provides:

(1) Where a local authority –

(a) is informed that a child who lives, or is found, in its area –

    (i)   is the subject of an emergency protection order; or

    (ii) is in police protection; or

(b) has reasonable cause to suspect that a child who lives, or is found, in its area is suffering, or is likely to suffer, significant harm, the authority shall make, or cause to be made, such enquiries as it considers necessary to enable them to decide whether it should take any action to safeguard or promote the child's welfare.

Alternatively, a local authority may be directed to investigate by a court. Section 37 of the Act provides:

(1) Where, in any family proceedings in which a question arises with respect to the welfare of any child, it appears to the court that it may be appropriate for a care or supervision order to be made with respect to him, the court may direct the appropriate authority to undertake an investigation of the child's circumstances.

However, although the primary responsibility for investigating rests with local authorities, they are not expected to investigate alone – it has long been recognised that the proper and effective investigation of child abuse and protection of children requires co-operation between all professions and agencies with staff that are in direct contact with children and families. These may include the police, health authorities, family practitioner committees, local education authorities, the probation service, the NSPCC and other voluntary agencies. Obviously, not all agencies will be involved in every case, but the list gives an indication of the many possible combinations of agencies that may play a part in investigating abuse and protecting children from further abuse. If the best interests of the child are to be served, these agencies and the various professions involved within them must work together towards the common goal of protecting the child. The need for such joint involvement was stressed by the Cleveland Report which recommended:

> 'The development of inter-agency co-operation which acknowledges no single agency – health, social services, police or voluntary organisation – has the pre-eminent responsibility in the assessment of child abuse generally and child sexual abuse specifically. Each agency has a prime responsibility for a particular aspect of the problem.'[1]

Local authorities and health authorities have long been required to co-operate with one another in order to 'secure and advance the health and welfare of the people of England'.[2] However, this requirement has been described as being 'of no practical value' because it was written in such general terms.[3] The report of the enquiry into the death of Jasmine Beckford concluded that there were powerful reasons why this duty to co-operate should, in the context of child abuse, be made more specific.[4] The Children Act 1989 imposes such a duty in section 46, requiring, *inter alia*, any local education and housing authorities and any health authority to assist a local authority when conducting enquiries under section 47 of the Act if required to do so, unless it would be unreasonable in the circumstances.[5]

Several other agencies have statutory duties and/or powers, and all agencies have specific functions and professional objectives. For example, the NSPCC's Royal Charter places upon it a duty 'to ensure an appropriate and speedy response to all cases where children are alleged to be at risk of abuse or neglect in any form'. The police, in addition to the many powers they share with the local authority for the protection of children, have a general responsibility for the protection of life and limb, the prevention and investigation of crime, and the submission of cases for criminal prosecution. Clearly, many agencies may have duties or powers which may assist in the investigation of cases of suspected child abuse. The willingness and ability of these different agencies to communicate and co-operate form the basis of investigating a case of suspected child abuse.

---

1   Butler Sloss, E (1988) 'Report of the Inquiry into Child Abuse in Cleveland 1987' Cmnd 412 London, HMSO p 248.

2   See, for example, section 22 National Health Service Act 1975.

3   Blom Cooper, L (1988) 'Roles of Good Law and Practice' in *Journal of Social Welfare Law* no 2 p 101.

4   Brent Area Health Authority (1985) 'A Child in Trust: Report of the panel of inquiry into the circumstances surrounding the death of Jasmine Beckford' London Borough of Brent 1985.

5   See also the duty imposed by section 27 of the Act requiring, *inter alia*, local education authorities, housing authorities and health authorities to assist local authorities in carrying out their functions under Part III of the Act

INTER-AGENCY CO-OPERATION – A NEW IDEA?

A recognition that inter-agency co-operation is required to deal with the problem of child abuse is not new. As long ago as 1950, a Government circular on the ill-treatment of children recommended the establishment of Children's Co-ordinating Committees.[6] In the 1960s the 'battered baby' syndrome was recognised and information began to be shared between doctors, the police and social workers. By the early 1970s, inter-agency co-operation had become commonplace. In 1972, the DHSS reported that most areas had in existence a review committee to plan local policy and management and to co-operate with adjacent areas. In May 1973, a study group was set up under the chairmanship of Dr A W Franklin. The group was composed of professionals involved with child abuse and saw itself as providing a link between the medical profession, the social services, the legal profession and the police.[7] The study group conference was attended by Sir Keith Joseph, then Secretary of State for Social Services, and a few days later, the Government announced an inquiry into the death of Maria Colwell who had died at the hands of her step father, despite a multitude of agencies being involved. As Franklin commented:

'While the timing of Maria Colwell and [the study group conference] was coincidental, the combination was explosive.'[8]

The inquiry into the death of Maria Colwell has been described as 'signalling the beginning of modern political, public and professional interest in child abuse'.[9] The report of the inquiry re-emphasised the necessity of multi-disciplinary co-ordination. In April 1974, the DHSS issued a circular on inter-agency working which contained three main recommendations – the formation of Area Review Committees (ARCs) where they did not already exist (now designated Area Child Protection Committees), the holding of case conferences (now designated child protection conferences) in every case involving suspected non-accidental injury and the establishment of a register of cases.[10] Developments in the investigation of cases of suspected child abuse over the past two decades show that substantial progress has been made in establishing arrangements for inter-agency co-operation.

---

6   Hallett, C & Stevenson, O (1980) *Child Abuse: Aspects of Inter-professional Co-operation* London, Allen & Unwin.

7   Franklin, AW (1975) *Concerning Child Abuse: Papers presented by the Tunbridge Wells Study Group on non-accidental injury to children* Edinburgh, Churchill Livingstone.

8   Ebeling, NB & Hill, DA (eds) (1983) *Child Abuse and Neglect: A Guide with Case Studies for Treating the Child and Family* Boston.

9   Parton, N (1991) *Governing the Family, Child Care, Child Protection and the State* London, Macmillan.

10   DHSS [1974] LASSL (74)13.

'WORKING TOGETHER' – THE PRACTICAL FRAMEWORK

The Children Act 1989 imposes a statutory duty to co-operate, but the agencies involved are given guidance as to the arrangements for inter-agency co-operation in 'Working Together under the Children Act 1989 – A guide to arrangements for inter-agency co-operation for the protection of children from abuse', which was prepared jointly by the Department of Health, the Home Office, the Department of Education and Science and the Welsh Office and published in 1991. The guidance consolidates previous guidance on procedures for the protection of children and recommends developments aimed at making these more effective. It does not attempt to provide guide lines on the practice of individual professions in the recognition of child abuse or subsequent care or treatment but is concerned with inter-professional and inter-agency co-operation.

Area child protection committees

The forum for inter-agency co-operation in each area is the Area Child Protection Committee (ACPC), whose role is to establish local inter-agency guide lines on procedures to be followed in individual cases and to oversee policy and practice within a geographical area, usually that covered by the local social services department and the district health authority. The composition of each committee includes representatives of social service departments, the NSPCC, the police, the local health authority, the family health services authority (including general practitioners), the probation service and the education service. Members are accountable to the agencies which they represent and these agencies are jointly responsible for the ACPC actions. The main tasks of the ACPC are detailed in 'Working Together':

(a) to establish, maintain and review local inter-agency guide lines on procedures to be followed in individual cases;

(b) to monitor the implementation of legal procedures;

(c) to identify significant issues arising from the handling of cases and reports from inquiries;

(d) to scrutinise arrangements to provide treatment, expert advice and inter-agency liaison and make recommendations to the responsible agencies;

(e) to scrutinise progress on work at preventing child abuse and make recommendations to the responsible agencies;

(f) to scrutinise work related to inter-agency training and make recommendations to the responsible agencies;

(g) to conduct reviews whenever child abuse is a known or suspected factor in the death of any child in the area;

(h) to publish an annual report about local child protection matters.

Each ACPC is responsible for producing local procedural handbooks, which should be available to the public (for instance through local libraries), accessible in constituent agencies to all members of staff, and to independent practitioners in direct contact with children and families. There are no nationally agreed procedures binding all local authorities. However, 'Working Together' recommends that the structure and content of local procedural handbooks should be standardised and provides an outline of the basic content and format.

Stages of work in individual cases

'Working Together' identifies six stages of work:

(i)   referral and recognition;

(ii)   immediate protection and planning the investigation;

(iii) investigation and initial assessment;

(iv)   child protection conference and decision making about the need for registration;

(v)   comprehensive assessment and planning;

(vi)   implementation, review and, where appropriate, de-registration.

However, these stages should be seen as a guide line only. As 'Working Together' points out, they do not necessarily stand alone nor are they clearly divided in time. There is likely to be some overlap. The sequence should, however, assist professionals to see more clearly the focus of work at each stage.

The referral and recognition of cases of suspected abuse has already been discussed (see Chapters 1 and 2). The issue of immediate protection of the child has also been discussed (see Chapter 3). In extreme emergencies the child may be taken into police protection or an application for an emergency protection order may be made. Alternatively the protection of the child may be assured by removing the alleged abuser from the family home – either by voluntary agreement, by a civil injunction or by arrest. However, it is worth reiterating at this point the guidance contained in 'Working Together' that, except in cases when a child is in acute physical danger, it is essential that the timing of the removal of children from their homes should be agreed following consultation with all appropriate professionals. However, if it becomes apparent at *any* stage of the investigation that the child is in need of immediate protection, the appropriate action to protect the child should be taken immediately.

Planning the investigation – strategy discussions

'Working Together' stresses that it is essential that there is an early strategy discussion, which may not require a meeting, between the statutory agencies, ie police and social services, to plan the investigation and in particular the role of each agency and the extent of joint investigation. Such strategy decisions are often the vital first link in the chain of inter-agency co-operation and it is the responsibility of the agency receiving the referral to initiate these. The guidance contained in 'Working Together' seems to suggest that discussions will take place between the statutory agencies concerned, but, whereas the police and social services will undoubtedly play a central role, they will not necessarily be the sole participants and will often need to call on other agencies and professions who may have information about the child, for example general practitioners, health visitors, probation officers, paediatric services, psychiatric and psychological services and school personnel. The latest guidance produced by the Joint Working Party of the Department of Health, BMA and Conference of Royal Medical Colleges[11] suggests that the main participants in strategy discussions should be determined at local level and a named senior person in each participating discipline should ensure that advice is available, as appropriate, for the purpose of strategy discussions. Medical advice may be needed for the purpose of the strategy discussion and the planning of the investigation and it will certainly form part of the investigation itself. The guidance points out that medical advice will take different forms. For example, advice should be sought from the general practitioner who will have direct knowledge of the child and family, from other senior doctors involved in the child's care and from the designated doctor who can offer more general advice on child health and development, including the need for a comprehensive medical or psychiatric assessment.

The procedural guide lines issued by Area Child Protection Committees will dictate the steps to be taken, including consultation with other agencies

---

11 Department Of Health, British Medical Association and Conference Of Medical Royal Colleges (1994) 'Child protection: Medical Responsibilities' addendum to 'Working Together under the Children Act 1989'.

and professions. The strategy discussions will determine whether the social services should investigate alone, or whether a joint investigation should be undertaken by social workers and the police. Obviously, the police will be involved in the investigation if there is the possibility of a criminal offence having been committed against the child. A joint investigation will usually be undertaken in cases where there is a suspicion of serious physical abuse which has resulted in probable significant harm (in these circumstances the child may well already have been taken into police protection or an emergency protection order obtained), where sexual abuse is suspected or alleged, where the child has been exposed to the likelihood of significant harm as a result of parental neglect (dependent upon the severity and immediacy of the neglect), or in cases where the child is thought to have been severely emotionally abused. In other cases, where there is a suspicion of physical abuse which has not resulted in the child suffering significant harm or where there is a suspicion of neglect which does not fall into the category to warrant a joint police/social services investigation, the social services will usually investigate alone.

Investigation and initial assessment

A child abuse investigation can have a significant impact on the child and the family – as 'Working Together' points out 'the process of investigation is painful and difficult for those who undergo it' – and this must be borne in mind by all those involved in the investigation. The manner in which the child and the family are involved in the early stages of the investigation can be of crucial importance and may well have a significant impact on the eventual outcome of the case. The child, and anyone with parental responsibility for the child, should be informed about the purpose of the investigation and how it will be conducted. Wherever possible, the investigation should be undertaken with the consent and co-operation of the child and the family. The guidance issued to social workers[12] stresses that it is important that parents are given time and opportunity to talk about themselves and any problems they may have and to describe their view of the situation. Even initially hostile and unco-operative parents prefer openness and honesty and a social worker who shows concern and listens to their point of view. Indeed, 'Working Together' suggests that sometimes consideration should be given to the need to provide a separate worker specifically for the parent. However, if it becomes apparent that the investigation is being frustrated by the family or access to the child is being denied, but an emergency situation is not identified, an application for a child assessment order should be considered. The idea that investigations

---

12 Department of Health (1988) 'A Guide for Social Workers Undertaking a Comprehensive Assessment' London HMSO.

should be conducted in a spirit of openness and co-operation with all involved, particularly the parents, is to be applauded in theory. Yet the practical realities must often be very different. Allegations of child abuse raise strong emotions in all those concerned, including the parents. Although the professionals will be expected to ensure that their emotions do not affect the way in which the investigation is conducted, the same cannot be said of the parents and there will be many occasions when their consent and co-operation is simply not forthcoming.

Interviewing the child

One of the key elements in any investigation will be to talk to the child. The arrangements for this will depend primarily on the age of the child, the level and kind of abuse suspected and the evidence already available to the investigators. In cases where civil or criminal court proceedings either have been or are expected to be instigated, a substantive interview with the child will be necessary.

Location and timing of the interview

Twenty years ago, it was not uncommon for child victims of abuse to be interviewed by police officers from the Criminal Investigation Department with no specific training. The officers concerned were usually female because it was felt 'it was a woman's job'. The interviews would often take place in the stark surroundings of a police interview room, furnished with a table and hard chairs and sometimes even with bars on the window! Such a scenario is unthinkable today. It is now recognised that interviews held in such surroundings will not elicit the best information and will undoubtedly be traumatic for the child. As 'Working Together' states 'awareness of the needs of the child should focus the enquiry on the child'. Today, interviews will rarely be held in police stations, but will generally take place in a purpose-built interview suite located either in a hospital, family centre or in special units – commonly referred to as family support units – now established by many police forces, where video recording facilities and possibly facilities for medical examinations are available (see Chapter 5). Every effort should be made to help the child relax and 'Working Together' suggests that consideration should be given to the child having a parent, relative, friend or supporter present during the interview as the circumstances of the case determine. However, guidance for those involved in video recording interviews (see below) suggests that limiting the number of people present at the interview should lessen the possibility of the child feeling overwhelmed by the situation and uncomfortable about revealing information, and that the presence of other people may distract or put pressure on the child. It goes on to point out that such considerations may be outweighed by the benefit of having a supportive accompanying adult available to comfort and reassure a very young or distressed child, particularly if the child requests it.

Occasions may arise when an immediate interview is necessary, for example, if the alleged abuser has been arrested by the police and further evidence is required before a charge can be made. However, in most cases the interview will be planned in advance, allowing adequate time to prepare a plan of the interview, including clearly defined objectives. This should, of course, be subject to the general presumption that delay is prejudicial to the child.

Video recording the interview – The Memorandum of Good Practice

One of the key advances in recent years has been the advent of video recording interviews with the child. The use of such video recordings in court will be considered in detail in Chapter 7, but at this stage it should be noted that such recordings may now be admitted in court in both civil and criminal proceedings. The Home Office, in conjunction with the Department of Health, has issued a guide for those making a video recording of an interview with a child witness – The Memorandum of Good Practice on Video Recorded Interviews with Child Witnesses for Criminal proceedings (the Memorandum). Part 1 of the Memorandum contains general advice on when and where to make a video recording, considerations about suitable equipment and the legal conditions which must be satisfied before a criminal court will accept the recording. Part 2 gives advice about what should be done before the interview and sets out basic questions which should be addressed by those involved. Part 3 concerns the conduct of the interview (see below) and Part 4 gives guidance about matters which need to be dealt with once the recording has been made, including the arrangements for the proper storage, custody and disposal of the tapes. Although intended primarily for those recording interviews where it is intended that the result should be acceptable in criminal proceedings, the Memorandum acknowledges that a video recorded interview in accordance to the guidelines will also be of benefit in civil proceedings.

The interviewer

The selection of staff for interviewing is of crucial importance. The development of inter-agency co-operation in recent years has been combined with an appreciation of the specific skills required to elicit the most reliable information from the child, whilst ensuring that the child is not subjected to undue stress by the interview. Emphasis is now firmly placed on the needs of the child and the skills of the interviewer. 'Working Together' states that staff should not be selected for interviewing unless they are of acknowledged competence and have undergone appropriate staff development and training (see below). The Memorandum suggests that the interviewer should be a person who has, or is likely to be able to establish, rapport with the child, who understands how to communicate effectively with him or her, particularly during disturbed periods, and who also has a proper grasp of the basic rules of evidence and the elements of criminal offences. This latter point highlights the emphasis in the Memorandum on criminal proceedings and concerns have been raised that this emphasis could mean that the child's immediate needs may take a secondary place to evidentiary requirements and cases in the civil courts could possibly be weakened, reflecting the different professional ideologies and aims and objectives of those involved.[13] The Memorandum accepts that this is a formidable job specification and some compromise will probably be necessary. A rigid definition of the roles of police and social service professionals is not likely to be possible or desirable and a high degree of flexibility and responsiveness within the joint investigating team is required in the interests of an effective interview.

Structure of the interview

As the Memorandum states, the basic aim of the interview is to obtain a truthful account from the child, in a way which is fair and in the child's interests and acceptable to the courts. It is recommended that the interview be based on a phased approach, although other interview techniques are not precluded.

The first phase of the interview is designed to build a rapport between the interviewer and the child. No reference should be made to the alleged abuse – the discussion should be centred around non-related events in the child's life such as school or television programmes. This helps the child to feel relaxed and enables the interviewer to supplement existing knowledge about the child's social, emotional and cognitive development, and particularly about his or her communication skills and degree of understanding.

The second phase is the free narrative account. Before being invited to volunteer information about the alleged abuse, the interviewer should convey to the child the need to speak the truth and the acceptability of saying 'I don't know' or 'I don't understand'. Once this has been done, the child will be asked to give an account of what has happened in his or her own words. The interviewer may prompt the child with open-ended questions such as 'did anything else happen?', but specific question should not be used.

The third phase involves questioning the child, beginning with open-ended questions such as 'could you please tell me more about ...', then moving on to specific, but non-leading questions which allow the interviewer to clarify earlier information such as 'what colour was ...'. If the specific but non-leading questions are unproductive, the interviewer may obtain more specific answers

---

13   Lyons & de Cruz (1993) '*Child Abuse*' Family Law 2nd ed Bristol.

by using closed questions, perhaps by giving the child a limited number of alternative responses such as 'was it ... blue or yellow or another colour'. There is a danger, however, that such questions will be considered leading questions – ones which imply the answer or assume facts which are likely to be in dispute – and this may affect the admissibility in court of any video recording of the interview.

The final phase is that of closing the interview, where the interviewer may need to go over the important parts of the child's account, using the child's language, before moving back to the neutral topics which were discussed in the initial rapport phase to close the interview.

Throughout the interview, the interviewer will need to have regard to the legal constraints which may affect the admissibility of any video recording, including avoiding the use of leading statements, hearsay evidence and references to the character of the accused. These issues are discussed in more detail in Chapter 7.

Medical examinations

In many cases, a medical examination or assessment of the child will be necessary. One of the main criticisms of the Cleveland Report was that children had been subjected to repeated medical examinations and that this was, in itself, a form of abuse of the child. Medical examinations or assessments should therefore be kept to a minimum and carried out by experienced paediatricians or police doctors, preferably with the consent of the parents and the child. (See further Chapter 5 on the role of the doctor in diagnosing abuse and Chapter 6 for the child's ability to consent to medical examinations and treatment.) In cases where a court order has been made, provisions now exist for the court to control and give directions regarding medical or psychiatric examinations or assessments. If an emergency protection order has been obtained in respect of the child, the limited parental authority vested in the local authority does not extend to allowing such examinations or assessments to take place unless the court itself has given a specific direction to this effect.[14] If access to the child is being frustrated by the parents, it may well be appropriate for the local authority to apply for a child assessment order, and the court may give specific directions as to examinations and assessment if the order is granted.[15] Similar directions may also be given if the court makes an interim care or supervision order.

---

14   Section 44(6)(b) Children Act 1989.
15   Section 43(9) Children Act 1989.

CHILD PROTECTION CONFERENCES AND DECISION MAKING

Function of the child protection conference

'Working Together' describes the conference as the prime forum for professionals and the family to share information and concerns, analyse and weigh up the level of risks to the children and make recommendations for action. However, the only *decision* to be taken at the conference is whether or not to register the child and, if registration is agreed, to allocate a key worker.

Convening the conference

If the initial investigation indicates that there is cause for concern in relation to the child and that a decision has to be made about further action, a child protection conference should be convened. The responsibility for this usually rests with the principal social services officer. However, the guidance produced by the joint working party[16] suggests that there appears to be a wide variation in the criteria used to decide whether a conference should be convened and points out that there is evidence that some agencies apply very strict criteria for the convening of a conference whilst others are more lax in the drawing up of guide lines. The guidance suggests the following criteria for convening a child protection conference:

(1) when there is enough evidence, which is not rejected during the investigation, that a child (living or as yet unborn) is likely to suffer significant harm, so that a child protection plan may be needed;

(2) when information is made available to the social services department or any other child protection agency concerning the pregnancy of a parent whose previous child had been very seriously harmed or died as a result of unexplained injuries or proved child abuse;

(3) when the agreed child protection plan cannot be implemented or is ineffective. For example, when a child whose name is already on a child protection register in another area moves into the locality;

(4) when there is strong dissent following investigation about the need for a child protection conference.

The time between referral and the child protection conference will vary according to the needs of each individual case. Initial conferences should normally take place within eight working days of referral unless there are special reasons why information from the investigation which would lead to a better decision is not available, in which case a maximum of 15 working days is recommended.

---

16   See note 11.

Chairing the conference

The conference must be chaired by a member of staff from the social services department (or the NSPCC if there is a local arrangement to this effect). The skill of the chair is crucial to the effectiveness of the conference and those appointed should have a good understanding and professional knowledge of child protection. The Joint Working Party (JWP) emphasised the need for consistency and independence in conference chairing. Independence will normally mean independence of line management of anyone with case responsibility and will command the confidence of all participants. The provision of a consistent chair in relation to any one child or family will yield positive benefits in terms of building confidence and clarifying lines of communication. A sound knowledge of the issues and personalities involved is likely to lead to better informed decisions being made on a continuing basis.

Attendance at the conference

The major criterion governing attendance at a child protection conference is that those who attend should be there because they have a contribution to make. Unnecessarily large meetings tend to inhibit discussion and can be overwhelming, especially to parents and children (see below). 'Working Together' suggests that all the agencies which have specific responsibilities in the child protection process should be invited to send representatives, including the social services, the NSPCC (when operational in the area), the police, the education authority (when the child is of school age), the health authority, the general medical practitioner, the health visiting service, the probation service, appropriate voluntary organisations, and a representative of the armed services in each case where there is a service connection. The key participants are likely to be those who have been involved in the recognition and referral, strategy discussion and investigative stages of the process and who have been active in the decision to convene a conference. The guidance issued by the JWP suggests a practical way of cutting down numbers attending, that is, for health professionals to work together so that, where appropriate, their views and reports could be represented collectively.

Written reports

Although the personal attendance of those with a contribution to make to the conference is obviously desirable, this will not always be possible. The medical profession, especially general practitioners, have particular problems in attending conferences, which are often convened at times when they would otherwise be in surgery or attending out-patient or clinic sessions. Research has shown that medical attendance at child protection conferences is poor, with general practitioners and other doctors attending 19% and 20% of conferences respectively in a particular sample. Health and developmental concerns were, however, discussed at 83% of the child protection conferences.[17] A suggestion that doctors, and general practitioners in particular, might attend for only part of the conference, to make their contribution and then leave, did not find favour with the JWP, which expressed the view that doctors should be part of the full decision making process of the conference and present throughout to add a medical perspective to discussions and to contribute to the weighing up of risk to the child. However, on occasions a written report may be submitted if a professional cannot attend in person. Ideally the author of the report should have an opportunity of discussing the content of the report with the chair of the conference prior to the meeting so that the chair can reflect accurately the views of the professional providing the report. In the case of medical reports it is important that the author discusses the report with the parents and, where appropriate, with the child, before submission whenever this is practically possible.

The involvement of children, parents and carers

The general principles underlying the Children Act 1989 emphasise that the welfare of the child is the paramount consideration and that professionals should work in partnership with parents and carers – parents and children having a right to be consulted and involved when decisions about their future will be made. These principles underpin all child protection work and, as a result, parents and responsible children are increasingly included in child protection conferences. The child, if of sufficient age and understanding (see Chapter 6), must be invited to attend the whole or part of the conference if it is consistent with safeguarding and promoting his or her welfare. The parents, or others who have parental responsibility, must be invited to attend if this is consistent with promoting and safeguarding the welfare of the child.

Studies indicate that the professionals, including doctors, consider that parental participation in child protection conferences is beneficial and that their attendance has a positive effect on conference proceedings.[18] However, there may be circumstances when it will not be right to invite one or other or both parents or a responsible child, although exclusion should be kept to a minimum and needs to be especially justified. The only basis for the decision to exclude is that the presence of one or both of the parents or the child would jeopardise the safeguarding and promoting of the child's welfare and interests. This could include situations where the presence of parents could seriously disrupt the conduct of the conference and lead to possible intimidation and violence. However, 'Working Together' makes it clear that the possibility that one of the parents may be prosecuted for an offence against the child does not in itself justify exclusion.

---

17 Department Of Health, British Medical Association and Conference Of Medical Royal Colleges (1994) 'Child protection: Medical Responsibilities' Draft Guidance PL\CO(93)2 para 10.1

18 Ibid para 10.6.15.

The decision to exclude rests with the chair of the conference, who should provide adequate opportunity for the professionals involved in the conference to share their views. If a decision to exclude is made, the decision and the reasons for making it should be recorded on the child's file and must also be recorded in the conference minutes.

Objectives of the conference

The first stage of the conference will centre around information sharing, to allow the participants to share current causes for concern and identify whether those causes for concern have been established. This stage will also allow the sharing of information about the child, the family and their circumstances and provide an opportunity to identify other causes for concern. This will be followed by an analysis of the risk to the child, which will be based both on information about child abuse known through research and practice knowledge, and also on information specific to each child who is the subject of the conference. The conference will then move to the decision making stage, where it will be decided whether the child needs to be the subject of an inter-agency child protection plan and placed on the child protection register (see below). Statistics issued by the Department of Health suggest that between March 1992 and March 1993, of the 42,600 children who were subject to initial child protection conferences in England, 24,700 were registered.[19] Yet how this decision is reached is not altogether clear. Obviously, if a consensus view has been reached at this stage in the meeting, few problems arise. However, it is acknowledged that not all conferences will lead to such clear-cut decisions and the decision whether or not to register a child may be contentious. The JWP noted that in some conferences, the participants may be asked to vote on the issue, although it is not known how widespread this practice is. The JWP concluded that the decision whether or not to register a child should be based on a thorough weighing up of risk, but that ultimately the decision should rest with the conference chair. The members of the JWP do not support the concept of voting at child protection conferences.[20] Any dissent over the registration decision should be recorded in the conference minutes.

If a decision is taken not to register the child because allegations or suspicions have not been substantiated, 'Working Together' stresses that this should be made clear to parents and that any inconvenience or distress caused is acknowledged. However, in some cases there may nevertheless be a need for inter-agency working and the provision of services; the conference should

---

19 Department of Health (1994) 'Children and Young Persons on Child Protection Registers Year Ending 31 March 1993 England' prepared by the Government Statistical Service.

20 Note 17 para 10.6.26.

then make recommendations to this effect. If it is thought that a decision cannot be reached on the information available, but suspicions remain, the conference may recommend an application for a child assessment order. If a decision is taken to register the child, it must be decided which category of registration should be used and the final stage of the conference will be to formulate an inter-agency child protection plan.

CHILD PROTECTION REGISTERS

The purpose of the register is to provide a record of all children in the area for whom there are unresolved child protection issues and who are currently the subject of an inter-agency protection plan and to ensure that the plans are formally reviewed every six months. 'Working Together' sets out the requirements for registration and the categories of abuse. Before a child is registered the child protection conference must decide if there is, or is a likelihood of, significant harm requiring a child protection plan. One of the following requirements needs to be satisfied:

(1) there must be one or more identifiable incidents which can be described as having adversely affected the child. They may be acts of omission or commission. They can be either physical, sexual, emotional or neglectful. It is important to identify a specific occasion or occasions when the incident has occurred. Professional judgment is that further incidents are likely; or

(2) significant harm is expected on the basis of professional judgment of findings of the investigation in this individual case or on research evidence.

The conference will need to establish, so far as they can, a cause of the harm or likelihood of harm. This could also be applied to siblings or other children living in the same household so as to justify the registration of them. Such children should be categorised according to the area of concern. (The categories of abuse for registration were discussed in Chapter 1.) In brief there are now four categories – neglect, physical injury, sexual abuse and emotional abuse.

Formulating an inter-agency child protection plan

Once a decision has been reached to place the child's name on the register, the conference will appoint a key worker, establish an initial child protection plan and make recommendations for a core group of professionals to carry out the inter-agency work. The key worker, who will be a social worker from the social services department or the NSPCC, has two main tasks – to fulfil the statutory responsibilities of his or her agency (including the development of a multi-agency, multi-disciplinary plan for the protection of the child) and to act as lead worker for the inter-agency work (to provide a focus for communication between the professionals involved and co-ordinate contributions). The key worker must also ensure that parents and children are fully engaged in the implementation of the child protection plan. The core group of professionals who will be primarily responsible for carrying out the plan will include the child's general practitioner, health visitor (if the child is five years of age or under) and a representative from school (if the child is of school age). The plan may involve an immediate application for an emergency protection order, or for an interim care or supervision order. In all cases where a decision is taken to register the child, even if immediate action is not called for, a comprehensive assessment of the child and family will be carried out.

COMPREHENSIVE ASSESSMENT AND PLANNING

Comprehensive assessment

Initial decisions about immediate action to protect the child are likely to have been based on limited information. The purpose of a comprehensive assessment is to acquire a full understanding of the child and family situation in order to provide a sound basis for decisions about future actions. The assessment will require careful planning and consideration will have to be given as to how it will fit in with any court action in relation to the child and possible criminal prosecution of the abuser. Guidance on an approach to assessment has been issued by the Department of Health[21] which describes a comprehensive assessment with eight components covering:

- the causes for concern;
- an assessment of the child (including emotional and physical development);
- family composition;
- individual profiles of parents/carers (those who have been or are to be significantly involved with the care of the child);
- the couple relationship and family interactions;
- networks (the role of the extended family);
- finance and physical conditions.

---

21 Note 12.

It is obvious from this that a comprehensive assessment cannot be undertaken without the knowledge and involvement of the family and a key task in undertaking the assessment will be gaining the parents' co-operation and commitment to the work. The guidance acknowledges that the timescale of the assessment will vary according to the complexity of the situation and the requirements of the legal process, but estimates that 6 – 10 sessions will be required.

Planning

The comprehensive assessment will inform the child protection plan. 'Working Together' makes it clear that a written plan will need to be constructed with the involvement of the carers/parents in the light of each agency's statutory duties and will identify the contributions each will make to the child, other family members and the abuser. The child and the parents should be given clear information about the purposes and nature of any intervention together with a copy of the plan. If immediate action has been taken to protect the child, and the initial suspicions of abuse have been substantiated during the investigation and assessment, it is likely that the plan will involve the initiation of care proceedings. Proceedings may also be instigated where the investigation and assessment reveal there is cause for concern and the statutory criteria for a care or supervision order are satisfied, although the child remains at home. Not all children who have been abused, or are considered to be at risk of abuse, are removed from parental care even on a short-term basis. Even if a care order is made and the local authority thereby acquires parental responsibility for the child, the child may remain at home (or within the wider family) with professional intervention and/or support networks provided. The Department of Health guidance suggests that factors influencing the decision to leave the child at home would include abuse of an essentially superficial or minor nature, having regard to the age of the child, an acceptance of responsibility and an acknowledgement of the inappropriateness of the behaviour and the need for future work, a protective stance taken by the non-abusing parent, the presence of supportive networks, evidence of basic stability and good standards of care and love for the child.

In more serious cases, the plan may involve the prosecution of the abuser. However, care proceedings should not generally be adjourned pending the outcome of criminal proceedings. The welfare and the avoidance of delay principles which underlie the 1989 Act generally require care proceedings to proceed as quickly as possible.[22] 'Working Together' acknowledges that the child protection plan may change significantly if the abuser goes to prison, but stresses that the plan should recognise that the abuser may want to return home after prison and it should make a statement about what will happen in this event.

---

22 *Re S (child abuse: cases management)* [1992] 1 FCR 31.

IMPLEMENTATION, REVIEW AND DE-REGISTRATION

Implementation and review

Once a child has been registered on the child protection register and a child protection plan agreed, the plan must be implemented and kept under regular review to ensure that it continues to achieve its objectives. Formal reviews are undertaken at least once every six months at a child protection review, which has the same format as the initial child protection conference (see above). As 'Working Together' states, the purpose of this is to review the arrangements for the protection of the child, examine the current level of risk and ensure that he or she continues to be adequately protected, consider whether the inter-agency co-operation is functioning effectively and to review the protection plan.

De-registration

The decision to remove a child's name from the register can usually only be made at a child protection review. 'Working Together' suggests that the reasons for de-registration can be grouped under the following headings (at para 6.45):

- The original factors which led to registration no longer apply – this would include:

  (a) a child who has remained at home but abuse or the risk of abuse has been reduced by work with the family and through the protection plan;

  (b) the child has been placed away from home and there is no longer access to the abusing adult or the access is no longer considered to present a risk to the child;

  (c) where the abusing adult is no longer a member of the same household as the child and there is no contact or such contact as occurs is no longer considered to be a risk to the child;

  (d) the completion of the comprehensive assessment and a detailed analysis of the risk has shown that registration is no longer required and child protection is not necessary.

- The child and family have moved permanently to another area and that area has accepted responsibility for the future management of the case.

- The child is no longer a child in the eyes of the law. This includes the child who reaches 18 years of age or the child who gets married.

- The child dies.

However, de-registration should not lead to the automatic cessation of services, and the professionals involved are encouraged to discuss with the parents and the child what services might be needed following de-registration. The Department of Health guidance stresses that a decision to disengage or close a case should not be taken without full multi-disciplinary consultation and suggests the factors influencing the decision will include:

(i)   a child free from abuse and developing adequately both in physical and emotional terms;

(ii) evidence of sustained, comparatively stable and reasonably sound relationships within the family;

(iii) evidence of support networks, personal or professional or both;

(iv) the family is generally settled, coping with the 'normal' crises of life without fundamental difficulties and would be willing to ask for help if necessary.

'WORKING TOGETHER' – CONFLICTING PROFESSIONAL IDEOLOGIES AND PROBLEMS OF MULTI-DISCIPLINARY WORKING

The framework for inter-agency co-operation is now clearly established. However, the practical outcome has been questioned. In 1988, Blom Cooper stated:

> '... the fact is that so often the collaboration we talk about is so wholly lacking when we get into the actual field. Time and again, if we look at child abuse inquiries, and there have been 30 of them since Maria Colwell in 1978, every one shows the failure in communication between the disciplines who are working to protect children ... there must be a sharing of responsibility ... the multi-disciplinary approach is simply not working well enough.'[23]

One of the main reasons for this failure would appear to be the different professional ideologies of child abuse and the differing aims of intervention. Each group of individuals will have their own perception as to the nature of the problem, and this in turn will be reflected in their preferred method of intervention. There is therefore, a danger of conflict. The problem has been explained thus:

> 'Each discipline is organised around a core of basic concepts and assumptions which form the frame of reference from which persons trained in that discipline view the world and set about solving problems in their field. The concepts and assumptions which make up the perspective of each discipline give each its distinctive character and are the intellectual tools used by its practitioners ... where the issues to be resolved are clearly in the area of competence of a single discipline, the automatic application of its conceptual

---

23   Blom Cooper, L (1988) 'Roles of Good Law and Practice' in *Journal of Social Welfare Law* No 2 p 99.

tools is likely to go unchallenged. However, when the problems under consideration lie in the interstices between disciplines, the disciplines concerned are likely to define the situation differently and may arrive at differing conclusions which have dissimilar implications for social action.'[24]

Child abuse is one such problem which lies in the interstices between disciplines. The 'basic concepts and assumptions' held by the different disciplines can be described as professional ideologies – general assertions that are held about human behaviour, its causes and how to change it. Failure to recognise different professional ideologies can lead to professional disputes and misunderstandings. It has been suggested that the various child abuse ideologies can be broadly classified into three alternative approaches to the problem – penal, medical and social welfare.[25]

The penal approach – child abuse as a crime

The penal approach presupposes that individuals are responsible for their own actions. When a child is abused, the act is viewed as a criminal offence and the abuser is regarded as answerable to society for his behaviour in the same way as any other form of criminal behaviour. This approach focuses attention on the act of abuse itself and regards the main aim of intervention as being the criminal prosecution of the abuser, with scant attention focused on the victim of abuse.

The medical approach – child abuse as an illness

In contrast to the penal approach, the medical approach does not regard abusers as responsible for their actions, but instead is concerned to identify the cause of the actions which is seen as being beyond the abuser's control. This approach asserts that mental illness, like physical illness, has an underlying disease process which needs to be identified before treatment can be directed at the abnormality. The aim of intervention will be the treatment of the abnormality to prevent the reoccurrence of the abuse.

The social welfare approach – child abuse as a symptom of family disfunction

In common with the medical approach, the social welfare approach presupposes that behaviour is determined and the main aim of intervention is seen as the treatment of the abuser as opposed to punishment. However, this approach takes a broader view than the medical approach and does not attempt to identify one major cause of the behaviour, conceding that a number of factors may contribute to the behaviour. Attention is traditionally focused

---

24 Mercer, quoted in Bourne & Newberger (1979) *Critical Perspectives on Child Abuse* Lexington, Mass, Lexington Books p 142.

25 Carter, J (1975) *The Maltreated Child* London, Priory Press.

on the abuser who is regarded as psychologically, emotionally and socially inadequate, and intervention takes the form of individual and family counselling and rehabilitation. A more radical form of the social welfare approach concentrates on society as a whole rather than the individual abuser. The abuser is regarded as a victim of society and the 'cure' is seen as being social redistribution rather than individual change.

Traditionally, police officers tended to adopt the first approach, social workers the third, while medical practitioners either adopted the second approach or were exclusively concerned about the threat to the child's health and development and failed to view the problem in any wider sense. Given the potentially polarised views each profession brings to the investigation and the differing aims of intervention, conflict is to be expected. There are obvious difficulties inherent in such concepts as 'treating a crime' or 'prosecuting an illness' or applying both strategies to a 'family problem'. The resulting conflict has the potential to affect the manner in which cases of child abuse are dealt with. To expect the professions to work together in the true spirit of inter-agency co-operation without first acknowledging and attempting to resolve the conflict is obviously totally unrealistic.

Additional problems of communication and decision making tend to be encountered during an investigation due to the differing organisational structures of the individual professions. Medical practitioners present few problems in this respect, but the police service tends to be extremely hierarchical in nature, with important decisions always being taken by senior officers. In practice, unless there was an emergency situation, investigating officers frequently have to report back to senior officers before action can be taken, whereas social services tend to delegate considerable decision making powers to social workers who are then frustrated by what they perceive to be unnecessary delay.

A child protection conference may only serve to highlight these problems. It will often be the first occasion on which all the professions come together. Their common link will be the abused child, but that in itself is not sufficient to ensure they work as a coherent team and develop sufficient cohesion and mutual trust to share sensitive information and agree future action.

Despite these problems, the agencies are expected to work together in investigating an allegation of abuse and agree a plan of future action. In recent years, radical changes have been made to the way in which cases of suspected child abuse are dealt with and close collaboration is expected between the professionals involved. However care needs to be taken in establishing arrangements for inter-agency co-operation. As Tibbets argues:

'Organisational arrangements in themselves are not a sufficient condition for successful integration if personal inter-relationships between the professions involved run counter to them.'[26]

These are words of warning which should always be borne in mind when discussing arrangements for inter-agency co-operation and the investigation of cases of child abuse. It is all too easy to assume that once a framework for inter-agency working has been established, any underlying conflict between the professions will simply disappear. Potential conflict must be acknowledged and attempts at resolution made. Existing procedures need to be constantly reviewed to ensure that they are not merely 'cosmetic exercises designed to paper over the cracks'.

BREAKING DOWN THE BARRIERS – JOINT TRAINING

'Working Together' acknowledges that difficulties will be encountered in joint inter-agency investigations, but suggests that these difficulties can be minimised by the selection of specialist staff who undergo appropriate inter-agency training:

'Inter-agency training is essential if inter-agency procedures are to function satisfactorily.' (para 7.7)

It is recommended that agencies establish joint annual training programmes on child abuse issues with access for all professional groups in direct contact with children and families. The JWP Guidance points out that the identification of multi-disciplinary training needs and the provision of a comprehensive multi-disciplinary training programme is work which can be effectively undertaken by a sub-committee of each Area Child Protection Committee. The guidance continues:

'The value of multi-disciplinary training is that it extends the knowledge base, enables participants to understand and appreciate the skills of others, increases understanding of professional roles, and leads to a better understanding of the problems faced by other professional groups. Multi-disciplinary training will also promote the development of realistic joint working procedures based on a thorough knowledge and appreciation of the skills other disciplines possess and the difficulties faced in putting these skills into practice.'[27]

However, the effectiveness of multi-disciplinary training will depend to a great extent on the initial training received within an individual's own profession. The ethos of inter-agency co-operation and child protection procedures now form an integral part of initial police and social work training, with further specialist training being provided, both within the

---

26 Tibbets, quoted in Hallett, C & Stevenson, O (1980) *Child Abuse: Aspects of Inter-professional Co-operation* London, Allen & Unwin.

27 Note 11 Para 12.9.

individual professions and on an inter-agency basis, for those who are directly involved with investigating child abuse and protecting children (see below). But the initial training of medical practitioners gives rise to some concern in this respect. Historically, the undergraduate training of doctors concentrated almost exclusively on scientific subjects such as human anatomy, physiology and biochemistry, with scant regard being paid to wider issues of human behaviour and social sciences.[28] Whilst this may enable doctors to diagnose abuse, it does little to equip them to play a full role in child protection. The JWP has recommended that education and training should start at the undergraduate stage and should cover an awareness of factors predisposing to the abuse of children, risk evaluation, ways in which abuse presents itself, the physical and emotional signs and symptoms of abuse, the effects on the child's development and national policy and local procedures relating to all child protection matters. The content of the education received by doctors is overseen by the General Medical Council (GMC), which has long offered guidance to universities and other licensing bodies as to what it considers the content of an appropriate medical education should be. The Council has stressed that its role is to guide rather than prescribe and that universities are free to meet the recommendations as they see fit.[29] Although in recent years the guidance has acknowledged a greater recognition of the social and psychological aspects of medical knowledge and practice, it seems the advice given by the GMC is way ahead of much practice. As one previous lay member of the GMC commented, the study of some subjects (for example social sciences) has been honoured more in the breach than in the observance.[30] In 1988, a working party of the education committee of the GMC, set up to examine the uneven development of teaching in the behavioural sciences, general practice and community medicine, reported that in some schools there was cause for concern because one or more aspects of such teaching had still not become established or else had withered under recent economic strains.[31] Current undergraduate medical training is clearly limited in that there is a reluctance to expand the scope of courses to incorporate the suggested broader approach to medical training, but pressure for reform is growing. Gould found considerable sympathy within the medical profession for the suggestion that medical students might benefit if their pre-clinical training was of a broader and less job-orientated nature, and was shared with students from other disciplines. He concludes, rather optimistically it may be thought:

'Tomorrow's doctors will be better educated by means of an undergraduate curriculum which will fit them to be not just competent medical technicians but informed and understanding members of the society they serve.'[32]

28 Gould (1991) *Examining Doctors: Medicine in the 1990s* London, Faber & Faber.

29 GMC (1980) *Recommendations on Basic Medical Education* London, GMC.

30 Stacey, M (1992) *Regulating British Medicine* Chichester, Wiley p 111.

31 Crisp (1988) 'Medical Education', *GMC Annual Report* for 1987, London GMC.

32 Gould note 28 at p 143.

Whilst it is agreed that all medical practitioners should be provided with the basic training and education advised by the JWP, whatever the shortcomings of existing undergraduate medical training in this respect, perhaps the most crucial stage to incorporate such training is in the years following graduation when doctors are undergoing general professional and higher specialist training. The need is particularly acute in the training of paediatricians and general practitioners, but all doctors whose work brings them into contact with children should receive specific training in aspects of child abuse and child protection. Widespread structural reforms of postgraduate medical education are currently being considered. Now is an ideal opportunity to ensure that the newly formulated postgraduate medical education gives sufficient prominence to such training which is essential if medical practitioners are to play a full and effective role in child protection.

Joint investigation – police and social workers

More specific training will be required by those professionals involved in the actual investigation and interviewing of the child. The issue of joint training for police and social workers was raised in a Home Office circular of 1988 which advised chief police officers to discuss with their local directors of social services the establishment of joint training arrangements for members of the investigation teams.[33] As 'Working Together' points out, the aim of this training is to enable members of each service to understand one another's role fully, to learn how to work together on a joint interviewing team on cases which may lead to criminal proceedings and, above all, to learn how to interview children who may have been badly abused by other adults in such a way as to encourage them to provide information without further hurting them.

Joint training schemes for police and social workers have now been developed throughout the country. The courses are usually held over a period of between five and seven days. The latter part of the course deals with policy, procedure, legal provisions and interviewing skills based on the 'Memorandum of Good Practice'. But perhaps more significantly, the first part of the course generally focuses on self-awareness training, including confronting stereotyped attitudes of the professionals to each other's profession, increasing awareness of each other's unique skills and expertise, and increasing self-awareness of the nature of child abuse. It is this first part of the course which attempts to break down the barriers traditionally erected between police and social workers, and encourages each profession to accept and respect the role and functions of the other professions. This, it is hoped, will create an atmosphere of mutual respect and trust which should go some way towards resolving conflict between the professions and enable them to work effectively together in interviewing the child, gathering the evidence and making decisions.

---

33   Home Office (1988) 'The Investigation of Child Sexual Abuse' Home Office Circular 52/1988 para 23.

JOINT INVESTIGATION – IS THERE AN ALTERNATIVE?

Much effort is currently being expended on establishing procedures for the joint investigation of cases of suspected child abuse. The concept of joint training leads to the assumption that police officers and social workers will be knowledgeable about the legal implications of evidence, the requirement of corroboration and the use of leading questions ('legally trained social workers'?), and both will have received training about the nature of abuse and its effects, and the feelings that the victim of abuse may experience ('socially trained police officers'?). Given the traditionally very different roles of the two professions and the potential conflict between them, questions have been raised as to whether joint investigation by police and social workers is the most appropriate and effective method of investigation. It would appear that other jurisdictions have been somewhat more creative in their response to the investigation of cases of child abuse, either by maintaining a punitive approach to the abuser combined with a protective approach to the child, or by adopting an essentially therapeutic approach to the family.

The punitive/protective approach – Israel and the youth examiner

One such response was initiated in Israel nearly 35 years ago when a special legal arrangement was established with regard to the examination and evidence of children in sexual offences. In 1955, the Knesset (Israeli Parliament) enacted the Law of Evidence (Protection of Children). Its purpose was to protect children under 14 years of age from the adverse effects of interrogation as a witness, both in the investigative stages of a criminal offence and in the courtroom. The law established the office of 'youth interrogator' (perhaps more appropriately known as a youth examiner), and took the investigating powers away from the police in cases of child sexual abuse, giving them to the youth examiner. Subject to certain exceptions, a child victim of sexual abuse may now only be interviewed by a youth examiner. When the police in Israel receive a report of suspected abuse, they immediately notify the youth examiner who then begins his or her own investigation, including taking a decision as to whether a medical examination is necessary. At the conclusion of the investigation, the youth examiner and the police will decide if a criminal prosecution is appropriate. If a prosecution is instigated, the youth examiner has the power to decide whether the child should give evidence at the trial. Should the youth examiner decide against a court appearance, he or she is allowed to give evidence of the child's statement as an exception to the hearsay rule, although certain requirements of corroboration must be met (see Chapter 7).

Experience of the system in Israel has shown that the youth examiners fulfil a dual function. As Harnon points out:

'On the one hand, there is the forensic and police task of assembling data and taking evidence in order to apprehend the offender and convict him. On the other hand, there is the purpose of providing treatment in the nature of catharsis, thereby enabling the child to free himself of anxieties and fears. [Youth examiners] thus take advantage of the interrogation to provide "short-term family care" at the same time.'[34]

From this, it would appear that the youth examiner is fulfilling the roles of both police officer and social worker. Instead of training two professions to work together, which is the current approach being adopted in England and Wales, in Israel a third profession has been created – that of youth examiner. The statute that created the office made no provision as to the qualifications required. Appointments are made by the Minister of Justice after consultation with a committee consisting of a juvenile court judge, a mental health expert, an educator, a child and youth care expert and a high ranking police officer. It was initially suggested that the ideal would be for the youth examiner to combine in his or her personality a psychologist and a lawyer. Candidates are normally recruited from professions connected with child care – psychologists, educational advisers, social workers or youth probation officers. However, apart from a knowledge of child development and sexual abuse, they must also have a knowledge of the rules of evidence, legal proceedings and interviewing skills – thus they can be seen as both legally trained social workers and socially trained police officers or lawyers.

The therapeutic approach – the Netherlands and the confidential doctor service

A rather different response was initiated in Holland over 20 years ago. Initially the Dutch had two official systems for dealing with child abuse – criminal investigations and actions to protect the child brought before the civil courts by social workers. In 1972 the confidential doctor service was established as a third option. The service is based on the notion that parents who have abused or neglected their children should be able to come of their own free will to an agency which they are confident will give them help without the risk of being judged or prosecuted. The main aim of the service is to keep the family unit together by providing a therapeutic, compassionate response to cases of child abuse, without the threat of punitive sanctions or coercive intervention. The service now operates nationwide and is run independently of the welfare and criminal justice agencies. Each centre is staffed by doctors who work part time and who are assisted by a small group of social workers and administrators. A strict anonymity rule is adopted – the centres never disclose to the family the identity of the person who initially reported the case. The referrals include all forms of abuse, including physical and sexual. About half of all initial reports are made by teachers, a third by

---

34   Harnon, E (1988) 'Examination of Children in Sexual Offences – the Israeli Law and Practice' in *Criminal Law Review* [1988] 263.

doctors and the rest by relatives or friends. As soon as a report has been made, the staff at the centre begin an investigation – the medical staff will talk to the child, the family doctor and school medical service and the social workers make contact with the local welfare agencies. Although the aim of the service in keeping the family together is similar to the principles underlying the Children Act 1989 – that wherever possible children should be cared for by both parents, the methods of investigation differ considerably. The confidential doctor service investigations are often carried out without informing the parents, which seems to be in direct contrast to the approach adopted under the Children Act 1989, which encourages the involvement and participation of parents and carers as soon as initial suspicions are raised.

Once sufficient evidence has been collected, the suspected abuser is called in. There is no obligation to inform the police, although there is often informal liaison with the police. If the abuser denies the allegation, but the confidential doctor is convinced abuse has taken place, the case will then be handed over to the police, who will take over the investigation and a prosecution may result. If other members of the family try to protect the abuser and there are unresolved child protection issues, the case will be reported to the child protection board, which has similar powers and duties regarding child protection as local authorities in England and Wales. Nationally, only about 10% of confidential doctor cases are referred to the child protection boards and about 3% to the police. The remaining 87% of cases are dealt with by the confidential doctor. The abuser is not prosecuted and, although in some cases the abuser may agree to leave the family home for a period of time, in a large proportion of cases the family remains together and receives therapy – thus fulfilling one of the main aims of the service. Concern has been expressed that the investigations involve breaches of civil rights – case conferences are held without informing parents, investigations are carried out behind their backs and personal files are scrutinised without permission. Despite this, the service has the support of both the police and the judiciary. It seems that the service has been successful in encouraging the referral of cases of abuse by providing a response based on help, compassion and solidarity rather than the traditional punitive approach based on coercion, control, judgment and sanctions. In England and Wales in recent years the tendency has been to move away from a strict punitive approach. However, the threat of sanctions remains, albeit tempered by a growing realisation of the need for therapeutic treatment of the abuser, particularly in cases of sexual abuse (see Chapter 8).

CHAPTER 5

THE ROLE OF THE DOCTOR IN THE INVESTIGATION

BY DR MICHAEL KNIGHT

PRIMARY AND SECONDARY ROLES

Doctors may become involved in the identification and evaluation of child abuse in either a primary or secondary role. Doctors acting in a primary role, such as general practitioners or casualty officers in accident and emergency departments, may be faced with injuries to children which may be suggestive of non-accidental injury, which, by virtue of the role of the doctor, are emerging for the first time. Equally, the general practitioner or casualty officer might be the first professional of any agency to be faced with a case of child sex abuse. In general practice, cases may be referred to the doctor by other members of the primary health care team such as health visitors, practice nurses, midwives or, more rarely, community nurses.

'Working Together'[1] gives clear guidance as to how the general practitioner should then proceed:

> 'It is essential that whenever a general practitioner becomes suspicious that a child may be at risk of, or is the subject of abuse of whatever nature, the information is shared with the statutory services responsible for child protection, ie social services departments, the NSPCC or the police.' (para 4.32)

Despite this apparently definitive guidance, in practice, there are other avenues open to the general practitioner. Either he or she may be so certain that a child has been physically injured or sexually abused that he or she elects to admit the child directly to the paediatric ward of the hospital, or may seek an urgent outpatient appointment for the child with a consultant paediatrician if he or she is less sure of the diagnosis.

In such circumstances, in accepting the referral, the paediatrician will be acting in a secondary or expert role, and the responsibility for informing the statutory agencies will pass to the hospital services, although it may well be that the general practitioner has, in addition, already informed one or more of the appropriate agencies at the time of the admission or referral of the child.

Also acting in a secondary or expert role may be a police surgeon. The term 'police surgeon' is an historic one, and in order to define their role more accurately, many police surgeons now wish to be referred to as 'forensic physicians'. Other terms such as 'forensic medical examiner' in the Metropolitan Police District, and 'forensic medical officer' in Northern Ireland

---

1 'Working Together under the Children Act 1989 a guide to arrangements for inter-agency co-operation for the protection of children from abuse' 1991 HMSO.

are used by doctors working with the police to emphasise their clinical independence *from* the police, a point particularly relevant in Northern Ireland. However, the national body representing all doctors working in conjunction with the police, whatever their designation, remains the Association of Police Surgeons.

Police surgeons may be asked to give an opinion by the police on a case that has been referred directly to them, or may be invited by a consultant paediatrician to give an opinion on a case which has been referred to the paediatric department, either as in-patient or out-patient. Collaboration between paediatricians and police surgeons was encouraged by the then Department of Health and Social Security in 'Guidance for Doctors' published at the same time as the report of the Butler-Sloss enquiry into the Cleveland affair in 1988[2]:

> 'In some areas paediatricians and police surgeons are very successfully conducting physical examinations in collaboration. It is hoped that this method of working will extend so that the number of examinations to which a child is subjected is kept to a minimum.' (para 12.3)

There is therefore a strong argument for close co-operation, which is practised very successfully in many areas; if a case is referred to a police surgeon, he will invite the consultant paediatrician to be present at the examination, and vice versa. Although at first sight the examination of a child by two doctors appears to be an intrusion on the child's privacy, in practice if the examination is conducted sensitively, with either of the doctors taking the lead role and the other that of an observer, such intrusion is kept to a minimum.

The joint examination has several advantages. First, and most importantly, the child only has to submit to a single examination, which is particularly important in the case of suspected child sexual abuse. Secondly, a joint statement can be issued, which, if not in total agreement, can identify areas of disagreement at a very early stage in the investigation. Thirdly, each doctor can bring to the consultation his own particular expertise; in the case of the paediatrician, in addition to giving an opinion about possible injuries, he can direct his expertise to such considerations as the general health, welfare and development of the child, particularly in cases of alleged neglect, and can assist in the diagnosis of any underlying physical illness which may, for example, cause bruising. The forensic physician has expert skills in the identification and evaluation of injuries and particularly patterns of injuries, and in the case of sexual abuse will have the necessary skills to obtain appropriate samples for onward transfer to the forensic science laboratory, and will have knowledge of the way in which such samples should be handled so that the preservation of the evidence will not be challenged.

---

2   DHSS 'Diagnosis of Child Abuse: Guidance for Doctors' 1988 HMSO.

A final advantage of a joint examination is that the paediatrician can then continue to give medical care to the child, and support to the family, without being perceived to be a part of the investigative team. Hopefully the statement will be an agreed one, in which case the police surgeon, perhaps more used to court appearances, can give evidence if necessary, although of course the paediatrician may also be required to attend court.

With respect to the categories of child abuse, in cases of alleged neglect or emotional abuse, the lead medical role will be taken by paediatricians and child psychiatrists respectively; both groups of doctors will also have a role in the identification, evaluation and treatment of children subjected to sexual abuse, particularly long-term abuse.

PHYSICAL ABUSE

Whether acting in a primary or secondary role, a doctor will follow the 'medical model' in the investigation of a case of physical child abuse: a history is taken, an examination is conducted, investigations are carried out, an opinion as to diagnosis is reached and a report or statement is issued. There are certain features in the history, as given by the carer or the child, which might lead the doctor to suspect that he is dealing with a case of physical child abuse, as listed in Figure 1.

Figure 1

History is contradictory or discrepant.

History is unrealistic.

History is just plausible, but classical signs of abuse are present.

History changes from day-to-day.

Delay in reporting injury.

Thus the most important feature of a case of child abuse will be an inconsistency between the history and the physical findings. Either it is just not possible for the injury to have been sustained in the way described, or the injury is apparently of a different age to that given in the history, or the history varies from interview-to-interview or from day-to-day indicating that the story is untrue and that there is 'something to hide'.

The doctor will then move on to make an examination. Injuries sustained non-accidentally fall into the same groups as those sustained accidentally, as listed in Figure 2.

Figure 2

Bruises, lacerations, weals, scars.

Burns and scalds.

Bone and joint injuries.

Brain and eye injuries.

Visceral (internal) injury.

Bites.

Just as in the history certain features may suggest a diagnosis of child abuse, so, on examination, certain findings will also suggest such a diagnosis. Of particular importance is the finding of multiple injuries, of different ages, perhaps at different sites. Examples would be the co-existence of an ageing bite mark at one site, and a fracture of a bone at another, or the presence of multiple bite marks or burns of different ages at different sites, suggesting a repetitive pattern of injury indicative of punishment routines.

The doctor will then proceed to investigations, of which the most important are blood tests to exclude an underlying cause for "easy" bruising (such as leukemia, haemophilia, or other similar blood disorders) and X-rays to exclude the presence of previously undiagnosed bone injury. It is vital that a full skeletal survey is conducted, since the combination of a fresh fracture and old undiagnosed fractures, possibly multiple and at different sites, is diagnostic of physical child abuse.

In the course of a complete physical examination, particular attention should be given to the head, and the organs of special sense. Repeated trauma to the head can not only cause fractures of the skull, contusion of the brain, and life-threatening intra-cerebral haemorrhages, but can also cause damage to the eye and the ear: the lens of the eye may be dislocated; there may be internal bruising to the eye; and even retinal detachment. Repeated trauma to the ear, such as by slapping, may produce rupture of the ear drum, or the collection of blood behind the intact ear drum. Evidence of scarring from repeated injury may be seen on the ear drum.

In the examination of the mouth, in young babies, particular attention should be given to the frenulum, the small fold of skin connecting the inside of the upper lip to the upper gum. This structure can be damaged in forced bottle feeding of the edentulous child. If a teat is forced into the mouth against the closed gums, then it will divert upwards and may damage the frenulum. Damage to the frenulum can also occur in accidental injury, but this would also entail other signs of injury to the surrounding area, such as bruising or lacerations. In the *absence* of other injury, damage to the frenulum in the bottle-fed child is almost diagnostic of forced bottle-feeding, and may be an indicator of other physical abuse.

Bite marks on children can be inflicted by siblings or children of other families, but can also be inflicted by parents or carers, either out of frustration or as a means of control and restraint or as part of a repetitive punishment pattern. Bite marks leave a distinctive pattern of bruising, from which the injury can be given an approximate age, and from which a forensic odontologist can obtain a 'match' from the pattern of a suspect's impressions. In addition, particularly with respect to sexual attacks, saliva can be obtained from a fresh bite mark, with the subsequent identification of the perpetrator by DNA analysis.

Burn mark injuries on children may be sustained by forcible contact with a hot instrument such as a lighted cigarette or fire grate, or by scalding, either from a hot fluid poured on the child, or from forced immersion in a hot bath. Although such injuries may of course be totally accidental, it is the features of the injury as outlined above such as the history, the age, the number and the site which will give an indication that the burns may be non-accidental in origin.

Thus, it is the doctor who takes the lead role in the diagnosis of physical non-accidental injury and who can give an opinion, having first obtained the history, examined the child, undertaken investigations and made a *firm* diagnosis which he can present to a case conference, or to a court of law.

SEXUAL ABUSE

In the case of sexual abuse, the lead role of the doctor is less clear, but is certainly maintained in acute sexual injury, that is child rape or child buggery discovered within 72 hours of the occurrence. In these events, child protection is as much an issue as is physical abuse; there may be acute ano-genital injury in need of medical or surgical treatment, and, if emission has occurred, there is a possibility of obtaining forensic evidence by use of the appropriate swabs that would assist in the identification of the perpetrator by blood grouping and DNA typing. The management of a child once admitted to hospital, should be by co-operation between the paediatrician and the forensic physician as outlined above. Further discussion in respect of the examination of children under anaesthetic is to be found below.

Chronic ano-genital abuse may leave signs of permanent damage. Chronic vaginal abuse may lead to repeated injury to the hymen, with evidence of old scarring. In repeated 'rubbing' of the genital area, the hymen may become thickened and inflamed, but remain intact. The vaginal entrance and the labia may show signs of previous injury or may also be reddened and thickened by repeated 'rubbing'.

Whether it is a disclosure from the child or other evidence that has led to the examination, great care must be taken in the interpretation of genital findings, since similar appearances may be caused by disease or by the insertion of foreign bodies. There is also a great range of variation in normal appearances from a hymen that is absent to one which is imperforate, and the hymenal orifice itself may be of several configurations.

Acute trauma to the anus may leave fresh lacerations at the anal margin or a 'gaping' anus with surrounding bruising. Chronic anal abuse can result in multiple healed fissures and a decrease in the tone of the anal ring muscles which may lead to imperfect closure of the anus, and easy dilation of the anus when the buttocks are gently separated, so-called 'reflex anal dilatation'. Once again, care must be taken in the interpretation of anal findings, since some of the findings that can be produced by external penetration can equally be produced by the extrusion of a hard stool. Thus, the findings on examination must be taken into consideration and placed in perspective with other information that may have come to light and is to be shared at a multi-disciplinary case conference.

Findings on examination may be totally normal; this by no means precludes previous sexual activity since inter-crural intercourse (between the tops of the thighs) or movement of the penis within the cleft of the buttocks may leave no physical sign, but may be repetitive, with consequent emotional destruction rather than physical injury.

In cases where an allegation has been made, or a suspicion of sexual abuse has been raised, perhaps by abnormal behaviour, normal findings on an examination are greatly reassuring to both child and parent, and it is therefore imperative that *all* children should be medically examined when the possibility of sexual abuse has been suggested.

Facilities for examination

It is of the greatest importance that any victim of assault, and particularly children, should be examined in satisfactory surroundings. Suitable locations would include a general practitioner's consulting room, the children's out-patient department at a hospital, or a side room on a children's ward. Traditionally, children were examined by police surgeons in examination rooms at police stations, which were often part of the custody suite. Thankfully, this is no longer the case, and most police forces now have victim examination suites where the victims of physical or sexual assault, whether adult or child, can be examined in surroundings that are ideal. Such examination suites may be attached to a police station, or may be at an entirely separate location. Suites include medical examination rooms, interview rooms, with video equipment for evidential recording, facilities for showering or bathing and usually a small kitchen area where suitable drinks and snacks can be prepared. The units are staffed by experienced CID officers;

a typical team would consist of a detective sergeant, a male detective constable and two female detective constables. In a county such as Suffolk, units are situated in Ipswich, Lowestoft and Bury St Edmunds, the main population centres serving the surrounding area.

The great advantage of these suites is that other professionals, such as paediatricians, scene-of-crime officers and photographers, can be invited into the suite, so that the victim can be interviewed, medically examined, and photographed if appropriate, in the one building, and can then proceed to shower or bath and put on a clean set of clothes with suitable refreshment being supplied. The transfer of victims of assault from one place to another is not only traumatic for the victim, but may also result in the loss of vital trace evidence.

MUNCHAUSEN'S SYNDROME BY PROXY (MSBP)

Munchausen's Syndrome describes adults who tend to wander from hospital to hospital and doctor to doctor inventing symptoms, and provoking needless investigation, either in an attempt to attract attention or, on occasions, in a direct attempt to obtain drugs such as opiates by inventing symptoms of pain. The patient tends to be very well informed, and, by virtue of the condition, experienced. The patient will have sufficient knowledge to be able to give a classical account of the pain associated with, for example, an acute heart attack or renal colic, and the examining doctor, unless he has previous knowledge of the patient, or is extremely experienced, will probably treat the patient with the desired analgesia. These patients tend to present themselves at casualty departments where they are examined by doctors who may have only limited experience, perhaps at senior house officer level.

Munchausen's Syndrome by Proxy is defined by Meadow thus:

'For children affected by the Munchausen's Syndrome by Proxy, the Proxy is the mother who provides the false information. Child abuse results partly from the direct actions of the mother – for example, giving drugs to make the child unconscious – and partly from those of doctors, who arrange invasive investigations or needless treatment for the child at the mother's instigation.'[3]

The Munchausen's Syndrome by Proxy received much media attention at the time of the trial of Nurse Beverley Allitt, with considerable resultant confusion. Although Allitt herself suffered from Munchausen's Syndrome, and had '... made 24 visits to the hospital's casualty department between 1987 and 1990',[4] she went on, in a form of Munchausen's Syndrome by Proxy, to injure children by suffocation or the injection of dangerous substances, as a

---

3   Meadow, R (ed) The ABC of Child Abuse BMA Publications 1993.
4   'Children's Nurse Convicted of Murder' British Medical Journal News, vol 306 p 1431.

result of which four children died. Allitt received 13 life sentences for the murder of the four children and for the attempted murder of another three, and for causing grievous bodily harm with intent to six more children.

Allitt had therefore progressed through the Munchausen's Syndrome by Proxy, to become 'Britain's most prolific female serial killer this century'.[5]

A more typical presentation of Munchausen's Syndrome by Proxy is the repeated partial suffocation of a child by a parent, almost always the mother. Following the admission to hospital of the child, covert videoing of the child's room may reveal a definitive diagnosis of the condition if the child is seen to be suffocated or otherwise harmed by the mother during a routine hospital visit. Covert video assessment has a sensitivity of over 90% in suitably screened cases.[6]

The ethical use of such covert videoing techniques has been discussed in articles which expressed opposing opinions in the 'education and debate' section of the British Medical Journal.[7]

Foreman and Farsides took the view that:

'The technique presents several ethical problems, including exposure of the child to further abuse and a breach of trust between carer, child and the professionals. Although covert videoing can be justified in restricted circumstances, new abuse procedures under the Children Act now seem to make its use unethical in most cases.'

However the same authors, in their conclusion, stated that:

'The use of covert videoing in Munchausen's Syndrome by Proxy, while controversial, is ethical in restricted circumstances.'

A particular worry of Foreman and Farsides is that covert videoing is incompatible with the Children Act, which requires local authorities to ensure 'the welfare of the child and to protect the child', whereas 'covert video assessment is problematic because the child's safety is risked to ensure long-term protection'.

In an article immediately following, Southall and Samuels took the view that, since the primary objective of the Children Act is the welfare of the child, covert videoing is entirely consistent with the ethos of the Act, since:

'... it is incumbent on all agencies working together on cases of suspected suffocation to obtain the most objective and definitive information to ensure the best protection of the child. Uncertainty arising from insufficient information could lead to sudden death, cerebral injury or long-term hidden emotional and physical torment that the child and his or her siblings have little or no defence against.'

---

5 *The Times* 29 May 1993, p 3.

6 Samuels, M McClaughlin, W Jacobson, R Poets, C Southall, D 'Fourteen cases of imposed upper airway obstruction'. Arch Dis Child 1992; 67: 162–70.

7 *British Medical Journal*, Vol 307, 4 September 1993 p 611–614.

Foreman and Farsides expressed concern about '... a breach of trust between carer, child and the professionals'. Southall and Samuels regretted such a breach of trust, but stated that: '... in our view if a parent may be inflicting life threatening abuse on his or her child, this becomes justifiable'.

Thus, both sets of authors agree that covert videoing is acceptable in some circumstances; Foreman and Farsides do so within a restrictive and narrow framework, whereas Southall and Samuels accept a greater degree of paternalism.

The use of covert video surveillance (CVS) clearly raises difficult ethical questions for the medical profession. Evidence produced by CVS will generally be admissible in court in civil proceedings relating to the child, even if the evidence is held to be unlawfully or improperly obtained. However, in *Re DH (a minor) (child abuse)*[8] Wall J stressed that the court would not wish, as a matter of practice, to continue to sanction conduct which was in fact unlawful. In this case a two-year-old child was admitted to hospital having been diagnosed as having an upper respiratory tract infection. The consultant paediatrician suspected that the mother was responsible as a result of Munchausen's Syndrome by Proxy. CVS was used without telling the mother or seeking the father's permission. As a result of the surveillance the mother was arrested and eventually pleaded guilty to an offence of cruelty to the child. The local authority initiated child protection proceedings. In the Family Division, Wall J considered that CVS as practised on this occasion was lawful and did not require the consent of the father. He concluded at p 174:

'In my judgment the paramount concern is the welfare of the child. The protection afforded to the child by the categorical and incontrovertible discovery of the fact and source of assaults upon him in a clinical setting and surrounded by clear safeguards designed collectively to prevent him from the risk of serious harm greatly outweighs the temporary damage caused by the observed assault. In my judgment, therefore, if the doctor takes the view that CVS is essential for the treatment of his patient he is entitled to undertake it without parental consent, provided that he is satisfied that there is no risk that his patient will come to any serious harm.'

The decision is therefore one for the doctor to make. However, as Wall J pointed out, critical to this analysis is the foolproof nature of the monitoring process. If the process involves a risk of anything more than transient harm to the child, doctors would be wise either to seek the consent of the parent not suspected of MSBP or a person or body having parental responsibility or an order of the court, if need be on an urgent *ex parte* basis.

---

8   [1994] 1 FLR 679.

CONSENT

Before a doctor examines a child, thought to be the victim of physical or sexual abuse, he must first obtain appropriate consent. The law has long regarded examination as part of treatment, and therefore the same legal considerations which apply to treatment may also, broadly speaking, be applied to the issue of consent to examination

Jauncey LJ, said in *F v West Berkshire Health Authority*[9]:

'There are four stages in the treatment of a patient, whether competent or incompetent. The first is to diagnose the relevant condition. The second is to determine whether the condition merits treatment. The third is to determine what the merited treatment should be. The fourth is to carry out the chosen form of medical treatment.'

An essential part of the diagnostic process is examination, which must therefore fall under the general heading of 'medical treatment'. This proposition was supported by Mr Nicholas Wilson QC, sitting as a Deputy Judge in the High Court in *Re H (mental patient)*[10] who said:

'If diagnosis is not treatment, it is the essential precursor of treatment, and I see no reason to distinguish between proposed diagnostic procedures and proposed therapeutic procedures. The same criterion governs their lawfulness ...'

With regard to children under 16, judgment on the issue of consent to treatment was given in *Gillick v West Norfolk and Wisbech Area Health Authority*.[11] The legal aspects of the *Gillick* case are discussed in Chapter 6, and it is established that a 'Gillick competent' child can not only consent to medical examination, but also has the right to refuse examination and treatment, a right that is now embodied in the Children Act 1989.

From a practical standpoint, despite the rights of the child to refuse or consent to treatment, the doctor would be well advised to attempt to obtain consent from one or other of the parents to the examination of a child, in addition to the child's own consent, although in some cases, particularly in relation to child sexual abuse, to obtain parental consent might be either impossible or inappropriate.

Again, from the practical standpoint, it is the *incompetent* child who may present greater difficulties to the doctor. If a child is in need of urgent medical treatment, for example following the discovery of internal bleeding after an assault, then it is clearly right for the doctor to proceed to a course of treatment, including an operation if necessary, as to do so is obviously in the best interests of the child. However, a doctor must distinguish in his own mind between *therapeutic* intervention, during the course of which evidence

---

9 (1989) 4 BMLR 32.

10 *Re H (mental patient)* (1992) 9 BMLR 75.

11 [1986] AC 112.

may be obtained, and an examination which is purely for *investigative* purposes; in the case of the latter, consent to the examination may be given by either parent, by the court under the terms of a Child Assessment Order under section 43 of the Children Act 1989, or under the restricted wardship jurisdiction under section 100 of the Children Act 1989.

Occasionally, for example in cases of ano-genital bleeding following sexual abuse, an examination under anaesthetic is necessary. Again, during the course of such an examination, forensic samples and other evidence may be obtained, but, as a general rule, an anaesthetic would never be justified for the purposes of the *collection of evidence only*.

As is the case with all decisions regarding children, whether clinical or not, it is the welfare of the child that must be the prime consideration. The doctor must make decisions in the knowledge that they may have to justify those decisions upon challenge, either in the civil court where he or she may face an action for the tort of battery, the criminal court where he or she may face a charge of common assault or perhaps indecent assault, or before the General Medical Council where he or she might stand accused of serious professional misconduct. If the doctor can show that at all times he or she has acted in what was considered to be the best interests of the child, then he or she must be certain to survive such challenges.

CONFIDENTIALITY

Doctors who are involved in the investigation of child abuse in the secondary role, that is paediatricians and police surgeons, will rarely have a problem with confidential information, since by the time this stage of the investigation has been reached, much of the information concerning the child and the family will already have been shared amongst the agencies concerned. As discussed in 'Working Together':

> 'Arrangements for the protection of children from abuse and in particular child protection conferences, can only be successful if the professional staff concerned do all that they can to work in partnership and share and exchange relevant information, in particular with social services departments (or the NSPCC) and the police.' (para 3.10)

The issues may not be so clear in the case of a doctor acting in the primary role, particularly the general practitioner who may be faced with, say, a 15 year old girl who gives a clear history of abuse, but maintains the right to confidentiality with regard to the perpetrator of that abuse.

'Working Together' suggests that there is no such dilemma:

> 'It is essential that whenever a general practitioner becomes suspicious that a child may be at risk of, or is the subject of, abuse of whatever nature, the information is shared with the statutory services responsible for child protection, ie social services departments, the NSPCC or the police.' (para 4.32)

However, at para 3.12, under the heading 'Exchange of Information', 'Working Together' refers doctors to the annual report of the General Medical Council in 1987, which gives '... unequivocal advice on this matter in cases of child abuse, including child sexual abuse'.

On the recommendations of the Standards Committee, the General Medical Council in November 1987 expressed the view that:

'If a doctor has reason for believing that a child is being physically or sexually abused, not only is it permissible for the doctor to disclose information to a third party, but it is the duty of the doctor to do so.'[12]

This approach is strongly contested by groups such as the Children's Legal Centre,[13] which stated that:

'The medical profession has no general duty to break confidence and provide information on patients to any other agency (save in very exceptional and closely defined circumstances).' (para 3.1.3)

The guidance of the General Medical Council was reviewed in the annual report of 1991 where it was stated:

'The Council's annual report for 1988 included advice that doctors had a duty to inform an appropriate person or authority when they suspected that a child had been physically or sexually abused. In reviewing this guidance the Committee concluded that circumstances might arise where disclosure would not be in the best interests of the patient. For this reason the guidance allows doctors greater discretion in deciding whether or not to disclose information so that individual circumstances of each case may be taken into account. Where child abuse is suspected ... the medical interests of the patients must take priority and may require the doctor to disclose information.'

The different stance of the General Medical Council was subsequently reflected in their 'Guidance to Doctors Professional Conduct and Discipline: Fitness to Practise' of January 1993, where it was stated that:

'One such situation (deciding whether or not to disclose information) may arise where a doctor believes that a patient may be the victim of physical or sexual abuse. In such circumstances the patient's medical interests are paramount and may require the doctor to disclose information to an appropriate person or authority.' (para 83)

The guidance continues at para 84, where it is stated that:

'Difficulties may also arise when a doctor believes that a patient, by reason of immaturity, does not have sufficient understanding to appreciate what the treatment or advice being sought may involve. ... In all such cases the doctor should attempt to persuade the patient to allow an appropriate person to be involved in the consultation. If the patient cannot understand or be persuaded and the doctor is convinced that the disclosure of information would be

---

12   Annual Report of the General Medical Council 1987.

13   Child Abuse Procedures – the Child's Viewpoint, the Children's Legal Centre 1988.

essential to the patient's best medical interests, the doctor may disclose to an appropriate person or authority the facts of the consultation and the information learnt in it. A doctor who decides to disclose information must be prepared to justify that decision and must inform the patient before any disclosure is made.'

Thus the contemporary guidance given to doctors allows greater discretion in deciding whether or not to disclose information, so that the individual circumstances of each case may be taken into account. There is therefore a much less strict duty of care placed upon the doctor by the General Medical Council, in apparent contradiction to 'Working Together'.

The concept of making a 'balanced judgment' introduced by the guidance given by the General Medical Council is acknowledged in the guidance produced by a joint working party of the Department of Health, the British Medical Association and the Conference of Medical Royal Colleges and issued as an addendum to 'Working Together'.[14] The guidance states:

'At all stages, therefore, a doctor needs to make a balanced judgment between the justification for breaching confidence and the distress it might cause and the withholding of vital information obtained within the privileged doctor/patient relationship.' (para 4.2)

In the matter of confidentiality, as with consent, the doctor's paramount consideration must be the welfare of the child.

The child protection conference presents special problems for the doctor in the area of confidentiality. Many agencies will be represented at such conferences, which may not be bound so strictly in the matter of confidentiality as is the doctor. Practical advice is given in 'Child Protection: Medical Responsibilities':

'Doctors, like other professionals, may need direct access to the child protection conference chair before the conference takes place. Doctors may wish to discuss concerns about disclosing confidential information as a result of parental involvement in the conference or the involvement of people whom they consider inappropriate, including the child, and the reasons for their concerns, so that the appropriate forum for sharing their information can be agreed.' (para 3.13)

A doctor may feel the need to advise the chair of the child protection conference that consideration should be given to excluding either a parent or a child from part of the conference, particularly if it is his or her intention to discuss matters which, though relevant to the case under consideration, are drawn from the records of third parties such as the extended family.

---

14 Child Protection: Medical Responsibilites; Guidance for doctors working with Child Protection Agencies: Department of Health, British Medical Association Conference of Medical Royal Colleges (addendum to 'Working Together - under the Children Act 1989').

CONCLUSION

In general, the position of the doctor as either the reporter of possible child abuse, or as part of the team investigating a report of such abuse, has been greatly clarified by the *Gillick* judgment, the Children Act and ethical guidelines issued in association with the Act.

Although all doctors would acknowledge the great importance played by child protection conferences in the investigation of child abuse, and the formulation of management policies for the child, the timing and length of conferences pose problems for doctors, particularly the busy general practitioner, who may have much to offer the conference. Anecdotal evidence suggests that the duration of conferences and subsequent reviews has been extended by the presence of parents and children.

A significant change in clinical practice has been the involvement of the parents at a much earlier stage in the doctor's investigation. The doctor is now much more inclined to discuss the findings with parents either during the examination or immediately afterwards, rather than the parents becoming aware of the doctor's findings for the first time at a case conference, with consequent distress at the disclosure of such findings at the conference.

Good practice has always dictated that the child should be made aware of the doctor's findings, and this has been reinforced by the Children Act. Of particular reassurance to both child and parent are normal findings on examination, particularly in cases of alleged sexual abuse.

As far as the future is concerned, one of the greatest advances that would be of assistance to doctors, the courts and particularly the child, would be the acceptance by the courts of consensus reports. In practical terms, there is often little difference between the opinions of the examining doctors, be they police surgeons or paediatricians, and medical experts employed by the defence. If joint reports could be agreed, and accepted by the courts, then greater attention could be focused on those areas where there is a difference of opinion; such practice would not only speed up the legal process by identifying the really important areas of concern to the courts, but would also be in the best interests of the child since much material that would be embarrassing or damaging to the child could be agreed and therefore perhaps not discussed in court at all.

CHAPTER 6

THE VOICE OF THE CHILD

'A CHILD IS A PERSON AND NOT AN OBJECT OF CONCERN'[1]

For many years society paid scant regard to children as individuals. Children were generally not regarded as people in their own right and were usually given no opportunity to express their views or wishes. Even if they were given such an opportunity, little credence or weight was attached to what they had to say ('Children should be seen and not heard', it was often said). Children were seen as being the 'property' of their parents. It was generally thought that parents knew what was best for their child and were seen as having 'rights' over the child. If state intervention was justified, the 'right' to decide what was best for the child was passed to the social workers and courts. Furthermore, if a child made an allegation of abuse, if not supported by other evidence, the allegation was likely to be dismissed. Conventional beliefs suggested that children were more likely to lie than adults and that they had poor recall and were more open to suggestion. The concept of parental rights and doubts over the credibility of children ensured that traditionally a child had no audible voice. However, in recent years children have gradually acquired a degree of autonomy and credibility. It is now recognised that children must not be treated as silent objects of concern, that children are people in their own right and that they have their own views and feelings which should be taken into account. The concept of parental 'rights' has changed to one of parental 'responsibility', which exists for the protection of the child and which yields to the child when he or she is old enough to understand the implications of a certain course of action. As Stone comments, there is an increased awareness that 'the child does not, on reaching the age of majority, spring like Minerva fully armed from the head of her parent'.[2]

It is also now recognised that even very young children can make credible, competent witnesses and that what they say should be taken seriously. As a result legal requirements regarding the admissibility of children's evidence are being relaxed and procedures in court are being reformed to enable more children to give evidence in court (see Chapter 7). It seems that children have now acquired a voice – a voice that is being listened to with increasing respect.

---

1   Butler Sloss, E (1988) 'Report of the Inquiry into Child Abuse in Cleveland 1987'. Cmnd 412, London, HMSO.

2   Stone, O (1982) *The Child's Voice in the Court of Law*, Canada, Butterworths.

AN INTERNATIONAL PERSPECTIVE – THE UNITED NATIONS CONVENTION ON THE RIGHTS OF THE CHILD

International attention was initially paid to the rights of children after the first world war when concern was expressed about the plight of children affected by the devastation of war. In 1924 the Fifth Assembly of the League of Nations adopted the Declaration of Geneva which emphasised children's material needs, but imposed no specific obligations on nations. In 1959 the United Nations, the League's successor, adopted a second world declaration – the Declaration of the Rights of the Child – which was based on the premise that 'mankind owes to the child the best it has to give'. The 10 principles outlined in the Declaration constituted a proclamation of general principles, but again imposed no specific obligations. The International Year of the Child, which at the time was described as the pinnacle of an international effort to promote the needs and rights of children, was celebrated throughout the world in 1979. In 1989 the General Assembly of the United Nations adopted the Convention on the Rights of the Child (the Convention). The Convention contains over 50 articles which can be broken down into three broad categories[3]:

(i)   Provision articles which recognise the rights of children to minimum standards of health, education, social security, physical care, family life, play recreation, culture and leisure;

(ii)   Protection articles which identify the rights of children to be safe from discrimination, physical and sexual abuse, exploitation, substance abuse, injustice and conflict;

(iii)   Participation articles which concern civil and political rights. They acknowledge the rights of children to a name and identity, to be consulted and to be taken account of, to have access to information, freedom of speech and opinion, and to challenge decisions made on their behalf.

The UK signed the Convention on 19 April 1990 and ratified it on 16 December 1991. It came into force in the UK on 15 January 1992. Ratification is said to ensure that the needs and interests of children are given a high profile across Government. Although in ratifying the Convention, the Government signified its intention to comply with its provisions, the Convention is not enforceable in the same way that the European Convention on Human Rights is enforceable – individual children cannot make applications alleging breaches of its articles and there are no direct sanctions that can be applied to ensure that the rights it contains are protected. The Government is obliged to report on the implementation of the Convention to a UN Committee on the Rights of the

---

3   Lansdowne, G (1992) 'UN Convention: Setting New Targets' in *Adoption & Fostering* 16(3) p 34.

Child. The Department of Health was given responsibility for co-ordinating UK's response and the first report was made in February 1994.[4] Article 4 of the Convention provides that states' parties shall undertake all appropriate legislation, administration, and other measures, for the implementation of the rights recognised in the Convention. The report notes that ratification of the Convention did not require any amendment to UK legislation, but accepts that there is a continuing need to take active measures to ensure that the aims of legislation are translated into everyday policy and practice throughout the country, citing the establishment of a strategy for monitoring the implementation of the Children Act 1989 as an example of such active measures. The report claims that the operation of the Act and its effect on children is subject to regular and public scrutiny by means of the Children Act Advisory Committee, which was set up to monitor the court-related aspects of the Act and reports each year to the Lord Chancellor, the Home Secretary, the Secretaries of State for Health and for Wales and the President of the Family Division of the High Court, and the reports to Parliament on the implementation of the Act from the Secretaries of State for Health and for Wales. In theory, the mechanics of the monitoring strategy seem sufficient to meet this aim. However, given the fact that the Convention confers no directly enforceable rights on individuals, there is the ever-present danger that the realities of life, in particular the financial constraints placed on local authorities, ensure that the rights of children are not accorded the status envisaged by the convention.

CHILDREN'S RIGHTS AND THE CONCEPT OF THE 'GILLICK COMPETENT' CHILD

The tendency to accord increased status to children reached a highpoint in the House of Lord's decision in the case of *Gillick v West Norfolk and Wisbech Area Health Authority*,[5] which has been referred to as a 'landmark of children's rights'.[6] The DHSS issued a circular, advising doctors that 'in the most unusual circumstances' it would be proper for them to give contraceptive advice and treatment to a girl under the age of 16 without her parent's knowledge or consent. Section 8(1) of the Family Law Reform Act 1969 specifically provides that minors who have attained the age of 16 years can give valid consent to surgical, medical or dental treatment. Section 8(3) provides that nothing in the section shall be construed as rendering ineffective any consent which would have been effective if the section had not been enacted, but there was no direct authority for children below the age of 16

---

4   'The UK's First Report to the UN Committee on the Rights of the Child' (1994) HMSO.

5   [1986] AC 112.

6   Bromley & Lowe (1992) Bromley's *Family Law*, 8th ed, London, Butterworths p 295.

years to give valid consent. Mrs Gillick, the mother of four daughters under the age of 16, sought a declaration that the circular was unlawful because it infringed her right, as a parent, to be informed and to veto any medical treatment of her children. The Court of Appeal ruled in favour of Mrs Gillick, holding that parents had an absolute right to decide questions affecting their minor children unless and until a court intervened. The majority of the House of Lords, however, ruled against Mrs Gillick. In the words of Lord Scarman:

> 'The underlying principle of the law ... is that parental right yields to the child's right to make his own decisions when he reaches a sufficient understanding and intelligence to be capable of making up his own mind on the matter requiring decisions.'

The decision of the Court of Appeal, although questionable in principle (why should a mature 15 year old girl not be permitted to make decisions regarding her own body if she understands the implications of the decision?), at least had the benefit of certainty. The ruling of the House of Lords places third parties in a potentially difficult position. When does a child reach sufficient understanding and intelligence to be deemed 'Gillick competent'? Whereas a competent adult is under no obligation to make wise, rational decisions, it may be thought that a child who purports to make a decision which an adult considers irrational and against the child's best interests would hardly be likely to be deemed competent to make that decision. The principle of the 'Gillick competent' child is to be applauded in theory, but the practical application of the principle, requiring subjective assessment of the level of understanding and intelligence of the child concerned in the light of the decision in issue, is not without its problems and requires careful consideration by all involved.

Despite the difficulty of dealing with the emerging autonomy of young people, the principles underlying the *Gillick* decision have been imported into the philosophy of the Children Act 1989. Furthermore, the Act gives children of sufficient age and understanding to make an informed decision *statutory* rights to *refuse* to submit to medical examinations or assessments contained in court directions in emergency protection orders, child assessment orders and interim care orders, thereby clearly indicating Parliament's intention that 'Gillick competent' children can not only consent to, but may also *refuse* to consent to, medical examinations and treatment. Recent decisions, however, indicate that the courts have taken it upon themselves to override the statutory right of refusal. Prior to the implementation of the Act, in the case of *Re R*[7] the Court of Appeal had overruled the refusal of a 15 year old ward of court to accept anti-psychotic treatment. On the facts of the case, the girl was deemed incompetent, but it was stated *obiter* that, even if she had been competent, her refusal would still have been overruled. Lord Donaldson in

---

7   *Re R (a minor) (Wardship: consent to medical treatment)* [1991] 3 WLR 592.

the Court of Appeal confirmed that the court acting in wardship can overrule the decisions of a 'Gillick competent' child and differentiated between powers to consent and powers to refuse treatment – whereas the competent child may consent to treatment, this did not mean that the child could refuse treatment which was deemed to be in her best interests. The reasoning in *Re R* was re-affirmed by the Court of Appeal in the later case of *Re W*.[8] The case concerned a 16 year old anorexic patient who was deemed competent (and therefore clearly had the power to consent to medical treatment by virtue of section 8 of the Family Law Reform Act 1969), but was overruled in her refusal of treatment. As the child was already the subject of a care order, the court was asked to exercise its inherent powers outside the wardship jurisdiction (see Chapter 3). The Court of Appeal ruled that, whereas section 8 of the 1969 Act allows 16 and 17 year olds to give valid consent, the provision does not address refusal of treatment and it does not empower them to refuse consent. Section 8(3) expressly preserves the validity of any other consent and the court interpreted this as allowing either parents, or the court exercising its inherent jurisdiction, to consent on behalf of a 16 year old who refuses to do so herself. The decision in *Gillick* was limited to its own facts – a 'Gillick competent' child may give valid consent to treatment, but no power of veto is conferred on the child. Although neither *Re R* or *Re W* was directly concerned with the statutory right of refusal conferred by the Act, the principles underlying these decisions seem to be in direct conflict with this statutory right.

Further inroads into a 'Gillick competent' child's autonomy over his or her body were made in the case of *South Glamorgan County Council v W & B*.[9] In the Family Division of the High Court, Douglas Brown J made an interim care order in respect of a severely disturbed 15 year old girl and gave directions under section 38(6) of the Act for the girl to undergo psychiatric examination and assessment at an adolescent unit. The girl purported to exercise her statutory right to refuse consent to the examination and assessment and the local authority brought proceedings to invoke the exercise of the inherent jurisdiction of the High Court to overrule the refusal and consent on behalf of the girl, on the basis that she was otherwise likely to suffer significant harm. After hearing psychiatric evidence, Douglas Brown J ruled that he was not prepared to find, on the evidence, that the girl was not competent within the meaning of section 38(6). However, relying on the authorities of *Re R* and *Re W*, he then ruled that the court could exercise it's inherent jurisidiction to override the refusal of a child of any age to submit to medical or psychiatric examination or treatment if it was in the best interests of the child, even if the child was deemed to have sufficient understanding to make an informed decision about the matter. This seems to be a classic case of giving with one hand and taking back with the other. Parliament's clear intention was to allow

---

8   *Re W (a minor) (Medical treatment)* [1992] 4 All ER 627.
9   *South Glamorgan CC v W & B* [1993] 1 FLR 574.

the competent child autonomy over his or her own body by giving the child the right to refuse any medical or psychiatric intervention. By deeming a child to be competent, and then overriding the child's refusal, the court is calling into question the whole concept of children's rights. Whilst the end result of the *South Glamorgan* case was undoubtedly correct – the facts of the case indicate that the girl was in urgent need of psychiatric help – the route taken to achieve the end result must be questioned. If the need for psychiatric intervention was so pressing that the court was prepared to override the child's right of refusal, why was the girl deemed to have 'sufficient understanding to make an informed decision' in the first place? As Parliament has given a competent child the right to refuse medical or psychiatric intervention, surely the preferred route to ensuring the child receives such intervention is by a conservative assessment of a child's competence. The more urgent the need for intervention, the slower the courts should be to find a child competent to refuse the intervention.

RESPECT FOR THE VIEWS OF THE CHILD

Older children who are deemed to be 'Gillick competent' have now been given a degree of autonomy in matters concerning their person, although the extent of such autonomy is by no means clear. Yet the process of maturing is a gradual one – a child does not become 'Gillick competent' overnight. Children are capable of forming their own views at a very early age and whilst the plaintive cries of a three year old that they do not want to go to bed may be ignored, the views of an eight year old as to where they want to live or who they want to care for them should not be dismissed out of hand. This is reflected in Article 12 of the Convention which provides:

(1) States' parties shall assure to the child, who is capable of forming his or her own views, the right to express those views freely in all matters affecting the child, the views of the child being given due weight in accordance with the age and maturity of the child.

(2) For this purpose, the child shall, in particular, be provided the opportunity to be heard in any judicial and administrative proceedings affecting the child, either directly, or through a representative or an appropriate body, in a manner consistent with the procedural rules of national law.

There is a growing awareness of the need to take account of the views of children, and this awareness is reflected in the 1989 Act.

The need to consult the child

Section 3 of the Children Act 1975 provided that, in reaching any decision relating to the adoption of a child, 'a court ... shall so far as practicable ascertain the wishes and feelings of the child regarding the decision and give due consideration to them, having regard to his age and understanding'. The Children Act 1989 extends this principle considerably. For the first time, apart from adoption law, statutory effect is given to the principle that the child's wishes and feelings should be taken into account. For example, before providing accommodation for a child by virtue of the duty imposed by section 20 of the Act, a local authority is required, so far as is reasonably practicable and consistent with the child's welfare, to ascertain the child's wishes regarding the provision of accommodation and give due consideration (having regard to his or her age and understanding) to such wishes of the child as it has been able to ascertain (section 20(6)). A similar duty is imposed on local authorities before making any decision with respect to a child whom they are looking after, or proposing to look after (section 22(4) & (5)). Children, if of sufficient age and understanding, will usually be invited to attend any child protection conferences. Local authorities are required to tell children what plans they have made about their placement and before conducting reviews of these arrangements they are required to seek and take into account the wishes of the children concerned. In contested section 8 applications and in all cases where a court is considering whether to make, vary or discharge a care or supervision order, the court is directed to have regard in particular to, inter alia, the ascertainable wishes and feelings of the child concerned (considered in the light of his or her age and understanding) (section 1(3)(a)). Interestingly, if a police officer takes a child into police protection there is an obligation to take such steps as are reasonably practicable to discover the wishes and feelings of the child (section 46(3)(d)), but apparently no obligation to take such wishes and feelings into account – presumably because of the limited time and choice of action available in such an emergency situation. The provisions of the Act therefore ensure that the child is consulted whenever possible and due regard is given to any views expressed whenever state intervention is justified. Nevertheless, in the absence of any state intervention, parents, and those exercising parental responsibility, have no legal obligation to ascertain or have regard to children's wishes before making decisions, even major ones, which affect the child. Within the family, it seems, a child has no guarantee his voice will be heard. Undoubtedly, in practice, many parents and carers do listen to the child's views and place due weight on what they hear. The weight, of course, will vary depending on the importance of the matter involved and the age and maturity of the child. This is surely a natural part of parenting. After all, democratic and harmonious family life generally revolves to a large extent around compromise, but the decision as to whether or not to accord precedence to the child's view is ultimately one for the parent or carer. Some conflict is inevitable, as every parent of teenage children will agree, but, if the conflict cannot be resolved within the family, does the child have a voice that can be heard outside the family?

For the first time, children now have a right to make an application to the court for leave to apply for a section 8 order. This is a significant change in the law which recognises the importance of children being heard on matters affecting their future. The popular press would lead one to believe that this gives children the right to 'divorce' their parents. Whilst this is technically inaccurate, children can now apply for leave to seek a residence order (which would settle the arrangements as to the person with whom he or she is to live), a contact order (which would govern the contact he or she has with specified persons) or a specific issue or prohibited steps order (which would decide what should be done about a particular aspect of his or her upbringing) – thereby giving the child the right to ask the court to chose between alternative lifestyles that may be available. However, section 10(8) provides that where the child makes such an application, the court may only grant leave if it is satisfied that the child has sufficient understanding to make the proposed application for the section 8 order, thereby effectively restricting the provision to older children. Such applications for leave must now be made or transferred to the High Court[10] – a move which may in itself place an additional psychological obstacle in the path of a child, for whom the local magistrates' court may be a more appropriate environment. The age and maturity of the child will obviously be the key factor in deciding if the child has sufficient understanding to make the proposed application. But even if the child does have the requisite understanding, the granting of leave is not automatic and the approach of the court has not been consistent. In Re C,[11] having decided a 14 year old girl did have the requisite understanding, Johnson J held that the question of leave was governed by the general principles of the Act and applied the welfare and non-intervention principles. However, in Re SC,[12] which again concerned a 14 year old girl who had the requisite understanding, Booth J held that the initial application for leave did not raise any question regarding the upbringing of the child and therefore the child's welfare was not the court's paramount consideration. The approach of Johnson J is more restrictive in that it involves the court inquiring into the merits of the substantive issues during the initial application for leave – thereby potentially refusing a child access to the courts at an early stage. Given the increasing voice being accorded to children this is difficult to justify. If a child has sufficient understanding to make the proposed application, surely that in itself should be sufficient. The qualification adopted by Booth J –

---

10   Practice Direction [1993] 1 All ER 820.

11   Re C (a minor) (Leave to seek section 8 orders) [1994] 1 FLR 26.

12   Re SC (a minor) (Leave to seek residence order) [1994] 1 FLR 96.

that the substantive application should not be palpably hopeless – is sufficient safeguard to ensure that leave will only be granted in appropriate situations.

Other jurisdictions have been somewhat more radical in their approach. In Finland, the Child Custody and Right of Access Act 1983 states that before a parent who has custody:

> 'makes any decision on a matter relating to the person of the child, he or she shall, where possible, discuss the matter with the child taking into account the child's age and maturity and the nature of the matter. In making the decision the custodian shall give due consideration to the child's feelings, opinions and wishes.'[13]

This appears to be taking the implementation of Article 12 to extremes. Whilst the imposition of such a statutory duty could arguably have the potential to influence behaviour, the duty must inevitably be vague and in reality must be unenforceable. It would also appear to constitute unwarranted intervention in family life. Certainly, children's participation in major decisions concerning themselves should be encouraged, but not to the extent of imposing legislative duties on parents and carers. It is only in circumstances where state intervention in family life is justified that there is sufficient justification for imposing a duty in order to ensure a child's viewpoint is heard.

Ascertaining the child's views – social workers and the initial investigation

During the initial stages of a child abuse investigation, the views of the child will be ascertained by the social workers, and sometimes police officers, involved. This will be done through discussion with the child. With young children, communication may be difficult, but the more mature the child, the more fully he will be able to enter into discussion and participate in the decision making process. However, although legally required to take children's wishes and feelings into account, in practice individual social workers may find they hold widely diverging views regarding children's abilities and their autonomy, and will have received differing amounts of training in direct work with children.[14] This means that the issues that social workers have to deal with are now much more complex than in the past. As Cooper suggests:

> 'Rather than simply 'rescuing' children from appalling and degrading conditions, as in the charitable work of the 19th and early 20th centuries, [social workers] must now combine knowledge of the importance of family links with an awareness of a child's developmental and emotional needs, taking into due account his own wishes and feelings.'[15]

---

13 Newell, P (1991) *The UN Convention and Children's Rights in the UK* London, National Children's Bureau, p 45.

14 Cooper, S (1994) *The Voice of the Child, Piaget and the Children Act Interpreted*, Social Work Monographs, Norwich.

15 Note 14 p 9.

However difficult their task may be, it is a crucial one and the child's wishes and feelings should be considered at every stage of an investigation and assessment. In many cases legal proceedings may not be initiated and so this will be the only opportunity for the child to put forward his or her views. Even if legal proceedings are initiated, the social worker may well be best equipped to describe to the court the consistency of a child's wishes and feelings.

Ascertaining the child's views – proceedings in courts

'The judge is greedy for information about the child and to hear the child's voice.'[16] However, it seems that the courts rarely hear the child's voice in person. It appears that magistrates in the family proceedings court hardly ever see a child privately, particularly where a welfare officer or guardian *ad litem* has been appointed. However, in the case of *Re M (minors)* 21 January 1993, unreported, authority appears to have been given to the interviewing of a child in private by magistrates, going against the pre-Children Act case law.[17] Judges in the county court and High Court have more freedom and it has been suggested that both judges and magistrates should see children more often and not be intimidated into thinking that only trained experts should be allowed direct access to the child's mind.[18] In many cases there can surely be no substitute for actually talking to the child in person. As long as any interaction between the child and magistrate or judge takes place in appropriate surroundings and is undertaken in a sensitive manner, it should cause no further trauma to the child and would help re-enforce the message of the Cleveland Report – the child is a person, not an object of concern. However, in practice, the principle sources of information for the court about the voice of the child are the professionals involved – social workers, welfare officers and guardians *ad litem*.

Welfare officers

Section 7(1) of the Children Act 1989 empowers any court, when considering any question with respect to a child under the Act, to ask a probation officer or local authority to report to the court 'on such matters relating to the welfare of that child as are required to be dealt with in the report'. This power is used most frequently in private law applications because, in the majority of cases of child abuse that reach court, a guardian *ad litem* will be appointed to represent the child and, as the Law Commission observed, such persons are better qualified to make independent assessments in care cases (see below).

---

16 Collins, P (1994) 'The Voice of the Child' [1994] *Family Law* 396.

17 The Children Act Advisory Committee Annual Report 1992/93 p 72.

18 Note 16 supra.

However, occasions may arise in public law proceedings where a court will ask for a welfare report to be prepared, for example if a welfare officer is already involved in a private law case and the court makes a direction pursuant to section 37 of the Act. Court welfare officers are qualified probation officers who are officers of the court and are therefore independent of the child and the parties to the proceedings. In preparing any report, the welfare officer undertakes an investigative role in order to provide factual background information to the court and is expected to visit and talk to the parties involved, including the child. The child's views will therefore usually be included in the report, along with the recommendations of the welfare officer. Although such recommendations are not binding on the court, the welfare officer's view commands great respect and if a court departs from a welfare officer's recommendation, it should state the reasons for so doing.[19]

The role of the guardian ad litem

The concept of the court receiving professional opinion concerning the interests of the child, expressed *independently* of the parents and local authority, came about as a result of the inquiry into the death of Maria Colwell.[20] The report of the inquiry expressed the view that it would have been of assistance to the court to have had the benefit of the views of independent social workers. The Children Act of 1975 made provision for the establishment of panels of guardians *ad litem* and reporting officers in adoption and care and related proceedings where conflict might occur between parents and the child, but the provision was not fully implemented until 1984. The role of the guardian *ad litem* has been considerably extended under the 1989 Act. The court is now required to appoint a guardian *ad litem* for the child in specified proceedings *unless satisfied that it is not necessary to do so in order to safeguard his interests* (section 41). Such an appointment will usually be made at the commencement of the proceedings and thus the guardian will be in involved in the case from the earliest opportunity. The specified proceedings are set out in section 41(6):

(1) applications for the making, variation or discharge of a care or supervision order and related appeals;

(2) where the court has given a direction under section 37(1) and has made, or is considering whether to make, an interim care order;

(3) where the court is considering making a residence order with respect to a child who is the subject of a care order;

---

19 Bromley & Lowe (1992) Bromley's *Family Law* 8th ed London, Butterworths p 381.

20 DHSS (1974) 'The Report of the Committee of Inquiry into the Care and Supervision Provided in Relation to Maria Colwell'.

(4) applications in respect of contact between a child who is the subject of a care order and any person;

(5) applications under Part V of the Act – which includes child assessment orders and emergency protection orders – and appeals against the making of, or refusal to make, such an order.

Guardians *ad litem* are usually qualified social workers and are always independent of the parties involved. A guardian will generally be appointed by the court from a panel held by the local authority in accordance with rules of court. The guardian is under a general duty to safeguard the interests of the child (section 41(2)). More specific duties are contained in Rules of Court:

(1) to advise the court whether the child is of sufficient understanding for any purpose including the child's refusal to submit to a medical or psychiatric examination or other assessment that the court has power to require, direct or order;

(2) to inform the court of the wishes of the child in respect of any matter relevant to the proceedings, including attendance at court;

(3) to advise the court of the appropriate forum for the proceedings;

(4) to advise the of court of the appropriate timing of the proceedings or any part of them;

(5) to advise the court of the options available to the court in respect of the child and the suitability of each such option including what order should be made in determining the application;

(6) to advise the court on any other matters on which the court seeks his or her advice or about which he or she considers that the court should be informed.[21]

The Department of Health has issued a guide entitled 'A Manual of Practice for Guardians *ad litem* and Reporting Officers' to assist the guardian in performing his duties. A guardian has a general discretion concerning what investigations to make, but in particular must contact or seek to interview such persons as he or she considers appropriate or as the court directs and obtain such professional assistance as is available and which he or she thinks appropriate or which the court directs him or her to obtain.[22] The guardian now has extensive rights to examine and take copies of any records of, or held by, a local authority in relation to the child, including child protection conference minutes (section 42(1) Children Act 1989 as amended by the Courts and Legal Services Act 1990, Schedule 16, para 18). If the guardian

---

21 Family Proceedings Court (Children Act 1989) Rules 1991, rule 11(4), Family Proceedings Rules 1991, rule 4.11(4).

22 FPR 1991, rule 4.11(9); FPC(CA)R 1991, rule 11(9).

inspects such records, he or she must tell the court and such other persons as the court may direct of all such records and documents which may, in his or her opinion, assist in the proper determination of the proceedings. Following the investigations, the guardian produces a written report for the court, advising on the interests of the child. The report is not used in deciding if a case has been proved, but will be considered in deciding what order to make, if any. Such reports, like welfare reports, although not binding, command great respect.

The official solicitor as guardian ad litem

The official solicitor represents minors and those adults incapable of managing their own affairs in a variety of family and other proceedings ranging from divorce to personal injury. In specified proceedings before the High Court, directions may be given that the role of the official solicitor should include the duty to act as guardian *ad litem* (section 41(8)). The Lord Chancellor's Department has issued guidance indicating that the official solicitor will consider acting as guardian *ad litem* for the child in cases where there is disputed medical evidence, or several variations in expert medical opinion (including psychiatric evidence), where the case involves a substantial foreign element, in cases involving special or exceptional points of law or where the official solicitor is already representing the child in other current proceedings.

Legal representation for the child and the guardian

In the specified proceedings mentioned above a child is entitled to be a party to the proceedings and a solicitor will usually be appointed to represent the child. If a guardian *ad litem* has been appointed, the guardian will be under a duty to appoint a solicitor.[23] Alternatively, the court may appoint a solicitor if no guardian *ad litem* has been appointed, or if the child has sufficient understanding to instruct a solicitor and wishes to do so (see below), or if it appears to the court that it would be in the child's best interests for him or her to be represented by a solicitor (section 41(3) & (4)). In many cases both a guardian *ad litem* and a solicitor will be appointed to act for the child. Provided that the guardian and the child do not have conflicting views, the solicitor must represent the child in accordance with instructions received from the guardian. It is envisaged that the solicitor and guardian will work together as a team, where the skills of one professional are explicitly acknowledged by the other. However, although the guardian will advise the court on the wishes of the child, his ultimate duty is to safeguard the interests of the child. As the Court of Appeal has pointed out:

---

23   FPR 1991, rule 4.11(2); FPC(CA)R 1991, rule 11(2)(a).

'[The guardian] has an independent function to perform, and must act in what he believes to be the minor's best interests, even if that should involve acting in contravention of the wishes of a minor who is old enough to articulate views of his own ... He owes a duty which has by its very nature to be divided: to the child whose views he must fully and fairly represent; and to the court, which it is his duty to assist in achieving the over-riding or paramount objective of promoting the child's best interests.'[24]

It follows that recommendations made by the guardian may conflict with the wishes of the child. Rules of court provide that, if it appears to the guardian that the child is instructing the solicitor direct, or intends to or is capable of conducting the proceedings on his or her own behalf, the guardian must inform the court. The guardian may then have legal representation, although they will not be eligible for legal aid, despite the recommendations of the Children Act Advisory Committee in their first annual report. In such circumstances, the solicitor can act independently of the instructions of the guardian if:

(1) he or she considers that the child wishes to give instructions which conflict with those of the guardian;

(2) the child is able, having regard to understanding, to give such instructions on his or her own behalf;

(3) he or she has taken into account the views of the guardian; and

(4) he or she takes into account any direction of the court as a result of the guardian informing the court of the conflict of instructions.[25]

If no guardian has been appointed and the child has sufficient understanding to instruct a solicitor and wishes to do so, the solicitor must act in accordance with the instructions received from the child. If the child is not competent to give instructions, the solicitor must act in the child's best interests. Therefore, as the Court of Appeal has pointed out,[26] the regime in public law cases contemplates that:

(i) there will normally be a guardian;

(ii) guardian and child may be separately legally represented;

(iii) the submissions made on behalf of the guardian must be directed to the child's best interests and may, in consequence, be different from those on behalf of the child;

(iv) the child's welfare will continue to be protected by the guardian.

The regime is complex, and has the potential to lead to a proliferation of professionals presenting the child's views to the court, on occasions in

---

24 Waite LJ in *Re CT (a minor)* [1993] 2 FLR 278 CA.

25 FPR 1991, rule 412(1)(a); FPC(CA)R 1991, rule 12(1)(a).

26 Bingham MR in *Re S (a minor) (Independent Representation)* [1993] 2 FLR 437.

addition to their own opinion as to how the child's welfare may best be served. However, as long as courts remain reluctant to hear the child in person, the regime at least has the virtue of ensuring that the child's voice is heard by the court and it is difficult to see how it could be simplified without the risk of suppressing the child's view in favour of those of guardian *ad litem*.

THE WELFARE OF THE CHILD v THE WISHES OF THE CHILD

It is now evident that children's wishes should be taken into account and decisions affecting a child are to be taken in the knowledge of the child's opinion. Yet, it is not easy to determine what weight should be given to those opinions. The dilemma was succinctly stated by the Master of the Rolls:

'The 1989 Act enables and requires a judicious balance to be struck between two considerations. First is the principle, to be honoured and respected, that children are human beings in their own right with individual minds and wills, views and emotions, which should command serious attention. A child's wishes are not to be discounted or dismissed simply because he is a child. He should be free to express them and decision makers should listen. Second is the fact that a child is, after all, a child. The reason why the law is particularly solicitous in protecting the interests of children is because they are liable to be vulnerable and impressionable, lacking the maturity to weigh the longer term against the shorter, lacking the insight to know how they will react and the imagination to know how others will react in certain situations, lacking the experience to measure the probable against the possible. For purposes of the Act, a babe in arms and a sturdy teenager on the verge of adulthood are both children, but their positions are quite different: for one the second consideration will be dominant, for the other the first principle will come into its own ...'[27]

Obviously, the older the child, the more weight is likely to be attached to his opinion, but it is also evident that the chronological age of the child is not the sole factor to be considered. Children mature at vastly differing rates and it is becoming increasingly apparent that each child needs to be assessed individually as to their mental and emotional maturity, intelligence and comprehension. In addition, children need to be given information on which to base their opinions. The Department of Health guidance[28] states 'all children need to be given information and explanations so that they are in a position to develop their own views and make choices'. However, this would seem to imply that children have the right to make decisions for themselves, which in the majority of cases is not so. Although the views of older, mature children are likely to be of considerable influence, in cases of child abuse

---

27 *Re S (a minor) (Independent Representation)* [1993] 2 FLR 437
28 'The Children Act 1989 Guidance and Regulations', Vol 3, Family Placements (1991) London, HMSO.

where state intervention is justified, it is the authorities and the court which retain the right to make decisions about the child and such decisions are to be based on the welfare principle – that the child's welfare is the paramount consideration. If the child's wishes conflict with what is thought to be in his or her best interests, the welfare principle prevails. Even in cases where the child has been given a statutory right to refuse medical or psychiatric examination or treatment, the courts have been prepared to override that right in what they consider to be the child's best interests. The child may well have been given a voice, but, understandably, he or she has not been given an unfettered *right* to decide what is best for him or her.

THE CREDIBILITY OF CHILDREN

As children have gradually achieved a degree of autonomy and greater respect has been accorded to their wishes and feelings, there has been a corresponding change in society's attitude towards the credibility of children. Increased awareness of the true extent of the physical and sexual abuse of children has been one of the factors which has influenced this change. In many cases of child abuse, the child victim will be the only witness. If the child is not believed the abuse will remain hidden at the bottom of the iceberg. Now that society is prepared to acknowledge the existence of abuse we must also be prepared to believe children who are the victims of abuse.

Psychological issues

'Children are more likely to lie than adults'

The old adage 'all little boys are thieves, cheats and liars' (presumably, therefore, so are all little girls?) clearly reflects conventional beliefs about children's veracity. But these traditional beliefs are now being questioned. Obviously, some children do lie some of the time – but so do adults, and the veracity of an adult is not normally doubted because members of the adult's peer group lie on occasions. The important consideration should be whether children are more likely to lie than adults. A Home Office review of children's evidence concluded:

> 'The question of whether children do lie more than adults cannot be answered from existing empirical evidence. There appears to be virtually no evidence of children's moral ability or propensity to tell the truth.'[29]

It seems that nobody really knows if children are more likely to lie than adults. In the case of very young children, it has been suggested that they do not possess the cognitive prerequisites to be able to lie and therefore it is said:

---

29 Hedderman, C (1987) 'Childrens' Evidence: The Need for Corroboration' London, Home Office p 21.

'Three year old children cannot lie ... [they] may be malleable, compliant or mistaken ... [but] they cannot intend to deceive.'[30]

This seems to be a very charitable interpretation of the capabilities of a three year old but, as children grow older, they clearly acquire the cognitive prerequisites to be able to lie – they believe that the listener is capable of being deceived. It also appears that older children generally acquire the ability to conceal a lie and therefore 'if any children are to be distrusted it is older rather than younger ones as older children are more able to deceive'.[31] Perhaps young children are generally thought of as more likely to lie simply because they are more likely to be found out when they do lie. But given the fact that there is no evidence to support the belief that children are more likely to lie than adults, the word of a child should be accorded just as much weight as that of an adult, on the assumption that if the adult lies the adult will be more able to conceal that lie.

'Children have poor powers of recall and are more open to suggestion than adults'

The alleged inferiority of a child's power to recall previous events increased the traditional tendency to disregard statements made by children, particularly if the abuse was disclosed some time after the alleged event. But psychological research suggests that a child's power of recall is far more extensive than previously thought and correct interview techniques can result in a marked increase in the amount of information recalled. Admittedly, research shows that very young children have comparatively little free recall. When asked to relate an event, without prompting, the younger the child, the more details will be omitted. The amount of information freely recalled increases as the child grows older, until the age of 13 or 14 years when adult levels of recall are reached. But however little information is freely recalled, that information is extremely accurate.[32] In one study[33] children between the ages of eight and 12 years were found to be as accurate as adults in recalling a live event by free recall or in response to general, open-ended questions, but the children were less accurate when asked specific, 'leading', questions. These results are consistent with an earlier study[34] which concluded that while young children were less capable of providing detailed descriptions of events, they were as accurate as adults in answering objective questions, and that five year olds were no less competent or reliable as eye-witnesses than adults when responding to direct and objective questions. A much earlier study, undertaken in 1910, found that when interviewing children aged

---

30 Morton, J (1988) 'When can Lying Start?' in Davies, J & Drinkwater, J (eds) (1988) *The Child Witness: Do the Courts Abuse Children?* Leicester, British Psychological Society for the division of Criminological and Legal Psychology p 35.

31 Note 29 p 5.

32 Naylor, B (1989) 'Dealing with Child Sexual Abuse' in *British Journal of Criminology* vol 29 no 4 p 396.

33 Dent (1988) quoted in *Naylor* (1989) note 32 p 398.

34 Mann (1979) quoted in *Hedderman* (1987) note 29 p 20.

between seven and 18 years, leading questions resulted in an average error score of between 25% and 30%, whereas the average error rate associated with free recall was between 5% and 10%.[35]

Clearly, the child's age must be a factor which affects the child's power of recall, although, as in determining the weight to be attached to the child's opinion, other factors such as cognitive maturity are relevant. But it would appear that very young children from the age of three or four years are capable of giving accurate and truthful accounts of events in response to objective questioning.[36] The possibility that children are more open to suggestion than adults is also borne out by these studies, although there is no consistency whether this tendency decreases with age. While studies have shown that both adults and children are susceptible to suggestion,[37] the possibility remains that children are more susceptible than adults because of social conformity ie because the child will be more likely to agree to a suggestion made by an adult who will generally be seen by the child as an authoritative figure.

As a result of these research findings, new interview techniques are being adopted by those responsible for investigating child abuse. Such techniques stringently avoid the use of leading questions, but rely on the child's free recall of events, helped by objective questioning or prompts (see Chapter 4).

'Children frequently fantasize about abuse and are unable to distinguish fantasy from reality'

The traditional doubts about children's veracity, accuracy and suggestibility are common to all children. In the case of child victims of sexual abuse, these doubts are exacerbated by additional beliefs – namely that children fantasize about abuse, and are then unable to distinguish their fantasies from what has actually occurred in reality. The belief that children fantasize about abuse is commonly attributed to the theory of Freud. Freud originally contended that adult female neurosis was attributable to childhood sexual trauma, but later changed this contention because he was unable to believe that the large number of adult females he saw as patients had all been sexually abused as children. Thus he claimed that his patients had all fantasized about childhood abuse and this view became generally accepted. Once accepted, this view became difficult to change. It was far easier for society to believe that children fantasized about abuse than to believe that large numbers of children were actually being abused. But given the fact that society now seems prepared to acknowledge a far wider prevalence of child sexual abuse, Freud's original contention seems socially unacceptable in society today. Indeed, once it is

---

35   Stern (1910) quoted in *Hedderman* (1987) note 29 p 19.

36   Berliner, L & Barbieri, MK (1984) 'The Testimony of the Child Victim of Sexual Assault' in *Journal of Social Issues* 40(2) p 125 at p 131.

37   Zaragoza, MS (1987) 'Memory, Suggestibility and Eyewitness Testimony in Children and Adults' in CECI, SJ Toglia, MP & Ross, DF (eds) (1987) *Children's Eyewitness Memory* Berlin, Springer.

accepted that child sexual abuse is generally under-reported there seems even less reason to disbelieve those children that do come forward with allegations of abuse.

Clinical experience in the US suggests that fabrication of abuse is rare and that the high rates of reporting in communities that have visible treatment programs for sexually abused children have not been accompanied by an increase in false reporting.[38] But establishing the truthfulness of such allegations by empirical evidence has proved difficult because there is no absolutely reliable test of the occurrence of abuse. The only study available to date concluded that 7.8% of 576 sexual abuse cases were based on fictional allegations, 6.25% of these fictional allegations had been generated by adults and 1.56% were fictions generated by children.[39] The proposition that adults are more likely to generate false allegations of abuse than children coincides with the relatively recent concern that children are being used as 'pawns' in the breakdown of a relationship. A decade ago it was not uncommon for one parent to allege ill-treatment of the child by the other parent in an effort to obtain custody on the breakdown of the relationship. More recently, with increased awareness of child sexual abuse, it is feared that one parent may be tempted to make allegations of sexual abuse in order to obtain a residence order knowing that sexual abuse is far more difficult to establish on a medical basis than physical abuse.

One rather extreme suggestion to test the accuracy of claims of abuse is the use of polygraph tests (lie detectors). One study in the US reported that out of 147 who alleged abuse and underwent a polygraph test, only one child was judged to have made a false allegation.[40] But in the current climate of concern for the victim, it is unthinkable that such tests would ever be used in this country. In any event, a polygraph test would be of no assistance in the case of a child who could not tell fantasy from reality. In such circumstances, the child surely believes the abuse occurred whatever happened in reality.

It seems that research on children's ability to tell fantasy from reality has failed to reach any firm conclusions. However, it has been said that:

'... people working in the field of sexual assault ... have found little evidence to support the claim that children genuinely fail to distinguish fact from fantasy.'[41]

---

38 Note 36 at p 127.

39 King, MA & Yuille, JC (1987) 'Suggestibility and the Child Witness' in Ceci, SJ Toglia, MP & Ross, DF (eds) (1987) *Children's Eyewitness Memory* Berlin, Springer.

40 Note 29 at p 24.

41 Note 32 at p 398.

The credibility of children – legal issues

'When are we going to give up, in all civilised nations, listening to children in courts of law?'[42]

This remark, made in 1911, reflected the traditional beliefs that children do not make reliable, competent witnesses. Therefore, it was argued, why waste the court's time in listening to them? Events in recent years have resulted in a dramatic change in society's attitude towards children as witnesses. Although children are rarely heard in civil courts, we are now doing our utmost to encourage children to be heard in criminal courts.

Age and the oath

For many years a child was deemed to be an incompetent witness, and therefore unable to testify in a court of law, merely by virtue of age. In early canon law, a child below the age of puberty was barred from giving evidence in the ecclesiastical courts. The common law originally would not allow a child under the age of seven years to give evidence, but in 1779 it was acknowledged that:

'[There] is no precise or fixed rule as to the time within which infants are excluded from giving evidence ...'[43]

Thus age itself ceased to be a bar to competence. But at the same time it was made clear that the judge always had a duty to determine a child's competence by questions to ensure the child understood the 'danger and impiety of falsehood'. At this time a child was only permitted to give evidence on oath and it was a commonly held belief that to lie on oath meant that the perjurer was certain to go to hell. So questioning a child witness to determine competence involved the child asserting that he or she believed that to lie meant he or she would 'go to hell-fire'. This, in turn, was said to lead to a 'crash course' of religious instruction before the child was questioned by the judge to ensure the child was fully conversant with the dangers of lying on oath and the attendant consequences of hell-fire if the child did so lie – at least children no longer have to be terrified of the devil and hell-fire before being allowed to testify! In criminal trials, the Children and Young Persons Act of 1933 permitted children who were not competent to take the oath to give unsworn evidence, if 'in the opinion of the court, he is possessed of sufficient intelligence to justify reception of the evidence, and understands the duty of speaking the truth'. However, this formal competency requirement – that children understood the duty of speaking the truth – meant that young children were precluded from giving evidence in court because, while four

---

42   Goodman, GS (1984) 'Children's Testimony in Historical Perspective' in *Journal of Social Issues* 40(2) p 9.
43   *R v Brasier* [1779] 1 Leach 199.

and five year olds may be perfectly reliable as witnesses, they were not always able to explain abstract concepts like 'duty' and 'truth'. In 1958, Lord Goddard, the Lord Chief Justice, commented that it was 'ridiculous' to suppose that any value could be attached to the evidence of a five year old child.[44] This sentiment was repeated by the courts over the next few decades, causing considerable concern amongst those involved in investigating cases of child abuse. As a result of the recommendations of the Advisory Group on Video Evidence, the Criminal Justice Act of 1991 now provides that all children are presumed to be competent witnesses. Children under 14 years give their evidence unsworn, while those over 14 give sworn evidence.

In civil cases, children are less likely to be required to give evidence in open court (see Chapter 7). However, the Children Act 1989 provides for the first time that a child may give unsworn evidence in civil proceedings, provided he understands that it is his duty to speak the truth and he has sufficient understanding to justify his evidence being heard [section 96].

Corroboration

In criminal proceedings, there was an additional barrier; the belief that children do not make reliable witnesses has traditionally been reinforced by the requirement of corroboration or supporting evidence. Prior to the enactment of the Criminal Justice Act in 1988, there existed a total ban on convicting a defendant on the uncorroborated evidence of a young child who gave unsworn evidence. In the case of a child who gave sworn evidence a conviction was possible, but only after the judge had warned the jury that it would be 'dangerous' to convict on such evidence without corroboration.

Section 34 Criminal Justice Act 1988 has now removed the corroboration requirement for both the sworn and unsworn evidence of children. The enactment of this section was presumably influenced by a Home Office review in 1987 of children's evidence and the need for corroboration.[45] The review concluded that:

> '... a general legal requirement that children's evidence be corroborated does not appear to be necessary.'

The abolition of the corroboration requirement for children's evidence is certainly a step towards according more respect to children as witnesses. However, quite how effective the abolition will be remains to be seen. At common law, in cases which do not, strictly speaking, require the jury to be warned of the danger of convicting on uncorroborated evidence, the judge has always had a discretion to emphasize to the jury that evidence from a particular source has, in previous cases, been shown to be unreliable. For many

---

44 *R v Wallwork* [1958] 42 Cr App Rep 153.

45 Note 29.

years, judges have treated the evidence of children with suspicion. It is commonly acknowledged that 'old habits die hard' and it is quite possible that judges will continue to use this discretion to show children's evidence in an unfavourable light.

One major obstacle remained in cases of child sexual abuse. Although there was no longer be any need to give a corroboration warning solely because the witness was a child, at common law, a corroboration warning had always been required where the witness is a complainant in a sexual case, and this common law requirement was unaffected by the Criminal Justice Act 1988. Therefore, in any prosecution in cases of child sexual abuse, the judge was required to warn the jury that it would be dangerous to convict on the evidence of the complainant alone. The judge was required to explain what was meant by corroboration and point out any evidence that was capable of amounting to corroboration. Once they had been so warned, the jury were then free to convict the defendant whether or not they decided the evidence of the complainant had, in fact, been corroborated.

Precisely what evidence is capable of amounting to corroboration is governed by highly complex, technical rules. To amount to corroboration, evidence must come from a source independent of the witness[46] and must implicate the accused.[47] Traditionally, corroboration may not consist of an accumulation of pieces of evidence, each one of which fails to satisfy the two criteria. An example was given by the Advisory Group on Video Evidence:

'... on a complaint of rape the accused and the complainant might have been seen together in an isolated spot, the complainant might have been seen in a distraught state shortly afterwards and have alleged that the offence took place, a doctor might have confirmed that rape had occurred after a medical examination and the accused might have refused to make a statement to the police or give evidence. In such a case there would be insufficient independent evidence relating each of the material particulars of the offence to the defendant and the complainant would not be corroborated.'[48]

If this supposition – that cumulative corroboration is not sufficient – is correct, corroborating many allegations of child sexual abuse would be little short of impossible. But the Advisory Group on Video Evidence does not appear to have had regard to a decision of the Court of Appeal in which Lord Lane, the Lord Chief Justice, said that corroboration may be cumulative and illustrated the point with an example:

'... in a rape case, where the defendant denies he ever had sexual intercourse with the complainant, it may be possible to prove (1) by medical evidence that she had sexual intercourse within an hour or so prior to the medical examination, (2) by other independent evidence that the defendant and no

---

46   *R v Whitehead* [1929] 1 KB 99.

47   *R v Baskerville* [1916] 2 KB 658.

48   Home Office (1989) 'Report of the Advisory Group on Video Evidence' London, HMSO para 5.22.

other man had been with her during that time, (3) that her underclothing was torn and that she had injuries to her private parts. None of these items of evidence alone would be sufficient to provide the necessary corroboration, but the judge would be entitled to direct the jury that if they were satisfied so as to feel sure that each of these three items had been proved, the combined effect of these three items would be capable of corroborating the girl's evidence.'[49]

In practice, however, the very real problem remained that, in the majority of cases of child sexual abuse, there were very few pieces of potentially corroborative evidence available. The Advisory Group on Video Evidence recommended that the need for a corroboration warning to be given in cases involving sexual offences should be abolished entirely – a move which would not only make the conviction of child abusers more likely, but would also benefit all victims of sexual offences, young and old alike. This recommendation has now been enacted in section 32 of the Criminal Justice and Public Order Act of 1994, which was brought into force on 3 February 1995.

WRONGFUL ACCUSATIONS – HAS THE PENDULUM SWUNG TOO FAR?

The Children Act 1989 and reforms of the criminal justice system go some considerable way to ensuring that children are given the opportunity to be heard and to be believed. Whilst these are generally welcome innovations, a certain amount of caution is advisable. Whereas the majority of children richly deserve their newly acquired status, there will inevitably be some children who abuse it and concerns have been expressed that the pendulum has swung too far in favour of the child. Teachers, in particular, have become increasingly concerned at the impact of recent reforms in schools and argue that 'streetwise' children are taking advantage of their new found voice to hit back at teachers without justification. As one teacher commented:

'A comforting hand on the shoulder, physical help in gymnastics or the administration of medicine can all lead to allegations of abuse.'[50]

Statistics compiled by one of the largest teaching unions – the National Association of Schoolmasters/Union of Women Teachers – show that the number of allegations of improper behaviour by teachers towards pupils rose for the second successive year in 1993. In 1991 the union instructed solicitors to represent 71 members who faced allegations of physical and sexual abuse. In 1992 the number rose to 134 and in 1993 to 158.[51] After investigation, the majority of these allegations were said to have been unfounded. Only 9 of the teachers were convicted of criminal offences in 1993, but no statistics are

---

49   [1988] Cr App Rep 26 at 31.

50   *The Times* 7 April 1994.

51   *The Times* 13 January 1994.

available on the number that were found to be substantiated on the civil standard of proof and it must be remembered that comparatively few allegations of abuse result in criminal prosecution. However, many of the teachers were suspended during the investigations and some never resumed their careers, even after being cleared. Baroness Blatch, the education minister, has acknowledged the scale of the problem, which she said derived from the over-zealous application of the Children Act and commented:

'We are looking at ways of making this legislation work, both in the interests of protecting children and allowing teachers to do their job properly.'[52]

Getting the balance right is inevitably a difficult task. Children have been given a voice – the older the child, the more likely he or she is to be heard. Inevitably, some children will try to abuse the use of their new-found voice. The abolition of the requirement of corroboration of children's evidence is to be welcomed as an indication that children as a class are not untrustworthy, but allegations of abuse must be evaluated in each individual case. The pendulum must not be allowed to swing too far. Children are, after all, still children, many of whom will not realise the full implications of a wrongful allegation. It is only to be hoped that a minority of children who abuse their voice will not thereby cast doubt on the voice of the majority of children in need of protection.

---

52   *The Times* 7 April 1994.

CHAPTER 7

TRIALS AND TRIBULATIONS – PROCEDURES IN COURT

THE NATURE OF THE TRIAL AND BASIC PRINCIPLES OF EVIDENCE

The adversarial trial

In England and Wales, in accordance with the common law traditions of open justice and the primacy of oral evidence, trials generally take the form of an adversarial contest consisting of a 'day in court' when both sides present oral evidence in one continual presentation and the function of the court is to decide who has 'won'. Judges and magistrates take no part in the preliminary investigations; they give no help to either side in presenting their case; and take no active steps to discover the truth, which is supposed to emerge from the clash of conflicting accounts – 'like referees at boxing contests they see that the rules are kept and count the points'. In contrast to the adversarial system of trial, most continental countries adopt an inquisitorial system of trial where the court is viewed as a public agency appointed to get to the bottom of the disputed matter. The court takes the initiative in gathering information as soon as it has notice of the dispute and builds up a file on the matter (the dossier) by questioning all those it thinks may have useful information to offer. The court then looks at the material it has collected, applies its reasoning power and determines where the truth lies.

It is commonly argued that the accusatorial system is rational and fair. But, whereas the historical development of the system may explain what many consider to be the stubborn adherence to outdated and illogical rules of evidence in some cases, it does little to engender a sense of rationality and fairness. Adversarial systems have their roots in trial by ordeal – one of the parties to a dispute would accuse the other and a court would decree that one party should undergo some form of ordeal – to be thrown into the village pond or branded with a hot poker. The rationale of the ordeal was to enable God to show whose cause was just – the judgment was deemed to be that of God, not the court. Of course in practice if someone accused of witchcraft floated in the pond, they were guilty and burned at the stake. If they sank they were innocent, but they were also frequently dead because no one had pulled them out of the water in time – so much for being rational!

At the beginning of the 13th century, the church withdrew its support for trial by ordeal, causing trial procedures to be reviewed throughout Europe. In Britain, the traditional adversarial pattern was maintained, but the judgment of God was replaced with the judgment of a group of neighbours called upon to give their verdict on the matter – the neighbours were compelled to take an oath and say whose cause was just on the basis of their local knowledge, or their hunch if they did not have any local knowledge. But on the continent a move was made to a system whereby the state appointed an inquisitor to find out the truth of the matter by asking questions and applying his power of reasoning to the answers. At this stage the inquisitorial system seemed far more rational. However, over the years the jury system developed into its present form – far from being a group of local people the jury became a group of independent assessors who learnt the facts from witnesses called by the parties. At the same time the inquisitorial system was called into question when the inquisitors took to torturing witnesses to overcome their reluctance to answering questions. This led to praise of the adversarial system as being 'the envy of the world'.

Yet, as juries developed into the group of independent assessors, the judges adopted a paternalistic attitude towards them – they were afraid that these 'lay' people would not be capable of discounting what was commonly considered to be unreliable evidence and so rules of evidence evolved to prevent certain evidence being admitted in the court room. Evidence is generally something which tends to prove or disprove any fact or conclusion. In an ideal world, it may be thought that *any* evidence which is relevant and tends to prove or disprove any fact that has to be decided by the court would be heard and this is what actually happens in some Scandinavian countries, for example, where a system of 'free proof' is adopted. The parties are free to prove a fact in any way they can – there are very few rules of exclusion and no one mode of proof is given preference over another. In contrast to this, in England and Wales a system of 'controlled proof' has long been adopted whereby the way in which facts can be proved before the court is subject to controls with many rules of exclusion.

The rules of exclusion originally applied to both civil and criminal trials, but the use of the jury in civil cases has declined considerably in recent years and there has been a corresponding move to abolish many of the rules in civil proceedings. Indeed, in civil cases concerning the welfare of a child, there is an increasing tendency to treat the proceedings as inquisitorial in nature. Wilson J in the county court recently commented:

'The game of adversarial litigation has no point when one is trying to deal with fragile and vulnerable people like small children. Every other consideration must come second to the need to reach the right conclusion if possible.'[1]

In upholding the judge's ruling that the general legal professional privilege attached to an expert's report must yield to the greater value to be attached to the child's welfare, Steyn L J in the Court of Appeal explained:

---

1   *Re D and M (minors)* (1993) 18 BMLR 71.

'[Since 1962] ... our system of civil justice has become more open. Judges have had to become more interventionist ... it is of particular importance to note that in the Family Division, care proceedings do not have an essentially adversarial character ...'[2]

The move away from the adversarial contest in civil cases concerned with the welfare of a child is indicative of the increased significance attached to the welfare principle and to the recognition of the rights and needs of children and, as such, is to be welcomed. However, the adversarial mode of trial, together with the associated rules of exclusion, are still firmly entrenched in criminal proceedings. Many of these rules of exclusion seem totally illogical – the only explanation offered is that they are totally illogical. It is sometimes very difficult, if not impossible, to justify some of the rules and decisions. To take a classic example, in the case of *R v Sparks*,[3] a white man was charged with indecently assaulting a child. Shortly after the assault the child told her mother that her attacker was a coloured man. The child did not give evidence at the trial and, because of the exclusionary nature of the rules of evidence, the mother was not allowed to give evidence in court of what the child had told her. The white man was convicted – despite the fact that the victim had expressly stated that her attacker was a coloured man. The case was appealed to the Privy Council, where the appeal was allowed on other grounds, but the judge commented:

'It was said that it was manifestly unjust to be left throughout the whole trial with the impression that the child could not give any clue to the identity of the assailant. The cause of justice is, however, best served by adherence to rules which have long been recognised and settled.'

This is an assertion which must surely cause considerable concern for anyone involved in the administration of justice. In cases of child abuse, despite recent procedural reforms of the criminal justice system (see below), the adherence to the adversarial form of trial means that, in practice, it is impossible to accord sufficient status to the welfare of the child.

The burden and standard of proof

The burden of proof

The term 'burden of proof' may at first appear to be self-explanatory. In fact there exists several different kinds of burdens and unfortunately no consistent terminology has been adopted by the judiciary or academic commentators in this area. The most significant burden – commonly called the legal burden – is the obligation placed on one of the parties to proceedings to prove a fact to the

---

2   *Re D and M (minors) supra* at p 84.

3   *Sparks v R* [1964] AC 964.

satisfaction of the court. As a general rule 'he who asserts must prove'. The facts which require proof are to be found in the relevant substantive law. Thus a local authority applying to a court for a care order bears the legal burden of proving to the court that the relevant conditions of section 31(2) of the Children Act 1989 are satisfied. Similarly, if the local authority applies for a child assessment order, it would bear the legal burden of satisfying the court that it has reasonable cause to suspect that the child is suffering or is likely to suffer significant harm (section 43(1)(a)). In criminal trials, the prosecution bears the legal burden of proving every element of the crime charged in order to establish the accused's guilt. There also exists a second burden – commonly called the evidential burden – which is the burden of adducing sufficient evidence to raise a particular issue. At the start of a trial, the legal and evidential burdens will generally be placed on the same party. Although the legal burden remains with that party throughout the trial, the evidential burden may shift to the other party during the course of the trial. Thus in care proceedings, the local authority will initially bear both the legal and evidential burdens. Once evidence has been adduced to satisfy the court that the conditions in section 31(2) do exist, the evidential burden then shifts to the other party – the parents, the child or the child's representative – to adduce evidence to counter the local authority's case. In criminal trials, both burdens will initially rest on the prosecution. If the accused wishes to rely on a defence, he or she will bear an evidential burden to adduce sufficient evidence to raise the defence. Once this evidential burden has been discharged, the prosecution will generally bear the legal burden of disproving the defence. It is only in exceptional circumstances that a legal burden is placed on a defendant.

The standard of proof

The standard of proof relates to how the party who bears the legal burden of proving any particular issue can discharge that burden by satisfying the court. As a general rule, in civil proceedings, the court must be satisfied on the balance of probabilities. As Lord Denning explained:

> 'If the evidence is such that the tribunal can say: "we think it more probable than not", the burden is discharged, but if the probabilities are equal it is not.'[4]

In criminal proceedings, where the legal burden rests on the prosecution, the standard of proof is beyond all reasonable doubt. (In exceptional cases where the legal burden rests on the accused, the standard is the lower, civil standard on the balance of probabilities.[5])

The different standards of proof in civil and criminal proceedings have raised problems when allegations of criminal conduct are made in civil cases.

---

4   *Miller v Minister of Pensions* [1947] 2 All ER 372.

5   *R v Carr Briant* [1943] KB 607.

In *Re H; Re K*,[6] Butler Sloss LJ held that, in cases involving children, the appropriate standard of proof was on the balance of probabilities. However, she went on to suggest that if a serious allegation was made which amounted to criminal conduct, the degree of probability must be 'commensurate with the occasion' or 'proportionate to the subject matter'. Similar reasoning seems to have been applied in the earlier case of *Re G*,[7] where Sheldon J held that a higher degree of probability was required to satisfy the court that a father had been guilty of sexual misconduct with his daughter than would be needed to justify the conclusion that the child has been the victim of such behaviour, of whatever nature, and whosoever might have been the perpetrator. The Court of Appeal in *Re W*[8] has since reinforced this view. Beldam LJ explained:

'... charges of sexual abuse made against the father ... involved as grave an imputation as could be levelled at a father; though acquitted of them in a criminal trial, if in civil proceedings they were found to have been proved against him, the stigma and disgrace would not be less than if he had been convicted. Thus, although it is now settled that in civil proceedings such charges do not require proof beyond reasonable doubt, the standard of proof to be required is nevertheless commensurate with the serious nature of the issues raised. So they must be proved beyond a mere balance of probability but not necessarily a standard as demanding as the criminal standard.'

The Court of Appeal ruled that the trial judge had erred in finding, on the balance of probabilities, that the children concerned had been sexually abused when the only possible perpertrator was the father – a higher standard of proof should have been applied. On the facts it was found that the judge's refusal to permit contact with the children had not depended solely on his findings as to sexual abuse and the order had been fully justified, whether or not the finding as to sexual abuse could stand, and so no child protection issues turned on the decision in this case. However, this will not always be so. Whilst it is understandable that the courts should be cautious when faced with an allegation of abuse which amounts to a criminal offence against a parent, it must be remembered that child protection proceedings are civil proceedings, the object of which is to protect the child not to establish the guilt of an alleged abuser. The question of guilt or innocence should be determined in the criminal courts, where the standard of proof will be beyond all reasonable doubt. Concerns about 'stigma' and 'disgrace' should not be allowed to cloud child protection issues in civil proceedings where the paramount consideration must be the welfare of the child.

In assessing the likelihood of future abuse, as opposed to finding as a fact that abuse has occurred, it seems that the court merely has to be satisfied that there is a real possibility of risk, which is arguably a lower standard than the

---

6   [1989] 2 FLR 313.

7   [1987] 1 WLR 1461.

8   *Re W (minors) (sexual abuse: standard of proof)* [1994] 1 FLR 419.

balance of probabilities. The Court of Appeal in *Newham LBC v AG*[9] made it clear that the wording of the threshold criteria – that the child is 'likely to suffer' – is not to be equated with 'on the balance of probabilities'.

The rule against hearsay evidence

Any hearsay statement is *prima facie* inadmissible in a court of law and, if strictly adhered to, the rule against hearsay evidence would have a dramatic effect on both civil and criminal proceedings involving child victims of abuse. Hearsay evidence is any out of court statement (ie a statement other than one made by a witness in the course of giving evidence in the proceedings in question), by any person, however made which is offered as evidence of the truth of its contents. There are two elements to hearsay evidence. First it must be an out of court statement – something said or done outside the witness box. For example, any third party, such as a social worker or police officer, repeating a child's account of abuse to a court would be repeating an out of court statement. However, such evidence would only be hearsay evidence if the second element is satisfied – it must be related in order to prove the truth of the statement. There may well be other reasons for repeating an out of court statement, for example to show a child's use of age-inappropriate language, and this would not infringe the rule against hearsay. There are numerous common law and statutory exceptions to the rule against hearsay, particularly in civil proceedings (see below). However, the existence of the rule continues to present a potentially insurmountable barrier in criminal proceedings.

Evidence of opinion and expert witnesses

As a general rule, witnesses are not permitted to express opinions – they may only speak of facts which they personally perceived. There are, however, two exceptions to this rule. In civil proceedings, a witness may express an opinion if it is expressed as a way of conveying relevant facts personally perceived by him.[10] Thus, in care proceedings, a child's physical condition may be described in terms of a witness' opinion as a way of conveying to the court what the witness saw. There is no express statutory provision for criminal proceedings and, technically, it seems the general rule applies. However, in practice the rule is easily evaded by the careful use of words and is sometimes simply ignored.[11]

The second exception is of more importance in cases of child abuse. A witness may be deemed to be an expert witness if, in the opinion of the judge, he or she has the required expertise in any given area, which may have been

---

9   [1993] 1 FLR 281.

10   Section 3(2) Civil Evidence Act 1972.

11   Keene, A (1989) *The Modern Law of Evidence*, London, Butterworths p 380.

acquired through study, training or experience. An expert witness may give evidence of opinion on a matter calling for expertise. As Lawton LJ explained:

'An expert's opinion is admissible to furnish the court with scientific information which is likely to be outside the experience and knowledge of a judge and jury. If, on the proven facts, a judge or jury can form their own conclusions without help, then the opinion of an expert is unnecessary.'[12]

An expert witness may, of course, testify to relevant facts of which he has personal knowledge in the same way as any other witness. But if the matter to be decided falls outside the experience and knowledge of the court, an expert may also use his skill and knowledge to assist the court in drawing inferences from facts, by giving his opinion on the proper inferences to be drawn. Thus, for example, a doctor could express an opinion as to the cause of injuries sustained by a child as this would be a matter outside the experience and knowledge of the court. However, the credibility of a witness is not thought to be such a matter, and the courts usually refuse to allow evidence concerning a child's credibility as a witness to be given by psychologists or psychiatrists.

In many circumstances an expert witness may wish to express an opinion on an 'ultimate issue' – ie one which the court itself has to determine – for example, whether or not a child has been abused. At common law this was prohibited because it was feared the expert witness would usurp the function of the court. In civil proceedings statutory provisions now expressly permit this.[13] There is no corresponding provision in criminal proceedings and, technically, it seems that an expert will be prevented from expressing an opinion on an ultimate issue. However, in practice, it seems the prohibition is often ignored as long as there is no danger of the jury according the testimony undue weight. Thus, whilst an expert may be permitted to express the opinion that a child has been abused, an opinion that the accused was guilty of the abuse would not be admitted.

PROTECTING THE CHILD – PROCEEDINGS IN THE CIVIL COURTS

Making the application

Which court?

One of the principles underlying the Children Act 1989 was to unify the laws and procedures relating to children and the Act created a three tiered court – the High Court, county court and family proceedings court (see Chapter 3). As

---

12   *R v Turner* [1975] QB 834 at 841.

13   Section 3 Civil Evidence Act 1972.

a general rule all public law applications concerning children are commenced in the family proceedings court. When applying for a care or supervision order, the only exception is where the application is being made following an investigation directed by the court under section 37 of the Act, in which case the application will be made to the court that made the initial direction.

The transfer of cases between courts is governed by the Children (Allocation of Proceedings) Order 1991 (SI 1991/1667). On receipt of an application, the family proceedings court will consider whether the proceedings should be transferred to another court. The court will have regard to the principle that any delay in determining the case is likely to prejudice the welfare of the child (section 1(5)) and, if it considers that the determination of the proceedings would be accelerated, it must transfer the proceedings to another family proceedings court. Alternatively, the case may be transferred, either upon a party's application or the court's own motion, to a county court if such a transfer is deemed to be in the best interests of the child and:

- it would significantly accelerate the determination of the proceedings (and no other method of doing so, including transfer to another family proceedings' court, is appropriate), or;

- there are other pending family proceedings in the county court and it would be appropriate for the proceedings to be heard together, or;

- the proceedings are exceptionally grave, important or complex.

Once transferred to a county court, the case may be transferred to the High Court if the county court considers that it is in the best interests of the child and the proceedings are considered to be appropriate for determination by the High Court, for example, if a precedent is to be set or a major principle is involved. The President of the Family Division of the High Court has also indicated in a practice direction that child-initiated proceedings should be heard in the High Court[14] (see Chapter 6). Provision also exists for cases to be transferred downwards from the High Court to a county court, and from the county court to a family proceedings court where appropriate having regard to the avoidance of delay and the best interests of the child.

The procedures governing the transfer of cases between courts are detailed and complex, but the overall aim is that all suitable cases should be dealt with in the family proceedings court. Courts have indicated that when the estimated length of a hearing is more than two days, or at the most three days (which would make it difficult for justices to sit on consecutive days and would in any event indicate a certain degree of complexity), the case should be transferred to a county court for hearing.[15] However, consistency is by no means guaranteed, although the Children Act Advisory Committee carried

---

14   Practice Direction [1993] 1 FLR 668.

15   *Essex County Council v L (minors)* [1992] The Times 18 December FD.

out a survey of transfers and concluded that there was a 'reassuring degree of commonality' and where differences existed they seemed more a matter of communication and differing practices than questions of principle. Even so, it is evident that further guidance on the criteria for transfer is required and the Children Act Advisory Committee are in the process of producing a guidance note on transfer criteria,[16] which will hopefully ensure a greater degree of consistency. When cases are transferred, effective communication between the relevant courts and adequate administrative arrangements are essential. The Children Act Advisory Committee found that in 40% of cases no telephone contact was made between the family proceedings court and the county court prior to transfer and noted, with concern, that in 75% of the transfers surveyed no date for the next hearing in the court to which the case was being transferred was known at the time of transfer. Courts are encouraged to set up 'hot line' communications between the tiers of courts to ensure the efficient transfer of cases with the minimum delay possible.

Parties to the proceedings and legal aid

In most cases the applicant for a care or supervision order will be the local authority, although the NSPCC may also commence proceedings. The application form requires information about, *inter alia*, the child and his or her family, other proceedings concerning the child and any future plans for the child. Once an application has been made, it can only be withdrawn with leave of the court.[17] Notice of the proceedings must be given to:

- the respondents (see below) and;

- every person whom the applicant believes to be a party to pending relevant proceedings in respect of the child;

- every person whom the applicant believes to be a parent without parental responsibility for the child;

- the local authority (if not the applicant);

- persons caring for the child at the time the proceedings were commenced and;

- a refuge provider if the child is staying in a refuge.[18]

The applicant is automatically a party to the proceedings and the respondents will be the child and any person who has parental responsibility for the child.[19] In addition, any person may file a request in writing that he or

---

16   *The Children Act Advisory Committee Annual Report* 1992/93 p 50.

17   Children (Allocation of Proceedings) Order 1991 Article 6.

18   Family Proceedings Courts (Children Act 1989) Rules 1991 (SI 1991/1395) Schedule 2.

19   Family Proceedings Courts (Children Act 1989) Rules 1991 (SI 1991/1395) Schedule 2 and Family Proceedings Rules 1991 (SI 1991/1247) Appendix 3.

she be joined as a party to proceedings and the court may grant such a request without a hearing or after hearing representations from the other parties.[20] This provision allows, for example, grandparents and foster parents the opportunity to be joined as respondents. However, if it is clear that the person concerned wishes to apply for a section 8 order, the criteria set out in section 10(9) of the Act should be met[21] and, in any event, the Court of Appeal has made it clear that a request should only be granted if the person concerned has a separate view to put forward in the proceedings.[22] Thus, for example, grandparents whose views coincide with those of the parents will not be joined as parties, but may be called as witnesses for one of the parties. This is undoubtedly a sensible approach to take. As noted in the previous chapter, procedures regarding the appointment of guardians *ad litem* and solicitors for the child already present the risk of a proliferation of people representing their own and the child's views to the court, thereby making the proceedings more protracted (and, of course, increasing the costs involved). For these reasons, there should be no proliferation of parties to the proceedings without good cause.

Those who are automatically parties to the proceedings – ie the child, parents and anyone with parental responsibility for the child – will be granted civil legal aid and the usual means and merits tests will be waived.[23] If the case proceeds to appeal, although the means test will continue to be waived, the merits test will be applied by the legal aid board. Any person who applies to be joined as a party to the proceedings will be subject to the usual means test, although the merits test will be waived.[24]

Drawing up a timetable and direction appointments

A court will very rarely be in a position to decide an application at the first hearing, even if the application is not contested, and adjournments are inevitable. A guardian *ad litem* will usually be appointed at an early stage in the proceedings, but will require time to carry out investigations, instruct a solicitor and compile a report for the court (see Chapter 6). If the case is contested, respondents will also require time to prepare their case and obtain witness statements. One of the major objectives of the 1989 Act is to keep the number of adjournments to a minimum and to reduce the length of intervals between hearings. Guidance issued to courts suggests that, in public law cases, a full hearing should take place within 12 weeks, although this time will

---

20 Family Proceedings Courts (Children Act 1989) Rules 1991 (SI 1991/1395) rule 7 and Family Proceedings Rules 1991 (SI 1991/1247) rule 4.7(3).

21 *G v Kirklees Metropolitan BC* [1993] 1 FLR 805.

22 *Re M (minors)(sexual abuse: evidence)* [1993] 1 FLR 822.

23 Legal Aid Act 1988 (CA 1989) Order 1991 (SI 1991/1924).

24 Section 15 Legal Aid Act 1988.

inevitably vary depending on the facts of the individual case. In order to achieve this objective, in care proceedings and in family proceedings when section 8 orders are being considered, the court is required to draw up a timetable with a view to disposing of the application without delay and to give such directions as it considers appropriate for seeing that the timetable is adhered to (sections 32(1) and 11(1)). Direction appointments play a crucial part in reducing delay by allowing the court to plan the progress of the case through the court, to identify the issues and narrow the areas of dispute, to appoint a guardian ad litem or solicitor for the child, if one has not already been appointed, to avoid unnecessary adjournments and to deal with as many preliminary matters as possible before a final hearing takes place. Parties to the proceedings are also required to provide time estimates of the hearings to assist in the listing and disposal of cases in the most effective manner.[25] In *Re MD & TD*[26] Wall J stressed the importance of accurate time estimates for this purpose and envisaged that parties would liaise over estimates before they were presented to the court. Direction appointments have long been held in county courts, but provision now exists for directions to be given by the justices' clerk or the magistrates in the family proceedings court.[27] Normally at least two days' notice of the hearing must be given to the parties concerned and generally all parties or their legal representatives should attend, although the child need not attend if the court considers it in his or her interests (see below). In practice, in most courts the direction appointments are taken by the justices' clerk before the time of the normal sitting of the court.

Documentary evidence and disclosure

Prior to the 1989 Act, evidence in care proceedings in juvenile courts was given orally at the hearing. One of the more significant changes brought about since the Act has been a move towards more open proceedings with advance disclosure of evidence to all the parties. In accordance with the objective of unifying laws and procedures, affidavits previously used in the High Court and county court have been replaced by written statements of evidence, which are also introduced into the family proceedings court for the first time. Rules of court now provide that written statements of the oral evidence which a party intends to adduce at a hearing or direction appointment must be filed and served on the other parties to the proceedings and the guardian *ad litem*. Furthermore, a party must also file and serve copies of any documents, including expert reports, on which he or she intends to rely.[28] The statements

---

25 Practice Direction [1994] 1 All ER 155.

26 [1994] 2 FCR 94 (FD).

27 Family Proceedings Courts (Children Act 1989) Rules 1991 (SI 1991/1395) rule 14 and Schedule 3.

28 Family Proceedings Courts (Children Act 1989) Rules 1991 (SI 1991/1395) rule 17 and Family Proceedings Rules 1991 (SI 1991/1247) rule 4.17.

and documents must be filed and served by such time as directed by the court or, if there is no direction, before the hearing of the proceedings or the direction appointment. Any further evidence or documents can then only be brought with the court's leave. The rules on advance disclosure do not, of course, apply to *ex parte* applications, which will typically be made in urgent situations where there is not time for the preparation of documents. In all other cases, including interim care applications, the rules apply and thus all parties will usually have advance notice of the evidence to be called or relied on. There are, however, occasions when disclosure will not be made to all parties. In *Official Solicitor v K*[29] the House of Lords held that the court in wardship has the power to order that evidence should not be disclosed to a party if the court was satisfied, having balanced the interests of the child (which were paramount) against the requirements of natural justice, that such disclosure would be so detrimental to the welfare of the child under consideration as to outweigh the normal requirement for a fair trial that all evidence must be disclosed so that all parties could consider it and if necessary seek to rebut it. This principle has since been extended to proceedings under the Children Act 1989, but the courts have made it clear that this is an exceptional procedure that can only be invoked when the court is satisfied that real harm – as opposed to the less stringent test of a significant risk of harm – to the child must otherwise ensue from the disclosure.[30]

Instructing expert witnesses

In many cases of child abuse, the evidence of expert witnesses, particularly medical or psychiatric experts, is likely to play a significant role. However, the court has the power to control the use of expert evidence. As previously discussed, in proceedings for a child assessment order, emergency protection order or interim care order, the child may not be medically or psychiatrically examined or assessed without a specific direction from the court (see Chapter 3); these provisions clearly aim to prevent repeated examinations of the child. Rules of court also provide that a child should not be examined or assessed for the purpose of the preparation of expert evidence for use in the proceedings without leave of the court[31] and, if such leave has not been granted, no evidence arising out of an examination or assessment will be admitted without leave of the court.[32] Thus the court has ultimate control over the examination and assessment of the child. Furthermore, even if a child is not to be physically examined or assessed, leave of the court is required before the

---

29   [1956] AC 201.

30   *Re M (minors) (disclosure of evidence)* [1994] 1 FLR 760.

31   Family Proceedings Courts (Children Act 1989) Rules 1991 (SI 1991/1395) rule 17(3) and Family Proceedings Rules 1991 (SI 1991/1247) rule 4.17(3).

32   Family Proceedings Courts (Children Act 1989) Rules 1991 (SI 1991/1395) rule 18 and Family Proceedings Rules 1991 (SI 1991/1247) rule 4.18.

papers in a Children Act case can be shown to an expert.[33] The obvious dilemma faced by the court is the potential number of experts with whom the parties may wish to consult. It is now clear that the court has both the power and the duty to limit expert evidence to given categories of expertise and to specify the number of experts to be called. In the case of *Re G*,[34] in the course of protracted care proceedings with respect to a child victim of Munchausen's Syndrome by Proxy, the mother of the child was granted leave to disclose medical reports 'to experts'. The court was not told that the mother intended to instruct six experts. The reports of the experts arrived late and caused delay in the preparation of the case by the other parties. Wall J in the Family Division rejected arguments made on behalf of the mother that a party must be free to present his or her case as he or she is advised and the court should not seek to fetter the professional discretion of the lawyers advising the mother. He held that the overriding principle is that the confidentiality which requires that leave be sought before papers are disclosed is the confidentiality of the court. It is the duty of the court to ensure a fair trial; it is also the duty of the court to exercise control over the evidence which it permits to be adduced before it, in the interests both of justice and of the child or children with whom it is concerned. He gave definitive guidance on the granting of leave:

'(1)   Generalised orders giving leave for the papers to be shown to 'an expert' or 'experts' should never be made. In each case the expert or area of expertise should be identified.

(2)   As part of the process of granting or refusing leave either for the child to be examined or for papers in the case to be shown to an expert, the advocates have a positive duty to place all relevant information before the court and the court has a positive duty to inquire into that information and in particular into the following matters:

(a)   the category of expert evidence which the party in question seeks to adduce;

(b)   the relevance of the expert evidence sought to be adduced to the issues arising for decision in the case;

(c)   whether or not the expert evidence can properly be obtained by the joint instruction of one expert by two or more of the parties;

(d)   whether or not expert evidence in any given category may properly be adduced by only one party (for example by the guardian *ad litem*)or whether it is necessary for experts in the same discipline to be instructed by more than one party.

(3)   Where the court exercises its discretion to grant leave for the papers to be shown to a particular expert (whether identified by name or a particular area of expertise) the court should invariably go on to give directions as to:

---

33   *Re M (minors) (care proceedings) (child's wishes)* [1994] 1 FLR 749 and *Re MD and TD (minors) (time estimates)* [1994] 2 FLR 336.

34   *Re G (minors) (expert witnesses)* [1994] 2 FLR 291.

(a)   the timescale in which the evidence in question should be produced;

(b)   the disclosure of any report written by an expert both to the parties and to other experts in the case;

(c)   discussions between experts following future disclosure of reports;

(d)   the filing of further evidence by the experts of the parties stating the areas of agreement and disagreement between the experts.

(4)   Where it is impractical to give directions under para 3 above at the time leave to disclose papers is granted, the court should set a date for a further directions appointment at which the directions set out in para 3 can be given.

(5)   Where it is necessary to consider the estimated length of hearing at a directions appointment the number of expert witnesses and the likely length of their evidence should be carefully considered and the exercise ... set out in *Re MD and TD (Minors) (Time estimates)* [1994] 2 FLR 336 undertaken.

(6)   It is commonplace of care cases for the local authority to wish at the outset to carry out an assessment. When this occurs, the court should in my judgment adopt the following approach:

(a)   it should specify the time in which the assessment is to be carried out and direct that evidence of the outcome of the assessment be filed by a given date;

(b)   it should fix a directions appointment for a date immediately after the date fixed for the completion of the assessments to reassess the case and give further directions for a speedy trial;

(c)   once the local authority assessment is available, immediate thought should be given at the directions appointment following its disclosure to the evidence (expert and otherwise) required to bring the case speedily and fairly to trial. Any directions for expert evidence should identify the areas of expertise for which leave is given and lay down a timetable as per para 2 above;

(d)   where a date for the final trial can be fixed before the assessment is complete that should be done. More commonly, however, it will only be possible to assess the likely length of a case once the initial assessment is complete and the issues in the case emerge.'

Such clear judicial guidance on the approach to be adopted should be welcomed by all concerned. There has been increasing concern about the use of experts in child protection cases. No statistical information is available about the percentage of cases involving experts or the impact of expert evidence on proceedings, but research is currently being conducted on the use and views of guardians *ad litem* using experts in child care cases on the approach of the courts to the granting of leave for expert assessments and examinations and on the range of expert assessments and opinion sought.[35]

---

35   Brophy, J (1994) 'Experts and Care Proceedings' in [1994] Family Law 454.

However, even in the absence of research findings, some concern is surely entirely justified in cases like *Re G* (above) where one party instructs no less than six experts. Quite apart from the unnecessary proliferation of witnesses, there are financial implications to be considered. As Wall J commented, nearly all public law Children Act cases are publicly funded and the court owes a duty to the public to ensure that public funds are not wasted on unnecessary investigation.[36] Whilst parties should not be disadvantaged in the presentation of their case by unnecessary restrictions, the court must be actively involved in controlling the evidence before it and it is no hardship to require advocates to satisfy the court as to the need for expert evidence of a specific type.

Disclosure of reports of expert witnesses and legal privilege

As a general rule, communications passing between a legal adviser and his client are subject to legal professional privilege and may not be disclosed in legal proceedings without the consent of the client. The privilege extends to communications between the client or his or her legal adviser and third parties, the dominant purpose of which is the preparation for contemplated or pending litigation.[37] The rationale of these rules is sometimes said to arise from the adversarial nature of litigation – that the privilege is necessary to put the unskilled litigant, who needs the services of a lawyer, on the same footing as a skilled litigant-in-person who has no need to reveal his secrets to anyone.[38] Therefore, as a general rule, reports of experts made on behalf of a party to litigation on the advice of legal advisers are privileged documents and, in the absence of a waiver, no order for disclosure can be made. As Roskill LJ commented:

> '... so long as we have an adversary system, a party is entitled not to produce documents which are properly protected by privilege if it is not to his advantage to produce, and even though their production might assist his adversary if his adversary or his solicitor were aware of their contents and might lead the court to a different conclusion from that to which the court would come in ignorance of their existence.'[39]

Thus, in contested care proceedings for example, if the parents consulted an expert for a report to assist their solicitor in advising them on the proceedings, the resultant report would be privileged and subject to disclosure only with the parents consent, thereby allowing the parents to disregard a report which was unfavourable to their case. Given the fact that the leave of the court is required before documents in the case can be disclosed to an expert or before any

---

36 Note 34 at 297.

37 *Waugh v British Railways Board* [1980] AC 521.

38 Keene, A (1989) *The Modern Law of Evidence* London, Butterworths p 409.

39 *Causton v Mann Egerton (Johnsons) Ltd* [1974] 1 All ER at 460.

examination or assessment of the child concerned can take place (see above) and given the paramountcy of the child's welfare in such cases and the move away from an adversarial system in civil proceedings concerning children, it was inevitable that the ability of parties to withhold unfavourable reports should be called into question. Although authority existed to suggest that in wardship proceedings the court had the power to order the disclosure of material governed by legal professional privilege, there were conflicting authorities as to whether such a power existed in proceedings under the Children Act.[40] The Court of Appeal addressed the issue in *Oxfordshire County Council v M*.[41] In this case leave was sought to disclose documents to experts on the basis that, if the leave sought were to be granted, the parties would be under no obligation to disclose any reports consequently obtained, which would be subject to legal professional privilege. The Court of Appeal held that cases involving children fall into a special category where the court is bound to take all necessary steps to arrive at an appropriate result in the paramount interests of the welfare of the child. Therefore, the court clearly has the power to override legal professional privilege in relation to expert's reports when it gives leave to parties to obtain them and may ensure the disclosure of the reports by making it a condition of the leave granted. As Sir Stephen Brown commented:

'If a party, having obtained the leave of the court, were to be able to conceal, or withhold from the court, matters which were of importance and were relevant to the future of the child, there would be a risk that the welfare of the child would not be promoted as the Children Act requires.'

However, this does not directly address the issue as to whether there is a positive duty to make voluntary disclosure of adverse medical reports when leave of the court has not been required for the preparation of such reports. In *Essex County Council v R*,[42] Thorpe J said:

'For my part, I would wish to see case law go yet further and to make it plain that the legal representatives in possession of such material relevant to determination but contrary to the interests of their client, not only are unable to resist disclosure by reliance on legal professional privilege, but have a positive duty to disclose to other parties and to the court ... [If] parties initiate or are joined in proceedings, with or without leave, and within those proceedings seek to establish rights or to exercise responsibilities in relation to a child whose future is the issue for the court's determination, it should be understood that they too owe a duty to the court to make full and frank disclosure of any material in their possession relevant to that determination.'

In the later case of *Re DH (a minor) (child abuse)*[43] in the Family Division, Wall J commented:

---

40 See Douglas Brown J in *Barking and London Borough Council v O* [1993] All ER 59 and Thorpe J in *Re R (a minor) (disclosure of privileged material)* [1993] 4 All ER 702.

41 [1994] 1 FLR 679.

42 [1993] 2 FLR 826 at 828.

43 [1994] 1 FLR 679 at 704.

'In my judgment the clear thrust of the judgments ... in the *Oxfordshire* case is that the welfare principle enshrined in s 1 of the Children Act 1989 not only overrides professional privilege in relation to medical reports but also necessarily imports the duty described by Thorpe J. In my judgment, therefore, the practice in family proceedings should follow Thorpe J's judgment in the *Essex* case unless and until the Court of Appeal says otherwise.'

Such a conclusion is entirely logical and accords with the principles underlying the Children Act 1989. If the court is to decide what is best for the child, parties cannot be allowed to withhold reports which are unfavourable to their case. The court must have all available information if the child's welfare is to be secured.

Admissibility of evidence in court

Reference has already been made to the increasing tendency to treat cases involving children in a non-adversarial manner and how advance disclosure of witness statements and documents ensures that all parties are fully informed of the evidence before a full hearing takes place. The major distinguishing feature between civil and criminal proceedings is the admissibility of hearsay evidence in civil proceedings. Prior to 1991, the position was complex, with different rules governing different courts. Fortunately, the position has now been clarified. The Children (Admissibility of Hearsay Evidence) Order 1991 (SI 1991/1115) made hearsay evidence given in connection with the upbringing, maintenance and welfare of a child admissible in civil proceedings in the High Court, the county court and the family proceedings court. The scope of this order has now been extended to include all civil proceedings, including those under the Child Support Act 1991.[44] Therefore, hearsay evidence, including video recordings of interviews with the child and reports of experts not called as witnesses, will be admissible in all child protection proceedings in the civil courts. However, the Admissibility Orders only permit the court to admit hearsay evidence – it is for the court to decide what weight should be attached to hearsay statements which are not made on oath and cannot be tested by cross-examination.

Proceedings in civil courts

Privacy

Proceedings in the High Court or county court will normally be held in chambers, without the attendance of the press.[45] In the family proceedings court, the press may be in attendance, together with the officers of the court, the parties, their solicitors, counsel, witnesses and others directly concerned in the case. Any

---

44   Children (Admissibility of Hearsay Evidence) Order 1993 [SI 1993/621].

45   Family Proceedings Rules 1991 (SI 1991/1247) rule 4.16(7).

other person can only be present with the permission of the court.[46] However, the press may be excluded if the court considers this to be in the best interests of the child[47] and, in any event, there are strict limitations on the reporting of proceedings. No person may publish any material which is intended or likely to identify the child concerned unless the court or the secretary of state dispenses with the restriction, as may be done if the child is missing and publicity could assist his or her recovery.[48]

Court procedure

Despite the relaxation of the exclusionary rules of evidence, the procedure at a hearing is formal and takes the traditional form of witnesses giving examination-in-chief, then being cross-examined and, if appropriate, re-examined. The court can give directions as to the order of the proceedings, but in the absence of such directions, evidence will usually be adduced by the parties in the following order:

- the applicant;
- any party with parental responsibility for the child;
- other respondents;
- the guardian ad litem; and
- the child, if he or she is a party to the proceedings and there is no guardian ad litem.

Each party may address the court and call witnesses, who will be examined-in-chief by the party calling them. The witnesses may then be cross-examined by the other parties, in the order indicated above. The party calling the witness may then re-examine the witness, but only on matters raised in cross-examination. After the parties have adduced their evidence, the applicant may call evidence in rebuttal, but only if fresh evidence has been raised for the first time during the respondents' case and finally, the guardian *ad litem* may be called on to make a statement. The court will, of course, have various reports and documents at their disposal (see above) which must be read before the case is heard.[49] Having heard the evidence, the court must then decide if the necessary criteria for the order applied for have been met and will usually retire to consider all the available evidence. If the court is not satisfied that the case has been proved, no order can be made. However, even if the criteria are met, the court must also consider the check-list in section 1(3) of the Act – including the range of powers available to it – and the concept of

---

46   Section 69(1) Magistrates Court Act 1980.

47   Family Proceedings Courts (Children Act 1989) Rules 1991 (SI 1991/1395) rule 16(7).

48   Section 97 Children Act 1989.

49   *M v C (children orders: reasons)* [1993] 1 FCR 264.

'no order' in section 1(5) of the Act. When making any order, or refusing an application, the court must state any findings of fact and give reasons for the decision.[50]

Attendance of the child

In each case, consideration must be given to whether or not the child concerned should attend the hearing. In any proceedings under Parts IV and V of the Act (care/supervision orders and child protection), the court may order the child to attend at a specified stage or stages of the proceedings (section 95(1)). However, it is now recognised that in many cases, the child's attendance at court is unnecessary and may only cause further trauma to him or her. Rules of court therefore provide that proceedings may take place in the absence of the child if the court considers it to be in the interests of the child, having regard to the matters to be discussed and the evidence likely to be given, and the child is represented by a guardian *ad litem* or a solicitor.[51] If the child's attendance is ordered, section 95(4) of the Act contains what seem to be draconian powers for the court to make an order authorising a constable, or such other person as may be specified in the order, to take charge of the child and bring him or her to court, and to enter and search any premises specified in the order if the person has reasonable cause to believe that the child may be found on the premises. This conjures up visions of a reluctant child being dragged from under a bed by a police officer and being frog-marched into court! The primary consideration should be the wishes of the child and the guardian *ad litem* will usually be required to ascertain the child's wishes and convey these to the court. If a child of sufficient age and understanding clearly indicates that he or she does not wish to attend, the court should be very cautious in ordering his or her attendance.

Conversely, children of sufficient age and understanding who wish to attend the proceedings should be allowed to do so unless there are very clearly articulated reasons why they should not. In *Re C (a minor) (Care: child's wishes)*[52] a 13 year old girl, who was said to be young for her age, at her request, attended care proceedings in the family proceedings court, save for brief intervals when evidence was being given which her guardian *ad litem* thought it better for her not to hear, and was also present throughout an appeal hearing in the High Court. It was argued before the High Court that the child had a right to be present if she so wished, and that the court had no power to override that wish, even in the supposed best interests of the child. Since no opposition was raised to the child's presence by any of the parties

---

50 *W v Hertfordshire County Council* [1993] 1 FLR 118.

51 Family Proceedings Courts (Children Act 1989) Rules 1991 (SI 1991/1395) rule 16, Family Proceedings Rules 1991 (SI 1991/1247)FPR rule 4.16.

52 [1993] 1 FLR 832.

involved, although the local authority expressed some misgivings, the question did not arise for decision in the case, but Waite J expressed the view that it would be surprising if the High Court had no control over the presence or absence of the child at appeal hearings. Waite J was obviously uneasy about the child's presence at the appeal hearing. He said:

'... I think it would be a pity if the presence of children as young as this at the hearing of High Court appeals from magistrates in family proceedings were to be allowed to develop unquestioningly into a settled practice ... if guardians *ad litem* are proposing to arrange for a child as young as this to be present at an appeal, they should give that question very careful thought beforehand, and be prepared, if necessary, to explain their reasons to the judge.'

In this case it seems that the girl spent most of the hearing 'preoccupied with her toys and colouring books'. Waite J's unease may be justified if it is attributable solely to the fact that he thought that this individual child was too young to obtain any possible benefit from attending the proceedings and he therefore thought little weight should be attached to her views for that reason. It is, however, surely a cause for concern if his statement is taken to indicate a presumption against the attendance of a child who expresses a clear wish to be there, which must be rebutted by evidence from the guardian *ad litem*. Yet such a presumption seems to have been applied in the later case of *Re W*.[53] The proceedings in this case concerned the making of a secure accommodation order under section 25 of the 1989 Act and the child had expressed a wish to attend. However, the guardian *ad litem*, the local authority and the mother all believed that it would not be in his interests to do so. Ewbank J in the Family Division held that the court had the power under its inherent jurisdiction to prevent a child attending court and that the court should only allow children to attend if it was in their interests – which again seems to apply a presumption that a child should not attend unless it is proved to be in his or her best interests. Admittedly, in this case it was anticipated that the boy would be unruly if permitted to attend court and this may well have been a justification for excluding him, but the current trend towards requiring proof that attendance is in the child's best interests should be discouraged.

---

53   (1994) *The Times* 13 July.

PROSECUTING THE ABUSER – PROCEEDINGS IN CRIMINAL COURTS

The decision to prosecute

During an investigation of suspected child abuse, the primary concern of all those involved will be to protect the child and the overriding consideration will be the child's welfare. However, as 'Working Together' points out, police involvement stems from their primary responsibilities to protect the community and bring offenders to justice, the police focus will be to determine whether a criminal offence has been committed, to identify the person or persons responsible and to secure the best possible evidence in order that appropriate consideration can be given as to whether criminal proceedings should be instituted. In more serious cases of abuse, the prosecution process may well be instigated by the arrest of the suspected abuser early in the investigation. In other cases, initial consideration will be given to prosecuting the abuser during strategy discussions between police and social workers. 'Working Together' merely states that the decision whether or not criminal proceedings should be initiated will be based on three main factors – whether or not there is sufficient substantial evidence to prosecute; whether it is in the public interest that proceedings should be instituted; and whether or not it is in the interests of the child victim that proceedings should be instituted – without specifying who should make the decision. In an ideal situation, in the spirit of inter-agency co-operation, any decision should be taken jointly by all those involved in the investigation. However, as previously discussed, the differing professional ideologies of the professions may result in conflict (see Chapter 4). Guidance issued to the police on the investigation of sexual abuse after the Cleveland crisis states that:

> 'In reaching [the decision to prosecute] the police will wish to take full account of the views of the other agencies concerned with the case, in particular the social services department, on how a prosecution might affect the victim and other members of the family.'[54]

This suggests that, whereas the police will take the views of other professionals involved into account, any decision to prosecute will ultimately rest with them. However, the guidance concludes:

> 'The success of the police intervention ... is not to be measured in terms of the prosecutions which are brought, but of the protection which their actions bring to children at risk.'

This once again seems to emphasise that the primary concern of the police should be the protection of the child, not the prosecution of the abuser.

---

54 Home Office (1988) 'The Investigation of Child Sexual Abuse' Home Office Circular 52/1988 para 25.

The Crown Prosecution Service

Once the police investigation is complete and a decision is made to prosecute the abuser, the case will be handed over to the Crown Prosecution Service (CPS), whose primary roles are to provide an objective assessment of the results of the police investigation and to prosecute those cases which pass the tests laid down in the Code for Crown Prosecutors, issued pursuant to section 10 of the Prosecution of Offenders Act 1985. The decision to proceed with the prosecution will be based on two criteria:

- The evidential sufficiency criterion

  Any prosecution will only proceed if the CPS are satisfied that there is a 'realistic' prospect of conviction. There must be enough evidence for the court, properly directed in accordance with the law, to be more likely than not to convict the defendant of the offence charged. The CPS must evaluate the available evidence in terms of its admissibility, credibility and persuasiveness. The recent recognition of the potential credibility of children (see Chapter 6) and reform of the criminal justice system to facilitate the reception of evidence from young children (see below) will undoubtedly influence this evaluation. Failure to satisfy the evidential criterion means that the prosecution will not proceed, no matter how great the public interest may seem in having the matter aired in court.

- The public interest criterion

  The second criterion to be satisfied is that a prosecution must be in the public interest. The Code sets out common factors which tend in favour of a prosecution – which include the seriousness of the offence and its effect upon the victim – and those which militate against a prosecution – including the health of the defendant and the effect of a prosecution on him or her. In cases of any seriousness, there is clear guidance that the prosecution should continue unless the public interest factors against a prosecution *clearly outweigh* those in favour, thus creating a strong presumption in favour of prosecution if the offence charged is serious.

The public interest v the child's best interests

But the question remains, what of the child's best interests? It may well be safe to assume that it is in the public interest that child abusers should be prosecuted – to decide otherwise would be effectively to de-criminalise child abuse. Yet in many cases, once the child's protection has been assured, there may be a conflict between the public interest in pursuing a prosecution and the child's best interests in having the case dealt with in a manner which causes the least stress and disruption. The Royal Commission on Criminal Justice acknowledged the importance of the feelings of the victim, but stressed that it could not override public interest,[55] which suggests that the views of the child will not be taken into account in deciding whether or not the prosecution should proceed. However, the Memorandum of Good Practice states:

> 'In deciding whether to include a child's evidence, and whether it is in the public interest that a case should be brought to trial at all, the Crown Prosecution Service will take into account the interests and wishes of the child. Reports to the Crown Prosecution Service should always include clear information about the wishes of the child, and his or her parents and carers, about going to court.'(para 2.15)

Although the Code of Practice treats the two criteria as separate issues, in practice, the public interest criterion cannot be totally divorced from the evidential sufficiency criterion. Paradoxically, whereas in most circumstances the older the child the more weight is attached to their views, in deciding whether or not a prosecution should proceed, the reverse may be true. The older the child, the more credible they may appear as a witness and the stronger the prosecution case will be. Although the older child may have strong views against proceeding, if the CPS feel there is a strong case against the abuser, the public interest in prosecuting the abuser will prevail. Yet in the case of a young child, who may not be such a credible witness but who holds similar views against proceeding, even though there may be a realistic prospect of conviction, there is also a relatively greater likelihood of acquittal. The child's views may therefore be accorded more weight in deciding whether the prosecution is in the public interest.

The decision to proceed is not one to be taken lightly. Although there are arguably perceived benefits to the child, in that a prosecution is seen as society's denunciation of the abuse and confirms to the child that they are not responsible, there will always be factors militating against prosecution. Despite recent reforms (see below) a court appearance is likely to remain a traumatic experience for the child. If the abuser is acquitted, the child inevitably feels that he or she was not believed or that he or she was responsible in some way. Even if the abuser is convicted, the child may feel responsible for the breakup of the family and any punishment inflicted on the abuser. All these factors must be considered in deciding where the public interest lies. Whereas the views of the child victim should always be considered and the child should be kept fully informed of any decisions made, the child should never be given the right to determine the matter – no child should be burdened with such responsibility.

---

55 Report of the Royal Commission on Criminal Justice (1993) Cm 2263 HMSO, 79.

Proceedings in court

The court in which the trial takes place will be determined by the criminal offence charged (see Appendix). The more serious offences are designated indictable offences and must be tried before a judge and jury in the crown court. Minor offences are summary offences and can only be tried in the magistrates' court without a jury. There also exists a wide category of hybrid offences, which may be tried either at the magistrates' court or the Crown Court. The choice is usually made by the defendant, who cannot be denied his right to trial by jury, but may choose to be tried in the magistrates' court. The magistrates, however, have limited powers of sentencing and therefore have a discretion to commit the case to the Crown Court, either for trial or for sentence, if the seriousness of the case merits this. It therefore follows that in more serious cases of abuse, the trial will take place on indictment at the Crown Court.

'A long time to wait'

In the past, trials on indictment had to be preceded by committal proceedings in the magistrates' court which meant that there was often a delay of many months before the case reached trial and child witnesses could be called upon to give evidence and face cross-examination twice – once at the committal proceedings and once at the trial. The Advisory Group on Video Evidence (see below) concluded that, in cases which involve children, the existing committal proceedings were irredeemably flawed. As a result of recommendations made by the Advisory Group, section 53 of the Criminal Justice Act 1991 now authorises the Director of Public Prosecutions, in the case of certain offences,[56] to serve a 'notice of transfer' on the magistrates' court in whose jurisdiction the offence has been charged, certifying that he or she is of the opinion:

- that the evidence of the offence would be sufficient for the person charged to be committed for trial;

- that a child[57] who is alleged:-

    (i)   to be a person against whom the offence was committed; or

    (ii)   to have witnessed the commission of the offence;

will be called as a witness at the trial; and

- that, for the purpose of avoiding any prejudice to the welfare of the child, the case should be taken over and proceeded with without delay by the Crown Court.

---

56   The offences concerned are detailed in section 32(2) of the Criminal Justice Act 1988 and include sexual offences and offences involving violence or cruelty.

57   For these purposes a child is a person under 14 years if the offence charged involves violence or cruelty, and a person under 17 years in the case of a sexual offence.

This provision is designed to ensure the actual trial takes place as quickly as possible. It allows the case to proceed directly to the Crown Court 'for the purpose of avoiding any prejudice to the welfare of the child'. References to the welfare of the child have previously been associated with civil proceedings. Whereas previous statutory provisions allowed concessions for child witnesses in criminal proceedings, these generally required a 'serious danger to the juvenile's life or health'.[58] The express acknowledgement that the *welfare* of the child should be taken into account in the conduct of criminal proceedings relating to the abuser reflects the growing concern with children's needs and rights.

The provision initially only referred to child victims of the offence, but was extended during the passage of the Bill to include child witnesses who are not actual victims – an acknowledgement that participation in criminal proceedings can be traumatic for all child witnesses. Provision for more wide-ranging reform is now contained in section 44 of the Criminal Justice and Public Order Act 1994. Committal proceedings are to be abolished and replaced with a new procedure for transferring cases to the Crown Court for trial. This will not affect the existing procedures under the Criminal Justice Act 1991 for cases involving children and the new procedure will not be brought into force until extensive consultations have taken place with the courts and practitioners.

Face to face – confrontation or intimidation?

At common law, a defendant always had a right to confront his accuser – a right that is reflected in other jurisdictions and is contained in the 6th amendment of the US which gives the accused a right 'to be confronted with the witnesses against him'. It has been explained that confrontation:

- ensures that the witness will give his statements under oath, thus impressing him with the seriousness of the matter and guarding against the lie by the possibility of a penalty for perjury;

- forces the witness to submit to cross-examination, the 'greatest legal engine ever invented for the discovery of truth';

- permits the jury that is to decide the defendant's fate to observe the demeanour of the witness in making his statement, thus aiding the jury in assessing his credibility.[59]

However, precisely how far this right of confrontation extends has not always been clear. At the turn of the century it was generally thought that it included a right to face-to-face confrontation with a witness. But in 1919, the

---

58 See, for example, sections 42 and 43 of the Children and Young Persons Act 1933.

59 Haugaard, J and Reppucci, N (1988) *The Sexual Abuse of Children: A Comprehensive Guide to Current Knowledge and Intervention Strategies.* San Francisco, Jossey-Bass p 355.

Court of Appeal held that if there is a fear that the witness may be intimidated, the witness can give evidence out of sight of the accused.[60] Because one of the reasons for the right of confrontation is to allow the jury to view the witness' demeanour while giving evidence, it follows that the witness should be in the view of the jury, even if not in the view of the defendant. In 1919, the accused was required to sit on the stairs leading to the dock, where he or she could not be seen by the witness, but nevertheless could hear the evidence being given.

A somewhat more sophisticated method of achieving the same objective is the use of screens, which received the formal approval of the Court of Appeal in 1989. However, the use of screens is dependent on leave of the court. As the Lord Chief Justice commented:

'The learned judge has the duty ... of endeavouring to see that justice is done. Those are high sounding words. What it really means is, he has got to see that the system operates fairly; fairly not only to the defendants but also to the prosecution and also to witnesses.'[61]

Advances in video technology in recent years have led to further reform. Section 32 of the Criminal Justice Act 1988 now permits children, with leave of the court, to give evidence by live television link in trials for assault and sexual assault. An evaluation of the video link conducted by Davies and Noon concluded that two years after its introduction, the link enjoyed widespread acceptance among all those with experience of its use.[62] The research found that the majority of children (76%) were able to give evidence without being reduced to tears at any point and only one child in the whole study was visibly distressed at all stages of examination. The report suggests that, given the frequently harrowing nature of the evidence in cases of sexual or physical abuse, these observations are highly encouraging. The very fact that it can be thought 'highly encouraging' that a percentage of child witnesses can give evidence to a court without being reduced to tears is itself indicative of the urgent need for reform of traditional procedures to accommodate child witnesses. Unfortunately, very little research has been carried out on children testifying under traditional procedures, so comparison is difficult, but it is generally accepted that video links are, at least, a step in the right direction.

Whatever the practical consequences of the use of video links, it is argued by some that allowing evidence to be given in this way infringes the accused's rights and the ability of the jury members to gather all the information needed to reach the best decision. It has been suggested that the camera becomes the juror's eyes and that:

---

60   *R v Smellie* [1919] 14 Cr App Rep 128.

61   *R v X, Y, Z,* [1990] 91 Cr App Rep 36 at 40.

62   Davies and Noon (1991) 'An Evaluation of the Live Link for Child Witnesses' Report to the Home Office.

'composition, camera angle, light direction, colour renderings will all affect the viewer's impressions and attitudes to what he sees in the picture.'[63]

In addition, concerns have been expressed by the courts in the US about the phenomenon of 'status conferral'. It was claimed in 1984:

'... it is quite conceivable that the credibility of a witness whose testimony is presented via closed-circuit television may be enhanced by the phenomenon called "status conferral". It is recognised that the media bestows prestige and enhances the authority of an individual by legitimatising his status ... such considerations are of particular importance when, as here, the demeanour and credibility of the witness are crucial to the state's case.'[64]

While the concept may have some merit in the case of an adult witness, the suggestion that the status of a young child can be enhanced simply by appearance on a television screen must be questioned. Conversely, it has been argued that a screen image of a child lacks the power of a child's own presence, the accused being more real to the jury since they see him throughout the trial.[65] Davies and Noon even found that on occasions prosecution barristers, when faced with a particularly impressive and resilient witness, have quite deliberately opted for an in-court appearance on the grounds of its greater impact! Whilst this raises concerns about the exploitation of the child, lawyers are trained to communicate with witnesses in open court and constraints imposed by electronic communication may lead to problems in establishing and maintaining rapport with the child. As Davies and Noon point out, few courses for lawyers include any provision for training in interviewing children, let alone for using interactive television. It would seem important to introduce such training, either in the initial qualification, or more plausibly as part of a more specialised course for those who will conduct this work in the courts. Given the importance attached to training interviewers at the investigation stage and the detailed advice on video recorded interviews contained in the Memorandum of Good Practice (see Chapter 4), the appropriate training of lawyers should be seen as a priority.

Video recording the child's evidence – problems and possibilities

To many, the ultimate aim of reform would be to spare the child the trauma of a court appearance in any form, while still allowing the prosecution of the abuser. Such ideas are by no means new. In 1963 it was suggested:

'The ideal procedure from the point of view of the child's interests can be stated quite simply. He or she should be interviewed by an officer trained in social casework and child welfare, given (if necessary) a medical examination

---

63 Armstrong quoted in Haugaard, J & Reppucci, N (1988) *The Sexual Abuse of Children: A Comprehensive Guild to Current Knowledge and Intervention Stategies*, San Franciso, Jossey-Bass p 355.

64 *Hochiester v Superior Court* [1984] quoted in Haugaard J & Reppucci [1988].

65 McEwan, J (1988) 'Child Evidence: More Proposals for Reform' Criminal Law Review 813 at 820.

by a doctor experienced in this work, and thereafter should take no part in the subsequent proceedings.'[66]

In 1963 this suggestion did find limited support, most notably from Professor Glanville Williams who passed on the proposal to the Criminal Law Revision Committee in 1969. But as Professor Williams observed:

'I never had any great hope that a committee of lawyers would accept the proposal, and they did not. They rejected it after a very brief discussion, and, not being mentioned in the Committee's report, it sank without trace.'[67]

Advances in technology in the last 25 years have led to renewed interest in the proposal. During the passage of the Criminal Justice Act 1988 through Parliament[68] an Advisory Group on Video Evidence was set up, chaired by Judge Thomas Pigot QC. The Home Secretary, in his reference to the Advisory Group made it clear that the right of the accused to cross examine the child should remain. A further restriction placed on the Advisory Group was the rule against hearsay evidence. In most cases, it is generally assumed that to allow a child's original account of the abuse to be admitted at the trial in place of the child's oral evidence would require a further exception to the hearsay rule. The Advisory Group were of the opinion that:

'... the terms of our appointment postulate the continued existence of the hearsay rule in its present form and the focus of our deliberations has therefore been upon whether and how a special exception relating to video recorded evidence might be made.'(para 2.8)

But it has been argued that, in certain circumstances, the required exception to the hearsay rule already exists.[69] This argument centres on the provisions contained in sections 23 and 24 of the Criminal Justice Act 1988, which allow for the admission of documentary hearsay evidence, a 'document' being defined to include tape recorded and video recorded statements. If a child victim of abuse is interviewed by a social worker or police officer or both, and the child's account of the abuse is either recorded in written form or a video recording is made of the account, such a witness statement is potentially admissible under either section 23 or section 24 of the 1988 Act. Section 23, which deals with first hand documentary hearsay statements, requires that the maker of the statement be shown to be unavailable because of – *inter alia* – his bodily or mental condition, or, if the statement was made to a police officer, the maker does not give oral evidence through fear or because he or she is kept out of the way. Section 24, which deals with business documents and permits multiple hearsay, provides that, if

---

66 Gibbens, T and Prince, J, (1963) *Child victims of sex offences*, London, Institute for the Study and Treatment of Delinquency.

67 Williams, G (1987) 'Child Witnesses' in Smith, P (1987) *Criminal Law: Essays in honour of JC Smith*, London, Butterworths.

68 House of Commons 20 June 1988.

69 McEwan, J (1989) 'Documentary Hearsay Evidence - Refuge for Vulnerable Witnesses' *Criminal Law Review* (1989) 629.

the statement was prepared for the purposes of pending or contemplated criminal proceedings or of a criminal investigation (an 'investigation document'), similar conditions of admissibility as contained in Section 23 apply, or alternatively, that the person who made the statement cannot reasonably be expected (having regard to the time which has elapsed since he or she made the statement and to all the circumstances) to have any recollection of the matters dealt with in the statement. The admissibility of any such statement is limited by sections 25 and 26 of the Act. In the case of an 'investigation document', the statement will only be admissible with leave of the court. Clearly, the admissibility of the evidence ultimately depends on the discretion of the trial judge and clear guidance is contained in section 25 and 26. But if it is assumed that in the individual case psychological harm would be the result of a court appearance and medical evidence to that effect is available, a child's initial accounts of abuse are potentially admissible under these provisions.

The Advisory Group on Video Evidence seemed pessimistic about the potential of these provisions:

> 'We are not disposed to attempt to assess in any detail how far the 1988 Act will operate to allow video recorded interviews to be put in evidence ... we are satisfied that the provisions are unlikely to affect the admissibility of evidence by the generality of children and other vulnerable witnesses.'(para 2.7)

It is, perhaps, not surprising that the Advisory Group did not see fit to explore the potential of these provisions more thoroughly. Obviously, the major drawback as far as the accused is concerned is that, if a child's statement was admitted under these provisions, there would be no opportunity to cross-examine the child. However, there may well be exceptional cases where this is justified and those involved in the management of such cases may do well to remember the existence of these provisions.

The Advisory Group proposed in December 1989 that the law should be changed so that at trials on indictment for violent and sexual offences, video recorded interviews with children should be admissible. A scheme was proposed whereby the child would not be involved in the actual trial of the abuser. The Advisory Group envisaged that the trial judge would rule on the admissibility of the video at a pre-trial application. The accused's right to cross-examine the child would then be retained by holding a preliminary hearing which would be held in less formal, more comfortable surroundings than the court room, with only the judge and counsel for each side, the child and either a parent or supporter present. The accused would be able to hear and view the proceedings through closed circuit television or a one-way mirror and be able to communicate with his or her counsel so that they could direct him or her to put any required questions to the child. At the preliminary hearing, any video recording which had been allowed in evidence would be shown to the child witness, who may then be asked to expand on certain aspects of it. The child would then usually be cross-examined by defence counsel. The Advisory Group emphasised that these proceedings should be as informal as possible, and that the judge should control cross-examination with special care. The preliminary hearing would itself be video recorded. At the eventual trial, the initial recorded interview would be shown at the point in which the child would now give evidence-in-chief and the video recording of the preliminary hearing would be shown at the place where cross-examination would normally follow. Thus the child's personal involvement in the legal process would be concluded at the end of the preliminary hearing.

The recommendations of the Advisory Group were generally greeted with hope and enthusiasm. But when the Criminal Justice Act 1991 was introduced, those who anticipated full implementation of the proposals were disappointed. In specified proceedings,[70] the Act amends the Criminal Justice Act of 1988 to allow for a video recording of an interview conducted between an adult and a child[71] witness and which relates to any matter in the proceedings to be given in evidence, as an exception to the hearsay rule, with the leave of the court.[72] But the video will only be admitted at the actual trial, there is no provision for a preliminary hearing to be held. Furthermore, the Act makes it clear that the video will only be admitted if the child will be available for cross-examination at the trial. Thus, a child's first experience of the trial is cross-examination. As Spencer commented:

'the child is precipitated into the court for the nastiest bit of the court experience.'[73]

Admittedly, such cross-examination may take place via a video link, but how far this will go in ameliorating the stress suffered by the child is still open to debate.

Secondary victimisation – does the child as a witness suffer more than the child as a victim?

Appearing in court is acknowledged as being a potentially stressful and intimidating experience for adult witnesses, therefore, there can be little doubt as to the detrimental effect a court appearance may have on a child. Recent legislative reforms have come about after a long, hard battle fought by those convinced that subjecting a child witness to the trauma of giving evidence in open court itself amounted to abuse of the child and was therefore a form of

---

70   The proceedings are detailed in section 32A Criminal Justice Act 1988 and include, *inter alia*, trials on indictment for those offences detailed in section 32(2) of the Act (see note 56 above), appeals to the Court of Appeal in respect of those offences and proceedings in youth courts for any such offence and appeals to the Crown Court arising out of such proceedings.

71   See note 57.

72   Section 32A Criminal Justice Act 1988.

73   *The Guardian* 17 August 1994.

secondary victimisation. The 1991 Act has proved something of a disappointment to those who anticipated more radical reform and the movement for further reform is still gaining momentum. Yet alongside the much-publicised legislative reforms, there have been a number of changes in practice which are also aimed at reducing the trauma suffered by child witnesses. Of particular significance is the acknowledgement of the importance of preparing the child for the court appearance and supporting the child before, during and after the trial.[74] The NSPCC, in consultation with other agencies, has produced a child witness pack which is aimed at helping children cope with a court appearance and includes materials aimed directly at child witnesses and their supporters, providing information about procedure in court and the process of giving evidence.

The combined effect of legislative reforms and changes in practice in recent years have undoubtedly gone some way to reducing the stress suffered by children required to give evidence in a criminal trial. Whereas in civil proceedings concerning a child, the child's welfare will, quite rightly, be the paramount consideration, this cannot be the case in criminal proceedings where a balance needs to be struck between the rights of the accused and the best interests of the child. For a long time the balance has been firmly weighted in favour of the accused. Recent reforms have begun to redress the balance in favour of the child. A concerted effort is now needed to assess the practical effects of these reforms, both on the child and the accused. Only then can it be decided how best to balance the rights of the accused and the interests of the child witness.

---

74   See Aldridge and Freshwater (1993) 'The Preparation of Child Witnesses' Journal of Child Law [1993] 25 and O'Hara, M (1994) 'Supporting the Child Witness' *Childright* [1994] no 108 p 11.

CHAPTER 8

THE ABUSED AND ABUSER – RECOMPENSE, RETRIBUTION AND REHABILITATION

COMPENSATING THE ABUSED

Compensation in criminal proceedings

The primary consideration of the criminal courts following conviction will be the punishment of the offender (see below). However, the criminal courts also have the power to order an offender to pay compensation to the victim for any personal injury, loss or damage resulting from the offence.[1] Compensation may be awarded for distress and anxiety, and for mental as well as physical injury. The power to order compensation arises when a court is dealing with an offender for an offence (ie after conviction). Although the power to order compensation was introduced in 1972, comparatively few orders were made by the courts initially. In an effort to encourage the use of such orders, the Criminal Justice Act of 1988 introduced a requirement that if a court, having power to make a compensation order, chooses not to do so, it must give its reasons. Criminal statistics[2] show a sharp rise in the number of orders made immediately following the 1988 Act – 108,400 orders were made in 1988, rising to 126,400 in 1989 and 129,600 in 1990 but the number of orders made than decreased steadily and in 1993 96,500 orders were made. In 1993 14% of offenders sentenced in magistrates' courts and 13% of those sentenced in the Crown Court were ordered to pay compensation.

A compensation order may be made instead of, or in addition to, dealing with the offender in any other way for the offence, so an order can be combined with any other sentence the court may impose or may alternatively be made as a sentence in its own right.[3] The orders are not intended to punish the offender (that is left to the other sentencing options of the court), but to provide the victim with a:

> 'convenient and rapid means of avoiding the expense of resorting to civil litigation when the criminal clearly has the means which would enable the compensation to be paid'.[4]

Thus the ability of the offender to pay any compensation awarded is crucial. If the court is considering both compensation and a fine, but the offender would not have the means to pay both, it is specifically provided that

---

1   Section 35 Powers of Criminal Courts Act 1973.
2   Criminal Statistics 1993 HMSO 1994.
3   Section 67 Criminal Justice Act 1982.
4   *R v Inwood* [1975] 60 Cr App Rep 70.

priority should be given to the compensation[5] which indicates the importance attached to compensating victims when the money comes from the offender himself and can be contrasted with the attitude of the government towards compensating victims from public funds which is evident in recent reforms to the Criminal Injuries Compensation Scheme (see below).

Child abusers convicted of criminal offences may therefore be ordered to pay compensation to the child by the criminal courts. The procedure will involve no further trauma for the child – it is not necessary to attend court and make an application in person, the CPS will ensure the court has all the relevant information if the abuser pleads guilty and, if a full trial takes place, evidence relevant to the compensation will emerge during the course of the trial. Compensating personal injury is, of course, notoriously difficult. Yet the criminal statistics for 1993 show that in the magistrates' court compensation orders were made in 64% of cases when an offender was convicted of an offence of violence against the person, compared to 57% of cases involving criminal damage, 56% of cases involving fraud and forgery and 20% of cases involving theft and handling stolen goods. By comparison, compensation orders were made in only 13% of cases involving sexual offences, which perhaps indicates that the courts are more prepared to compensate physical rather than psychological injury. A similar pattern emerges in the Crown Court. In the past the courts have obtained guidance from the amounts paid by the Criminal Injuries Compensation Board in comparable cases.[6] Whether such comparison will continue to be made following the introduction of the new tariff scheme (see below) remains to be seen. The Home Office has sought to encourage the use of compensation orders for personal injury by issuing guidance as to suggested figures appropriate for common injuries; these range from up to £50 for a graze to £2,500 for a broken arm or leg.[7] No reference is made to psychological injury in the guidance. It seems that the majority of compensation orders are made for relatively minor injuries, which would not qualify for an award under the Criminal Injuries Compensation Scheme (see below). In 1992, the average compensation awarded was £118 in magistrates' courts and £445 in Crown Courts.

A compensation order made by a criminal court does not preclude the victim from commencing proceedings in the civil courts (see below). Any damages awarded in civil proceedings are assessed without regard to the compensation order, but the plaintiff may only recover an amount equal to the aggregate of any amount by which the civil damages exceed the compensation and a sum equal to any portion of the compensation which he fails to recover,[8] thereby ensuring that the victim cannot be compensated for the same loss twice. Similarly, any award made by the Criminal Injuries

---

5   Section 35(4A) Powers of Criminal Courts Act 1973.

6   *R v Broughton* [1986] 8 Cr App Rep 380.

7   Justice of the Peace [1993] 157(52) 828.

8   Section 38 Powers of Criminal Courts Act 1973.

Compensation Authority (see below) will be reduced by the amount of compensation ordered by a criminal court in respect of personal injuries.[9]

The obvious restriction on the use of compensation orders as a means of compensating child victims of abuse is that the abuser must be convicted of a criminal offence before an order can be made and in the past this has meant that very few victims of abuse were compensated in this way. The reforms to the criminal justice system (see Chapter 7) should result in more successful prosecutions being brought, thus potentially allowing more victims to be compensated. Despite this, the numbers will still be comparatively small, bearing in mind the extent of the problem of child abuse. In cases of intrafamilial abuse an order may only serve to heighten conflict within the family and reduce the possibility of rehabilitation. Although it could be argued that similar considerations would apply to any decision to prosecute the abuser in the first place, a compensation order could exacerbate the situation further since the compensation is paid by the abuser himself to the victim and, particularly if the order is to be paid in instalments, could serve as a continual reminder of an incident which all members of the family would rather put behind them. Even in cases of abuse outside the family, the use of compensation orders has been criticised, especially where the amount awarded is comparatively low. In July 1994, following a conviction for gross indecency and indecent assault on a six year old girl, the abuser was placed on probation and ordered to pay the child £50 compensation at £5 a week. The girl's mother described the ruling as a 'disgusting insult' and said she wanted to throw the money back into the molester's face.[10] The judge appears to have considered the award as a reward for the trauma involved in appearing in court rather than as compensation for the offence itself, which is a questionable use of compensation orders. The public outcry which followed was based partly on the fact that the judgment was seen as indicating that £50 was the 'going rate' for sexual assault on a child and partly on the fact that a custodial sentence was not imposed. The judge undoubtedly invited criticism by explaining that he would not impose a custodial sentence because the abuser would be ridiculed by fellow inmates due to the fact he had stunted growth and a glass eye!

Overall, although the use of compensation orders in criminal trials should be encouraged where possible and appropriate, such circumstances are likely to be rare in cases of child abuse.

---

9   Criminal Injuries Compensation Authority (1994) *Child Abuse and the Criminal Injuries Tariff Scheme* Issue no 1 (3/94) para 26.

10   *The Times* 29 July 1994.

The criminal injuries compensation scheme

The original scheme

The criminal injuries compensation scheme was introduced in August 1964 as a non-statutory scheme to provide payment from public funds to the innocent victims of crimes of violence and those injured in attempting to apprehend criminals or prevent crime. In introducing the scheme the government of the day made it clear that it did not accept that the state was liable for injuries caused to people by the acts of others, but it believed that the public felt a sense of responsibility for, and sympathy with, the innocent victim and it was, therefore, right for this feeling to be given practical expression by the provision of a monetary award on behalf of the community.[11] Awards were initially made on an *ex-gratia* basis and the scheme was administered by a non-departmental public body – the Criminal Injuries Compensation Board (CICB).

Provision for a statutory scheme

Provision was made in the Criminal Justice Act of 1988 for the scheme to be placed on a statutory basis. The terms and conditions upon which compensation could be awarded by the CICB were laid down and the basis of assessment of such awards and the powers and obligations of the Board in the discharge of its functions were specified.[12] Under both the initial non-statutory scheme and the statutory scheme provided for in the 1988 Act awards were assessed on the basis of common law damages – ie what an applicant in a civil suit could expect to receive from his attacker. There were two broad heads of damage for awards – general damages for pain and suffering for the injury plus any future loss of earnings, and special damages for past loss of earnings and other non-recoverable expenses (eg medical expenses). In the view of the present government, calculation of awards on this basis necessitated finely judged assessments of the degree of suffering and financial loss, which militated against speedy and consistent decision-taking and made it very difficult to predict the future costs of the scheme.[13] As a result, it was concluded that a scheme based on common law damages was inherently incapable of delivering a service which produces awards reasonably quickly, and in an understandable and predictable manner. Accordingly, it was decided to repeal the provisions in the 1988 Act when a suitable legislative opportunity occurred and to introduce a new scheme,

---

11 Home Office (1993) *Compensating Victims of Violent Crime: Changes to the Criminal Injuries Compensation Scheme* Cmnd 2434 London, HMSO.

12 Sections 108–117 Criminal Justice Act 1988.

13 Note 11 para 8.

based on a tariff or scale of awards for injuries of comparable severity, with no compensation being paid for loss of earnings. The new scheme was to be administered by a new, non-departmental public body, the Criminal Injuries Compensation Authority (CICA).

Challenging the legality of the tariff scheme

The proposed introduction of the new tariff scheme from April 1994 met with considerable opposition. Opponents claimed it was a cost-cutting exercise by the government, who had admitted that it hoped that the new scheme would save about £325 million a year by 2001. In March 1994, 11 trade unions, including the Fire Brigades Union and the Prison Officers' Association whose members claimed they faced the risk of violent crime daily and believed that they would be disadvantaged under the new scheme, began legal proceedings in an effort to stop the introduction of the tariff scheme. An application was made to the High Court for declarations that the Home Secretary had acted unlawfully both by failing or refusing to bring into force the statutory scheme in the 1988 Act and by implementing a new tariff scheme. In May 1994, the High Court rejected the claims and upheld the tariff scheme as lawful.[14] Applications at this time were being processed under the tariff scheme which had been brought into effect from 1 April 1994, but the recipients of awards were told that the awards were provisional. However, in November 1994, the Court of Appeal ruled that, although the Home Secretary had good grounds for delaying the implementation of the statutory scheme, while the statutory provisions for the scheme remained unrepealed although not in force, he was not free to establish a scheme which was radically different from the provisions which had been approved by Parliament.[15] The current status of the criminal injuries compensation scheme is thus uncertain. Leave to appeal to the House of Lords has been granted and it is to be hoped that there will be an early resolution. Should the House of Lords uphold the decision of the Court of Appeal, the government could, of course, attempt to repeal the relevant provisions of the 1988 Act and would thereafter be free to continue with the tariff scheme. It appears that this is the government's intention.[16] In the meantime, no awards can be finalised, although applications will presumably continue to be received by the CICA. The delays that the government were seeking to reduce will no doubt be exacerbated.

Criteria for an award

To qualify for an award, an applicant must have sustained 'personal injury directly attributable to, *inter alia*, a crime of violence'. The scheme does not

---

14   *The Times* 24 May 1994.

15   *The Independent* 10 November 1994.

16   *The Times* 12 January 1995

define a 'crime of violence'. In *R v Criminal Injuries Compensation Board ex parte Clowes*,[17] it was held that a crime of violence is one which contains an element of potential danger to personal safety. Guidance issued by the CICA in relation to child abuse states:

'Physical assault is the most obvious example [of a crime of violence], but the term may also include sexual abuse or interference which is not always thought of as a crime of violence. Rape, incest and buggery are further clear examples, but we can consider indecent assault too.'[18]

'Personal injury' includes physical injury and mental injury (ie a medically recognised psychiatric or psychological illness). However, compensation will not normally be payable for mental injury alone unless the applicant was, *inter alia*, the non-consenting victim of a sexual offence. Trivial injuries are excluded from the scheme as the injury must be serious enough to qualify for at least the minimum award available under the tariff – currently £1,000.

The CICA must be satisfied, on the balance of probabilities, that the events alleged actually occurred. Whilst it is not necessary that an offender should have been convicted before an award can be made, the CICA may withhold or reduce compensation if an applicant has not taken, without delay, all reasonable steps to inform the police or other appropriate authority of the circumstances of the injury with a view to bringing the offender to justice. On the face of it, this may preclude many claims by abused children, but the scheme makes it clear that every case is to be treated on its merits and a sympathetic view will be taken where the delay or complete failure to report the incident to the police is clearly attributable to youth, which rendered it difficult or impossible for the victim to appreciate what to do. Alternatively, the 'appropriate authority' may well be the child's parents, who will be expected to take action on the child's behalf, although the parents' failure to inform the police will not constitute a bar on the child's claim if it would have been unreasonable to expect the child to take the matter any further himself. Bearing in mind the reluctance of children to disclose abuse, particularly in the case of young children, such an approach is essential if child victims of abuse are to have access to the scheme.

However, victims of intrafamilial abuse face further hurdles. Prior to 1979, no compensation was payable if the victim and offender were living together at the time as members of the same family. The scheme was extended to include victims of violence within the family in October 1979, but claims based on abuse within the family before that date will necessarily fail,[19] regardless of problems encountered with time limits for making the claim (see below).

---

17 [1977] 120 Sol Jo 856.

18 Criminal Injuries Compensation Authority (1994) *Child Abuse and the Criminal Injuries Compensation Tariff Scheme* INF21 (4/94) para 2.

19 *R v Criminal Injuries Compensation Board ex p P* [1993] 2 FLR 600.

However, even under the extended scheme, where the victim and the person responsible for causing the injury were living in the same household at the time of the injury as members of the same family, compensation will only be paid if the person responsible has been prosecuted in connection with the offence, unless the CICA consider that there are practical, technical or other good reasons why a prosecution has not been brought. In such cases the CICA will require a full explanation on the child's behalf, but, since there are a number of reasons why a prosecution may not have been brought – including the strict evidential requirements and the high standard of proof in criminal proceedings (see Chapter 7) – in many cases a satisfactory explanation will be available and so the fact that a prosecution was not brought will not preclude an award being made. A finding of abuse made in family proceedings may well be sufficient to persuade the CICA that a crime of violence has taken place. However, no compensation can be paid unless the CICA is satisfied that the offender will not benefit, as may happen if the child and the offender are still living under the same roof.

In all cases, the CICA must be satisfied that it would not be against the child's interests to make the award. Little guidance is provided by the CICA as to when an award would not be in a child's interests, but the matter has, in the past, been considered by the courts, as leave of the court is required before an application for compensation can be made on behalf of a ward of court.[20] In such circumstances the courts have made it clear that they are acting as a filter and that it is not for the judge hearing the application for leave to try the very issue which is specifically within the remit of the CICA,[21] and so the courts consideration of the child's interests in this respect is of rather limited assistance. Nevertheless, it seems that if an award might jeopardise the chance of the family being reconciled, it may not be in the child's interests to make the award. In cases where there is no possibility of reconciliation, an award will usually be in the child's interests.

Time limits

Prior to the introduction of the new tariff scheme, applications had to be made within three years of the incident giving rise to the injury, although the CICB could waive this requirement in exceptional cases. Guidance issued by the CICB suggested that the Board adopt a sympathetic attitude towards late claims made on behalf of children or by children themselves when made within a reasonable time of reaching full age. In practice it seems the emphasis is on a 'reasonable' time. In *R v Criminal Injuries Compensation Board ex parte P*,[22] the applicant claimed she had been abused by her step father between 1967 and 1976.

---

20 *Practice Direction (Ward: criminal injury)* [1988] 1 FLR 183.

21 See *Re G (a minor) (a ward: criminal injuries compensation)* [1993] Fam Law 65 and *Re G (a ward) (Criminal injuries: compensation)* [1991] 1 FLR 89.

22 Note 19.

However she did not inform the authorities until 1988, and the step father was convicted in 1989. In 1990 her application to the CICB was refused because of her delay and because of the restriction, prior to 1979, that no compensation was payable if the victim and offender lived together as members of the same family. Her application for judicial review was dismissed by the Divisional Court on the second ground and so the question of delay was unfortunately not considered by the court. But a delay of 14 years between the last incident of abuse and the application for compensation could not fairly be termed a 'reasonable' time and it would be surprising if such an application were to be granted. This is particularly so in the light of recent changes to the scheme. The time limit for making the application has now been reduced from three years to one year. The sole justification offered for this reduction in time seems to be that:

'it will help the scheme administrators predict the work flow and future costs of administration and compensation more readily.'[23]

Admittedly, the CICA retain the discretion to waive the normal time limit in exceptional cases, and the indications are that it will normally be waived in respect of claims made either by, or on behalf of, applicants who are under 21.[24] But, even so, the reduction of the time limit is a cause for concern in respect of all victims, not only children. Many victims of violent crime are extremely traumatised by the incident and the time taken to recover from an attack should not be under-estimated. It seems that considerations of administrative convenience take precedence over the needs of victims in this respect.

Applications on behalf of children

Although the scheme itself makes no specific mention of applications on behalf of a person under the age of 18, guidance issued by the CICA indicates that such a claim must be made by an adult with parental rights over the child. (The reference to 'parental rights' rather than 'parental responsibility' is presumably attributable to the fact that the CICA is based in Glasgow and the law in Scotland continues to refer to parental rights. However, given the fact that the guidance is equally applicable to England and Wales, consideration should be given to amending the guidance to reflect the move away from 'rights' and towards parental 'responsibility' south of the border) The one explanation for this requirement provided by the CICA is that a child under that age cannot legally decide whether to accept the authorities determinations and, if there is no one to act for the child, there may be unnecessary delay before any compensation can be paid.[25] Usually, the

---

23 Note 11 para 27.

24 Note 18 para 3.

25 Ibid para 8.

person to act will be one of the child's parents, but, as the CICA point out, if the child has been subjected to abuse within the immediate family this may not be possible. If the child is a ward of court, the official solicitor will usually make an application on the child's behalf, after obtaining leave from the court to make a claim (see above). But the restrictions on the use of wardship by local authorities (see Chapter 3) will make this an unlikely scenario in the future. If the child is in care the CICA expect the claim to be lodged by, or on behalf of, the authority to whom care has been granted and, in other cases, will look to the person having parental rights over the child for the time being. This raises a potentially controversial point as to what happens if the appropriate person or authority fails to make such a claim and the child is thereby prejudiced. Local authorities are under a duty to safeguard and promote the welfare of children looked after by them,[26] which arguably includes a duty to make an application for compensation under the scheme where it has evidence of abuse, and an abused child could arguably have a claim in negligence against the local authority or for breach of statutory duty for failing to do so. Any such claim would encounter two major difficulties. First, the child would have to prove a cause of action which may be an insurmountable barrier, especially in view of the recent decisions (see below). Secondly, even if the child could prove a cause of action, a further difficulty would be encountered in time limits under the Limitation Act 1980 (see below). If, on reaching the age of 18, a victim of abuse realises that an application for compensation could have been made on her behalf during her minority, she may make the application herself and the CICA guidance indicates the normal time limit will be waived 'in respect of claims made either by, or on behalf of, applicants who are under 21', thereby obviating the need to sue the local authority or responsible person for the financial loss suffered as a result of their failure to make an application. But if this application is refused because of the delay, an action in negligence may be considered against the local authority. The usual time limit of six years from the date on which the cause of action accrued will apply (section 2), but the operation of the limitation period is suspended during a plaintiff's minority (section 28) – thereby giving the victim six years from attaining the age of 18 to sue. Whereas no one would wish to deny a victim of abuse the opportunity of redress, the prospect of victims of child abuse suing those who failed to make an application for compensation on their behalf many years after the abuse took place is not a happy one – involvement in litigation at any time is potentially traumatic and this must be especially so when the litigation takes place some considerable time after the events giving rise to the cause of action. One way to avoid this would be to encourage those concerned to make applications on behalf of the child victim. Both the police and local authorities are well placed to do this, but 'Working Together' makes no reference to

---

26 Section 22 Children Act 1989.

considering the possibility of making a claim for compensation on behalf of the child, or of advising those with parental responsibility of the existence of the scheme. It seems that in some areas, local initiatives have been developed by police and local authorities to do this,[27] but a concerted effort needs to be made nationwide if child victims of abuse are to be able to take full advantage of the compensation scheme.

Awards under the tariff scheme

Injuries are now assigned to one of 25 payment levels, ranging from £1,000 to £250,000. In the case of serious multiple injuries, the award will be the tariff award for the highest rated injury plus, where the injuries affect different parts of the body, 10% of the tariff value of the next most serious injury and, where appropriate, 5% of the tariff value of the third most serious injury. The tariff makes specific provision for the sexual and/or physical abuse of children:

Not involving rape or buggery:

Isolated incidents over a period of up to one year	£1,000
Pattern of abuse over period one to three years	£3,000
Pattern of abuse over period exceeding three years	£6,000

Involving rape or buggery:

Rape or buggery (single incident)	£7,500
Repeated rape or buggery over period up to three years	£10,000
Repeated rape or buggery over period exceeding three years	£17,500

The victim of an isolated incident of abuse which results in physical injury could claim the tariff for that injury – for example minor burns on the upper or lower limbs would attract an award of £1,500 whereas paralysis of all four limbs would attract the maximum award of £250,000. The scheme also provides compensation for shock or 'nervous shock', which is defined to include conditions attributable to Post Traumatic Stress Disorder, depression and similar generic terms covering such psychological symptoms as anxiety, tension, insomnia, irritability, loss of confidence, agoraphobia, pre-occupation with thoughts of self-harm or guilt, and related physical ones such as alopecia, asthma, eczema, enuresis and psoriasis. The shock must result in disability for more than six weeks from the incident and disability in this context includes impaired work (or school performance), significant adverse effects on social relationships, and sexual dysfunction. Where the disability is moderate (lasting for over six to 16 weeks) the award will be £1,000, rising to £20,000 for permanent disability.

---

27   Yates, C (1990) 'Criminal Injuries Compensation for Children' in *Journal of Child Law* [1990] 23.

Compensation is usually awarded as a lump sum, but *interim* awards can be made if the medical prognosis is uncertain. The CICA have the discretion to make payments to those with parental control, but indicate that substantial awards will usually be invested and managed by the authority during the child's minority. If the child is in care, the expectation is that the local authority will be responsible for investment and administration.

The criminal injuries compensation scheme represents a potentially fruitful source of financial compensation for an abused child. Even if the tariff scheme continues, the main criticism has been that awards will no longer be made for loss of earnings, which will have little relevance to children. Whilst it must be acknowledged that no amount of money can ever fully compensate for the abuse, and there may be exceptional circumstances where any benefit of an award to the child would be outweighed by a deterioration in family relationships as a result of the application being made, in many circumstances it will be in the child's interests to receive compensation. The number of applications from, or on behalf of, children under the age of 18 rose from a total of 4,825 in the year ending March 1990 to 6,822 in the year ending March 1992 and accounted for 5% of the total applications received.[28] Despite this rise in applications, there are clearly many occasions when no application is made, although the victim is eligible for an award. This may well be due to the fact that those responsible for making the claim are ignorant of the existence of the scheme. The problem can be addressed by increasing the public profile of the scheme and encouraging all those working with abused children to consider the possibility of making a claim. Unfortunately, the initiative for this is unlikely to come from the government or the CICA itself. The 28th Report of the CICB noted the recent rise in applications concerning children and indicated that it found the trend worrying (para 1.12). Quite why it should be 'worrying' is not clear from the report, which continues by stating that it is difficult to pin-point the reason for the rise in applications, but suggests that it may be simply that following recent high profile enquires into child abuse there is a greater awareness of the problem or it may be that local authorities have over recent years become more aware of their responsibilities to apply for compensation on behalf of children in their care. Whatever the reason, the fact that more applications are being made for compensation by, or on behalf of, child victims of abuse is surely to be applauded rather than identified as a worrying trend! The only possible 'worrying' factor could be the financial implications of the increase. The underlying thrust of recent reforms of the scheme is clearly one of concern about the rising cost of the scheme and administrative convenience. Concern for the victim obviously takes second place to these considerations.

---

28   Criminal Injuries Compensation Board (1992) 28th Report cmnd 2122 London, HMSO.

Claims in the civil courts

Claims against the abuser and the delayed discovery rule

In cases of physical or sexual abuse the abuser will, *prima facie*, incur civil liability for assault and battery (see further Chapter 1). However, civil actions brought by victims of abuse are rare.[29] In 1991, in the case of *Stubbings v Webb and another*,[30] Browne-Wilkinson VC commented:

> 'Over recent years, for the first time civil actions have been brought by victims of adult rape against their assailants. As to actions against child abusers, this is apparently the first time in which the alleged victim has sought to sue her abusers.'

Any action brought during the child's minority will be subject to the ordinary rules of disability, applying to all civil proceedings, which prevent a minor from bringing or defending any proceedings except by a next friend or guardian *ad litem*.[31] During the victim's childhood problems will often be encountered because there will be no one willing and able to sue on the child's behalf. Once the victim reaches the age of majority, he or she becomes, in theory, capable of bringing an action in his or her own right. Obviously, at this stage, the victim may well encounter insuperable problems of proof, particularly if the abuse occurred during early childhood, but if such problems can be overcome and the claim established, the victim will be awarded damages for any physical and mental injury suffered as a result of the abuse. Such damages may be substantial. In November 1993, for the first time a successful claim for damages for assault was brought by three sisters who were allegedly subjected to a catalogue of sexual abuse and beatings by their father. The High Court ordered the father to pay the girls, who were by this time in their 20s with children of their own a total of £39,699.[32]

Although the usual limitation period for an action in tort is six years, this period only begins to run once the victim reaches the age of majority and so, as long as the action is brought before the victim reaches 24 years of age, no problems with limitation will arise. Yet in many cases, particularly in cases of sexual abuse, the damage caused will be primarily psychological, and the victim may initially be unaware of the causal link between childhood abuse and mental and emotional harm suffered in adulthood, and only realise the link between the two in later life. In these circumstances, it is now clear that

---

29   Bryan, M (1994) 'Sexual Abuse: some common law and equitable responses' *Journal of Child Law* [1994] 6(1) 13.

30   [1991] 3 All ER 949 at 960.

31   RSC Order 80.

32   *The Times* 12 November 1993.

the victim will find any claim for compensation statute-barred. In the case of *Stubbings v Webb and another*[33] the plaintiff alleged that her adoptive father and brother had sexually and physically abused her between the ages of two and 14. Although she suffered psychological problems during her adulthood, she did not realise the problems were attributable to the childhood abuse for many years. Eventually, following discussions with a psychiatrist, a writ for battery was issued in 1987, some 16 years after the last of the alleged assaults had occurred and more than 12 years since she had attained her majority. The defendants claimed her cause of action was barred by the Limitation Act 1980, but the plaintiff alleged her claim was governed by section 11 of the Act which applies to:

> 'any action for damages for negligence, nuisance or breach of duty ... where the damages claimed by the plaintiff ... consist of or include damages in respect of personal injuries ...'

The basic limitation period under section 11 is three years, but the period can run from the date of knowledge of the person injured (the 'delayed discovery' rule).

The Court of Appeal found that, since the plaintiff only became aware of the link between the abuse and the harm suffered within three years of issuing the writ, her action was not barred by the statute. However, the House of Lords held that section 11 was inapplicable since the plaintiff's claim was for trespass to the person which did not fall within 'negligence, nuisance or breach of duty' as required by section 11. The House of Lords relied heavily on *Hansard* to ascertain Parliament's intention in passing the Act. As a matter of strict statutory interpretation the decision is clearly correct, although it has been argued that the possibilities of creative interpretive analysis of the Limitation Act are much greater than the House of Lords recognised.[34] The implications of the decision for victims of abuse are clear. The delayed discovery rule is not applicable to claims for rape, indecent assault, or indeed any trespass to the person. Any claim must be brought within six years of reaching majority, even if, during this period, the victim is unaware of the link between the abuse and the harm suffered in adulthood and only discovers it in later life.

It seems that other jurisdictions have been somewhat more creative in their application of delayed discovery rules.[35] For example, the law in California has recently been changed to allow victims of childhood sexual abuse to sue within three years after discovering their injuries, or eight years after reaching majority, whichever date occurs later.[36] Even if such a change were to be

---

33 [1991] 3 All ER 949.

34 Note 29.

35 See Lamm, J 'Easing Access to the Courts for Incest Victims: Towards and Equitable Application of the Delayed Discovery Rule' *Yale Law Journal* vol 100 2189.

36 California Civil Procedure Code 340.1.

enacted in this jurisdiction, which seems highly unlikely, the victim would still have to convince a court that she did not 'know' of her injuries for some considerable time after the abuse occurred. Statements made by Lord Griffiths in *Stubbings v Webb* suggest that this may be no easy task, particularly in cases of severe abuse. He said:

> 'Personal injury is defined by section 38 [of the Limitation Act 1980] as including "any impairment of a person's physical or mental condition" and I have the greatest difficulty in accepting that a woman who knows that she has been raped does not know that she has suffered a significant injury ... sexual abuse that goes no further than indecent fondling of a child raises a more difficult question.'

The irony of these statements seems to be that, even if the delayed discovery rule were to be applied, the more serious the abuse, the less likely any claim would be to succeed in later years. Any claim for negligence against the abuser will clearly fall within the remit of section 11, but such claims are likely to be rare (see Chapter 1). Overall, little encouragement can be found for victims of abuse seeking compensation from the abuser in the civil courts.

Claims against the professionals – negligence and breach of statutory duty

If the prospects for victims seeking redress from the abuser seem bleak, the prospects for victims seeking redress from any of the professionals involved in the investigation and diagnosis of abuse are worse. In previous chapters, much emphasis has been placed on the procedures for inter-agency co-operation and the guidance issued to the various professionals involved in cases of suspected child abuse. In an ideal world, if these procedures and guidance are adhered to, there should be no unwarranted intervention in family life, child abuse should be prevented wherever possible, but those children who are abused should be protected from further abuse. Finding the right balance is inevitably a difficult task and, while no-one would wish to impose unrealistically high expectations of the professionals charged with such responsibility, if the professionals act in such a way that falls below the standard expected of them, and the child, or indeed the alleged abuser, suffers harm as a result, some form of redress through the civil courts may well be expected. Liability of the professionals in negligence would depend primarily on whether a duty of care is owed to the child and/or the child's parents, and whether that duty was broken (see Chapter 1). Alternatively a local authority who fail to meet the required standard in investigating abuse may arguably be in breach of a statutory duty. In order to establish a breach of statutory duty, the plaintiff must prove that the relevant statute was intended to create civil liability, that the statute imposed a duty on the defendant which was owed to the plaintiff, that the defendant was in breach of the duty and the plaintiff suffered damage of a type contemplated by the statute.[37] Local authorities have long been under duties imposed by statute in relation to certain children[38] and the Children Act 1989 imposes several such duties.[39] If local authorities fail to discharge these duties, it may be thought an action would lie for breach of statutory duty.

However, a recent decision of the Court of Appeal[40] severely limits the potential for any such redress. In the case of *M and another v LB of Newham and Others*, the local authority were investigating a case of suspected child abuse involving a four year old child. Following an interview with a social worker employed by the local authority and a psychiatrist it was concluded that the child had been sexually abused by the mother's boyfriend, the child was made a ward of court and access by the mother was limited. One year later, the mother obtained a transcript of the interview from which it was apparent that the child had not identified the mother's boyfriend as the abuser, and the mother and child were subsequently reunited. The child and the mother complained that as a result of their enforced separation they suffered a positive psychiatric disorder diagnosed as anxiety neurosis. They brought an action against the social worker, the local authority and the psychiatrist alleging negligence, in that they failed to investigate the facts with proper care and thoroughness, and further contended that the local authority was in breach of its statutory duty. Their action was dismissed at first instance, the statement of claim being struck out as disclosing no reasonable cause of action, and an appeal by the mother and child was dismissed in the Divisional Court. A further appeal was then made to the Court of Appeal. At the same time, the Court also heard an appeal in the case of *P (minors) v Bedfordshire County Council*. In this case, during the period between November 1987 and October 1992, numerous reports were made to the county council concerning the possible neglect and physical, sexual and emotional abuse of the plaintiffs, five children aged between one and nine years. Both the mother and father of the children had at various times asked for the children to be taken into care, but although the three older children spent several periods of time with foster parents and the children were placed on a child protection register in June 1992, the county council only applied for care orders in October 1992. The children (suing by the official solicitor as their next friend) brought an action against the county council for negligence and/or breach of statutory duty, complaining that the council should have acted more quickly and more effectively and alleging that, as a result of the council's failure, they suffered ill-treatment and illness, their proper development was neglected and their health was impaired. On the application of the county council the proceedings

---

37 See further Harpwood, V (1993) *Lecture Notes on Tort* London, Cavendish.
38 See section 9 Children and Young Persons Act 1969.
39 For example sections 17, 20, and 47.
40 *M v LB of Newham, P v Bedfordshire* [1994] 19 BMLR 107.

were struck out as disclosing no reasonable cause of action. The children appealed to the Court of Appeal.

The Court of Appeal therefore had to decide whether a child may maintain an action for damages (whether for breach of statutory duty or common law negligence) against a local authority for steps taken or not taken in relation to the child by that authority as the responsible social services authority. The Court also had to decide whether a psychiatrist employed to give advice to a local authority in relation to a child owed that child or the child's mother a duty of care in relation to that advice.

In relation to the actions for breach of statutory duty, the Court unanimously held that the relevant statutory provisions which impose duties on local authorities do not give rise to a private law remedy in damages. It was said that the duties imposed are framed in terms too general and unparticular to lend themselves at all readily to enforcement by individuals, and local authorities are accorded so large an area for the exercise of their subjective judgment as to suggest that direct enforcement by individuals was not contemplated.

In relation to the actions for negligence, it was decided by the majority that no duty of care was owed by the local authority or the psychiatrist, either to the child or the mother, and the actions had therefore been correctly struck out. It was pointed out that a local authority has no power or duty at common law to intervene in relation to a child in their area and can only exercise a statutory function if they are to intervene. It was not thought to be fair, just and reasonable that a local authority should owe a duty of care to those concerned in the decisions they reach in the exercise of their statutory function. As far as the psychiatrist was concerned, the Court pointed out that the child had been referred to the psychiatrist by the local authority in order that advice be given to the local authority and it was never intended that the psychiatrist should give that advice to the child or the mother. The psychiatrist did not therefore owe the child or the mother a duty of care in relation to that advice.

This was clearly a policy decision by the majority aimed at preventing local authorities and other professionals being vulnerable to actions for damages in private law by aggrieved children and parents – both because there was concern the professionals would be forced to work 'looking over their shoulder' and because of the financial implications of such claims. As Gibson LJ commented:

> 'If the law were ... to recognise a duty of care owed to the children by the local authority in taking decisions on interventions, there is a significant risk of the exercise of such functions in a detrimentally defensive frame of mind ... Further, if litigation were encouraged by a duty of care being held to exist, a major diversion of resources to defending such actions is likely to ensue.'

Staughton LJ was of the same mind, stating he would not impose a private duty on local authorities performing their public law function of caring for children in need, nor would he impose a general duty of the same nature on doctors and health authorities participating in the same process. For the time being it seems that those involved in cases of child abuse in a professional capacity can rest assured that, in the absence of malice, they will not be faced with civil actions brought on behalf of the child. Any other outcome would undoubtedly have caused considerable concern amongst the professions and may well have had a detrimental effect on working procedures. However, in the *Bedfordshire* case, an appeal has been taken to the House of Lords and judgement is currently awaiting. One element of the case does present cause for concern. In the *Newham* case the professionals involved were at least taking positive steps to do their best for the child concerned, although one can sympathise with the mother and child and perhaps wish that more care had been taken. But the facts of the *Bedfordshire* case reveal a catalogue of omissions in the face of apparently cogent evidence of the need for action. The county council's failure to take action seems blatantly culpable. Whilst the denial of a right of action to the victims can be justified on policy grounds, it provides no assurance that the events will not be repeated, which is surely a serious cause for concern.

DEALING WITH THE ABUSER

Punishment and sentencing in the criminal courts

The concept of punishment

The primary aim of a criminal prosecution will be to punish the abuser, although it is also possible to compensate the victim through the sentence of the court (see above). Punishment has been defined as:

> '... the principled infliction by a state-constituted institution of what are generally regarded as unpleasant consequences upon individuals or groups adjudicated, in accordance with publicly and legally recognised criteria and procedures, correctly applied, to have breached the law, as a response to that breach, as an enforcement of the law and where that response is not inflicted solely as a means of providing compensation for the harm caused by the offence.'[41]

Those who view the problem of child abuse from a medical or social welfare standpoint (see Chapter 4) may well have opposed prosecuting the abuser during the initial stages of the investigation and similar opposition will undoubtedly be raised at the sentencing stage – if the abuser is not regarded as responsible for his behaviour, inflicting punishment on him will be regarded as unjustified. Yet those

---

41   Lacey, N (1988) *State Punishment: Political Principles and Community Values*. London, Routledge p 12.

who adopt a penal approach to the problem will be concerned to see the abuser punished following conviction.

To many, those who break the criminal law are punished simply because they deserve it. Punishment is seen as a form of retribution, and the 'just deserts' theory of punishment underlies present sentencing practice (see below). However, punishment may also be said to serve different objectives. It may act as a form of deterrence in that punishment, or the threat of punishment, deters both individuals and society as a whole from committing crime. Alternatively, it may act as a form of incapacitation in that some forms of punishment, most notably imprisonment, serve to incapacitate the offender and thus prevent him committing further offences during the period of incapacitation. Finally, and more controversially, it may be argued that punishment acts as a form of rehabilitation where the aim of the punishment is to reform the offender so that he becomes adjusted to the social order. Therefore, even between those who agree that abusers should be punished, there may well be different objectives or justifications for inflicting the punishment.

Whilst imprisonment certainly incapacitates the abuser, except in the most serious cases, the term of imprisonment will be finite and the incapacitation may be relatively short term. Few would argue that punishment has any significant deterrent effect on abusers. Indeed, it has even been suggested that the threat of punishment as a deterrent may seriously misfire because the abuser may use the threat as a way of persuading the child not to disclose the abuse: 'If you tell anyone I'll be sent to prison.' Glaser and Spencer thus argue that, rather than deterring the abuse, the threat of punishment (in particular the threat of imprisonment) seems more likely to deter reporting of abuse.[42]

It therefore seems that abusers are punished, either as a form of retribution or, arguably, as a form of rehabilitation. Originally, it was believed that reform could come of punishment itself – for example a period of solitude would induce remorse, repentance and reform. With hindsight, such a view seems incredibly naive. Yet in recent years, increasing attention has been paid to the idea of rehabilitating offenders, particularly those convicted of sexual offences against children (see below). As Search points out:

'In the vast majority of cases, the sexual abuse of children is a cycle of behaviour that goes on repeating itself, not only through the abuser's own lifetime, but possibly through his children's and his grandchildren's. In terms of human misery alone, when you think of the appalling damage that can result from child sexual abuse, it makes sense to try to break the cycle by tackling the problem at source.' [43]

---

42 Glaser, D & Spencer, J (1990) 'Sentencing, Children's Evidence and Trauma' *Criminal Law Review* (1990) 371 at p 380.

43 Search, G (1988) *The Last Taboo: Sexual Abuse of Children*. London, Penguin p 87.

However, whilst the rehabilitative ideal may be theoretically attractive, the importance attached by society to punishing the abuser as a form of retribution or 'just deserts' should not be underestimated. Given the feelings of revulsion and disbelief that are frequently expressed on hearing of cases child abuse ('how could anyone possibly rape a five year old child or burn a baby with cigarettes?) it is doubtful whether society would ever be prepared to forego what it sees as its right to see the abuser punished – to see the abuser suffer 'unpleasant consequences'. The question is, are retribution and rehabilitation mutually exclusive aims, or is it possible to achieve both by the same sentence of the court? Bernard Shaw once commented:

'To punish is to injure, to reform is to heal, you cannot mend a person by damaging him.'[44]

Yet, in many cases it seems that this is precisely what we are currently hoping to achieve.

Sentencing practice and sentencing guidelines

With the exception of murder, which carries a mandatory sentence of life imprisonment, for every offence there is a prescribed maximum sentence, but no minimum sentence. This does not, however, mean that the courts have complete discretion in passing sentence. The principle underlying the framework of sentencing contained in the Criminal Justice Act 1991 is that of proportionality – that the punishment should be proportional to the crime. A court may not pass a custodial sentence[45] unless it is of the opinion either that the offence, or the combination of the offence and one or more offences associated with it, was so serious that only such a sentence can be justified for the offence, or, where the offence is a violent or sexual offence,[46] that only such a sentence would be adequate to protect the public from serious harm from the offender.[47] The length of any custodial sentence imposed must be commensurate with the seriousness of the offence or offences, subject to the permitted maximum.[48] However, in the case of a violent or sexual offence, there is theoretically no requirement that the offence itself justifies a custodial sentence and the sentence imposed may be such that, in the opinion of the court, is necessary to protect the public from serious harm from the offender.[49] 'The public' includes a single individual or group of individuals.[50]

---

44 Bernard Shaw quoted in Berg, C (1959) *Fear, Punishment, Anxiety and the Wolfenden Report*. London, George Allen & Unwin Ltd.

45 If the offender is aged 21 or over, the custodial sentence will be one of imprisonment. Young offenders under 21 years of age but over 14 years (male) or 15 years (female) will be sentenced to detention in a young offender institute, but there are restrictions on the length of such sentences. See section 63 Criminal Justice Act 1991.

46 As defined by section 31(1) Criminal Justice Act 1991.

47 Section 1(2) Criminal Justice Act 1991.

48 Section 2(2)(a) Criminal Justice Act 1991.

49 Section 2(2)(b) Criminal Justice Act 1991.

50 *R v Hashi* [1994] Crim LR 618.

However, where the individual or group of individuals can be adequately protected by other means, the sentence must be one commensurate with the seriousness of the offence. In *R v S*,[51] the defendant had been convicted of various sexual offences against children of his family. He was sentenced to a total of seven years imprisonment, passed as longer than normal sentences necessary to protect the public. On appeal the sentence was reduced to one commensurate with the seriousness of the offences as there was no evidence that the offender had offended outside of the family circle, and there was no real likelihood that he would acquire another family circle. It therefore seems that in cases of intrafamilial abuse, longer sentences will rarely be justified as the child victim will usually be adequately protected by other means.

In exceptional circumstances, a sentence of imprisonment may be suspended for between one and two years.[52] If a court decides to exercise this power, it is required to consider whether the circumstances of the case are such as to warrant in addition the imposition of a fine or the making of a compensation order. The white paper preceding the Act explained that this was so that 'offenders do not seem to go unpunished'[53] – clearly the government was concerned that offenders should be seen to be punished as a form of retribution. Although the circumstances should be 'exceptional' before the sentence of imprisonment can be suspended, such circumstances may well be established in cases of intrafamilial abuse, as illustrated by the case of *Cameron*.[54] The offender had been convicted of assault occasioning actual bodily harm after slapping one of his three children, a five year old boy, causing extensive bruising on his face, arms and buttocks. The trial judge imposed an immediate custodial sentence of 12 months, but on appeal the Court of Appeal decided the sentence should be suspended. Although it was said that an assault on a defenceless young child was always a serious matter, the local authority had decided that it was in the best interests of the family (which presumably also included the best interests of the victim) if the abuser and the three children could be rehabilitated under supervision and, in the view of the Court of Appeal, this was sufficient to justify the suspension of the sentence.

If a custodial sentence is not justified, the court may consider a community based sentence, which may include a probation order, whereby the offender is placed under the supervision of a probation officer for a specified period of between six months and three years (see below), a community service order, whereby the offender is made to perform unpaid work in the community for between 40 and 240 hours, or a combination order which allows probation and community service to be combined in one order.[55] If a community based sentence

---

51   [1994] Crim LR 868.

52   Section 5(1) Criminal Justice Act 1991.

53   Home Office (1990) *Crime, Justice and Protecting the Public* Cmnd 965 London, HMSO para 3.22.

54   [1993] Crim LR 721.

55   Section 6–11 Criminal Justice Act 1991.

is not justified by the seriousness of the offence, the offender may be fined (in which case the court must take into account both the seriousness of the offence and the offender's means), or made the subject of a conditional or absolute discharge.

In an effort to ensure consistency of approach to sentencing, in June 1992 the Magistrates Association issued sentencing guidelines for use in magistrates' courts.[56] However, these guidelines which concentrate on levels of fines and compensation, are likely to be of limited assistance in sentencing abusers. More significantly, the Court of Appeal from time to time hands down guideline judgments which make generalised statements about sentencing for particular types of offence. For example in *R v Billam*[57] the Court of Appeal laid down guidelines for sentencing in rape cases, suggesting that, for rape committed by an adult without any aggravating or mitigating features, a figure of five years' imprisonment should be taken as the starting point in a contested case. Aggravating factors may include the age of the victim (where she is either very old or very young) and the effect upon the victim, whether physical or mental. Thus rape of a young child who is severely traumatised as a result will attract a higher sentence than that of a 20 year old who is not severly traumatised.

The role of the victim in the sentencing process

Before passing sentence, the court will be provided with information from various sources about the offender and the offence or offences committed. In all cases the offender's antecedent history, including any previous convictions, will be reported to the court and, in considering the seriousness of any offence, the court may take into account any previous convictions of the offender or any failure to respond to previous sentences.[58] Additionally, the court will usually, and in some cases must, obtain a pre-sentence report[59] – a written report made by a probation officer or a social worker with a view to assisting the court in determining the most suitable method of dealing with the offender. Guidance issued jointly by the Home Office, Department of Health and Welsh Office[60] suggests the report should address the current offence, relevant information about the offender and a conclusion, including, where relevant, a proposal for the most suitable community sentence. In addition to such reports the court may well be provided with specialist information in the form of medical or psychiatric reports prior to sentencing.

However, in many cases the court will have very little information available about the victim. In cases of intrafamilial abuse where a pre-sentence report has been prepared, reference may well be made in the report to the

---

56 The Magistrates' Association 'Sentencing Guidelines' 1992.

57 [1986] 82 Cr App Rep 347.

58 Section 29(1) Criminal Justice Act 1991 as amended.

59 Section 3 Criminal Justice Act 1991.

60 Home Office (1992) *National Standards for the Supervision of Offenders in the Community* .

relationship between the offender and the victim, and the effect of the abuse on the child as it relates to the abuser's attitude towards the offence. Yet in the usual case, the probation officer or social worker who compiles the report will not directly approach the child victim. The report is concerned with the offender not the victim. In cases of extrafamilial abuse, even this limited source of information will not be available to the court. Even if the court makes a compensation order, the victim does not have any right to intervene in the proceedings – the role of the victim is largely limited to that of witness for the prosecution and will play no part in the sentencing procedure. To some, this is clearly considered to be beneficial to all concerned. Duff is of the opinion that the 'introduction of the victim into the equation' can upset the delicate balance of rights and interests which has built up between offender and state.[61] Yet, whilst this view has some merit from the point of view of the offender, what of the rights and interests of the victim? Admittedly, in cases of child abuse, given the trauma associated with the trial, it could be argued that once the abuser has been convicted, it is in the child's best interests that he or she should play no further part in the sentencing procedure. But, particularly in cases of intrafamilial abuse, the child may hold very strong views about the eventual outcome of the case and, given the increasing importance being attached to the voice of the child (see Chapter 6), it can be argued that the child should be allowed to express those views to the court. Given the existing restrictions on the imposition of custodial sentences and the test of proportionality, the views of the victim would not enable the court to pass any more severe sentence than would be justified in the circumstance, and could therefore only operate in favour of the abuser.

Other jurisdictions have adopted a more radical approach to victim participation in the criminal procedure. For example, in the US, almost all states have introduced a victim bill of rights which typically introduces the right to be informed, to be consulted and to be compensated by the offender. The right of the victim to express his or her concerns to the judge is more controversial. 'Victim impact statements' are commonly used to provide the court with information about the victim's opinions, without the need for a further court appearance, but in some circumstances these have been ruled unconstitutional.[62] However, in West Germany, the victim even has a right to act as 'assistant prosecutor' and to make penal demands in that capacity.

The merits of involving victims to such an extent may be questioned. Certainly, in cases of child abuse, the prospect of the child victim making 'penal demands' is not one which would receive support in this country. But the concept of 'victim impact reports' deserves further consideration.

---

61   Duff, P (1988) 'The Victim Movement and Legal Reform' in Maguire, M and Pointing, J (eds) (1988) *Victims of Crime: A New Deal?* Milton Keynes, Open University Press.

62   Van Dijk, J (1988) 'Ideological Trends within the Victim Movement' in Maguire, M & Pointing J, (eds) (1988) note 61.

If the child has been put through the trauma of a prosecution (and despite recent reforms, the trial will remain a traumatic event for a child), the least the court can do is listen to the views of the child and consider the impact of both the offence and possible sentences on the child. This does not mean that the child should be permitted to make positive recommendations as to sentence. Indeed, to do so may make it harder for the child to overcome the feelings of guilt commonly encountered in such cases. But the court should at least be made aware of the child's feelings. At present, attention is focused exclusively on the offence and the offender in the sentencing procedure. The use of victim impact statements in other jurisdictions illustrates how the feelings of the child victim of abuse can be made known to the sentencer. As yet, this is an area which appears to have attracted comparatively little interest. A decade ago a similar lack of interest was apparent in all aspects of child abuse in the criminal courts, yet tremendous progress has been made over recent years. Perhaps in a further decade, similar progress will have been made concerning the child victim of abuse after conviction of the abuser.

Treatment within the criminal justice system

On the face of it, the sentencing options available to the court appear to offer little opportunity to rehabilitate or reform the offender. In sentencing an abuser, the emphasis will be on retribution. Yet it is becoming increasingly recognised that, if abusers are to be rehabilitated and further abuse prevented, they require some form of 'help' or treatment, either in addition to or as an alternative to traditional forms of punishment. As Scott comments:

> 'Unless we face the challenge ... we will achieve nothing more than our Victorian forbears 100 years ago who, as men of their times, could not have envisaged the possibility of rehabilitation beyond the vengeance of retribution and the illusion of deterrence.'[63]

In recent years, the criminal justice system has acknowledged this in relation to sex offenders and the opportunity now exists to offer such abusers treatment, either by means of a custodial sentence at an establishment participating in the Sex Offender Treatment Programme or by means of a probation order with conditions attached.

Treatment in custody – the sex offender treatment programme

In the past it was frequently argued that a term of imprisonment had no rehabilitative effect and, particularly in the case of those convicted of sexual offences, it was argued that imprisonment made an abuser more likely to commit further abuse on his release:

---

63 Scott, D (1989) 'Legally Enforced Treatment of the Incestually Abusing Parent: Problems of Policy and Practice' *Journal of Social Welfare Law* (1989) 217.

'... there is increasing evidence to suggest that the necessary herding of sexual abusers together under rule 43 [which allows prisoners to be segregated for their own safety] offers reinforcement in the form of opportunities for further sexual excitement and sharing of their sexual experiences.'[64]

Prior to 1991, the Home Office had no central policy on the treatment of offenders. However, amid increasing concern at the lack of treatment opportunities, in 1991 the Home Office took the initiative and set up a Sex Offender Treatment Programme (SOTP) as a nationally co-ordinated programme provided at prison establishments throughout the country.[65] The programme allows for the systematic treatment of large numbers of sex offenders, using a cognitive-behavioural model of treatment previously employed in Canada and the US. The aims of the treatment are to make the offender take responsibility for his offences, become motivated to engage in treatment as a consequence, and to equip him with behavioural controls to exercise against the temptation to re-offend.[66] The effectiveness of providing 'treatment' within a prison setting has been questioned. As Ditchfield and Marshall point out:

'The confines of a prison are far from ideal for the purpose of altering a person's sexual behaviour, largely because of the absence of contact with others in a normal social setting, which makes it difficult to put into practice the social skills training intended to normalise relationships with others, especially with the opposite sex. Moreover, changes in motivation and behaviour that have been achieved in a prison context may not be generalisable to real-life situations, where the offender is suddenly confronted with a full range of opportunities for re-offending. Finally, the rigid timescale of prison sentences does not lend itself to effective treatment – the treatment may end before the sentence, or vice versa, and both circumstances may cause problems.'[67]

In serious cases of abuse a custodial sentence following conviction will usually be inevitable, and therefore there is no alternative to the provision of treatment within a custodial setting. Yet alternatives now exist to provide treatment without imposing a custodial sentence.

Probation orders with conditions of treatment

The court may make a probation order and attach conditions of treatment. The purpose of a probation order is to either 'secure the rehabilitation of the offender' or to 'protect the public from harm from him and/or preventing

---

64　Glaser, D and Spencer, J (1990) 'Sentencing, Children's Evidence and Trauma' *Criminal Law Review* (1990) 371 at p 380.

65　See generally the articles contained in 'The Sex Issue' *Prison Service Journal* [1994] (94) 14–30.

66　Barker, M (1994) 'What do we know about the effectiveness of treatment for sex offenders' *Prison Service Journal* [1994] (94) 26.

67　Ditchfield and Marshall (1991) 'A Review of Recent Literature Evaluating Treatments for Sex Offenders in Prisons and Comparable Institutional Settings' *Prison Service Journal* [1991] (81) 24.

the commission by him of further offences'.[68] The offender must consent to the making of the order. The court has power to attach conditions to the order, which may include residential conditions and a condition that the offender undergoes a programme of treatment.[69] In the past, although this option was theoretically available to a court, in practice there were very few treatment programmes available. In recent years, with increasing emphasis being placed on rehabilitating offenders, particularly sexual offenders, probation services throughout the country have taken up the challenge and initiated treatment programmes.[70] In some areas, the programmes are run on a voluntary basis, on the assumption that therapeutic work can only be done with the active consent of the participant. However, most programmes take offenders on both a voluntary and statutory basis and many probation officers suggest that the availability of a programme, attendance at which can be made a condition of a probation order, has made courts more willing to sentence sex offenders to probation rather than a custodial sentence.

In some areas the probation service may refer offenders to treatment programmes offered by other organisations. The most commonly referred to is the Gracewell Clinic,[71] which has established a national reputation for work with sex offenders. If an offender has been convicted of a sexual offence and the court is considering imposing a custodial sentence, a probation order with a condition of residence at Gracewell may be considered as an alternative. Typically, the court will adjourn, ask for full reports and make it a condition of bail that the offender resides at Gracewell during the period of adjournment. During this period, full reports will be prepared (including a pre-sentence report – see above) together with an assessment of the offender's suitability for residence. At the following court hearing, a probation order may be made, with conditions of residence and treatment at Gracewell attached. As Ray Wyre, the Director of the clinic explains, such a scheme can offer benefits to the offender and his family which would not be available within prison. In particular, it takes the offender out of the home, offering a supportive, therapeutic programme within a residential setting, enabling the child or children to stay at home. It acknowledges that the offender is guilty, but also recognises that for many children it is important that the abuser, whom they both love and hate, is receiving help and yet still offers the security and protection the child needs. Wyre concludes:

'the programme clearly demonstrates how seriously offending is seen. It does not offer a soft option and neither does it ignore punishment issues ...'[72]

---

68 Section 2(1) Powers of Criminal Courts Act 1973 as amended by Criminal Justice Act 1991.

69 Schedule 1A Powers of Criminal Courts Act 1973.

70 Barker and Morgan (1991) 'Probation Practice with Sex Offenders Surveyed' *Probation Journal* 38(4) 171.

71 Wyre, R (1992) 'Gracewell Clinic' in Rogers, Hevey, Roche & Ash (1992) *Child Abuse and Neglect: facing the challenge* London, The Open University.

72 Note 70 at p 251.

Wyre is one of a growing number who believe that retribution and rehabilitation are not mutually exclusive and this belief is now reflected in the sentencing practice of the courts.

Efficacy of treatment

The effectiveness of treatment in preventing future abuse is not yet proven. Measuring rates of recidivism of sexual offenders is notoriously difficult due primarily to the 'dark figure' of unrecorded crime. A comprehensive review of the research literature on child abuse interventions concludes that, whilst many studies report positive effects of behavioural intervention on rates of recidivism, it is difficult to be sure that any changes are due to the treatment applied rather than other aspects of the offender's situation.[73] Concerns have also been expressed about inadequate training and support for tutors involved in such treatment.[74] In setting up the SOTP the Home Office evidenced its support of the concept of treatment for offenders. It is to be hoped that the support will be continued. A concerted effort now needs to be made to evaluate the effectiveness of treatment programmes and to ensure that those involved have adequate training and support.

PREVENTION IS BETTER THAN 'CURE'

Over the past decade a comprehensive legal framework and detailed guidance for professionals has evolved as a response to the recognition that child abuse is a significant social problem. Legal provisions allow professionals to respond to a case of child abuse – to protect the victim and other children from further abuse. Provision exists to compensate the abused and, as inadequate as money undoubtedly is as a form of compensation, it is arguably better than nothing. Society may inflict punishment on the abuser. In the past this has been primarily as a form of retribution, but increasing recognition is now paid to the concept of rehabilitation, although treatment programmes are aimed primarily at sexual offenders. Counselling may well be available on a voluntary basis for both abuser and abused and, in cases of intrafamilial abuse, the whole family may be offered therapy with the long-term goal of allowing the family to function effectively together as a unit with no further risk to the child.

Society has recognised a problem and developed a legal and practical framework in response. Much time and effort has been expended and

---

73 Gough, D (1994) 'Child Abuse Interventions: A Review of the Research Literature' Public Health Research Unit, University of Glasgow.

74 Sheridan, M (1994) 'The Training and Support Needs of Staff Involved in The Sex Offender Treatment Programme' *Prison Service Journal* [1994] (94) 20.

considerable progress has been made. However, the implementation of the Children Act 1989, the publication of 'Working Together' and the various reforms to the criminal justice system should not be regarded in any way as the fulfilment of an objective. The vast majority of children are now better protected than they have been in the past but further reforms are needed in many areas and existing working procedures need to be kept under constant review if the welfare of the child is to be secured in all cases.

The child protection system allows society to respond to abuse that has already happened. How effective the system is in offering a 'cure' to the problem is open to debate. It would be much better if child abuse could be prevented in the first place, or at least if the level of abuse could be reduced. The first step must be to identify the underlying causes of abuse, only then can effective steps be taken towards prevention. In March 1994 the NSPCC launched an independent national commission into preventing child abuse.[75] The 18 month enquiry hopes to highlight the causes of abuse and suggest strategies for prevention. Such a step is to be welcomed, but the initiative shown by the NSPCC should not be taken to relieve others – primarily the government – of the responsibility for initiating further research. It is unrealistic to suppose that child abuse can ever be completely eradicated – but this should not prevent us from seeking to achieve that millenium.

---

75   *The Times* 24 March 1994.

APPENDIX

CHILD ABUSE AND THE CRIMINAL LAW

PHYSICAL ABUSE AND NEGLECT

CRUELTY TO PERSONS UNDER 16:

Children and Young Persons Act 1933 section 1

(1) If any person who has attained the age of 16 years and has responsibility for any child or young person under that age, wilfully assaults, ill-treats, neglects, abandons, or exposes him, or causes or procures him to be assaulted, ill-treated, neglected, abandoned, or exposed, in a manner likely to cause him unnecessary suffering or injury to health (including injury to or loss of sight, or hearing, or limb, or organ of the body, and any mental derangement), that person shall be guilty of a misdemeanour ...

(2) For the purposes of this section:

(a) a parent or other person legally liable to maintain a child or young person or the legal guardian of a child or young person shall be deemed to have neglected him in a manner likely to cause injury to his health if he has failed to provide adequate food, clothing, medical aid, lodging for him, or, if having been unable otherwise to provide such food, clothing, medical aid or lodging, he has failed to take steps to procure it to be provided under the enactments applicable in that behalf.

...

(7) Nothing in this section shall be construed as affecting the right of any parent, teacher, or other person having the lawful control or charge of a child or young person to administer punishment to him.

MAXIMUM PENALTY: 10 YEARS' IMPRISONMENT

EXPOSING CHILD, WHEREBY LIFE IS ENDANGERED, OR HEALTH PERMANENTLY INJURED

Offences Against the Person Act 1861 section 27

Whosoever shall unlawfully abandon or expose any child, being under the age of two years, whereby the life of such child shall be endangered, or the health of such child shall have been or shall be likely to be permanently injured, shall be guilty of an offence ...

MAXIMUM PENALTY: 5 YEARS' IMPRISONMENT

ASSAULT

Common law

Any act by which the defendant, intentionally or recklessly, inflicts unlawful personal violence on another or causes another to apprehend immediate and unlawful personal violence.

MAXIMUM PENALTY: 6 MONTHS' IMPRISONMENT

ASSAULT OCCASIONING ACTUAL BODILY HARM

Offences Against the Person Act 1861 section 47

An assault which causes actual bodily harm [ie hurt or injury calculated to interfere with the health or comfort of another].

MAXIMUM PENALTY: 5 YEARS' IMPRISONMENT

GRIEVOUS BODILY HARM OR WOUNDING

Offences Against the Person Act 1861 section 20

Unlawfully and maliciously wound or inflict grievous bodily harm [ie breaking the victim's skin or causing serious bodily harm].

MAXIMUM PENALTY: 5 YEARS' IMPRISONMENT

GRIEVOUS BODILY HARM OR WOUNDING WITH INTENT

Offences Against the Person Act 1861 section 18

Unlawfully and maliciously wound or cause grievous bodily harm ... with intent to do some grievous bodily harm to any person ...

MAXIMUM PENALTY: LIFE IMPRISONMENT

MANSLAUGHTER

Common law

The defendant kills the victim and one or more of the following applies:

(i)   death was due to the defendant's recklessness;

(ii)   death was due to gross negligence on the part of the defendant;

(iii)   death was a result of an unlawful act on the part of the defendant, which he should have realised carried a risk of some harm;

(iv)   the defendants' mental responsibility was diminished at the time of the act [Homicide Act 1957 section 2]

(v)   the defendant was provoked [Homicide Act 1957 section 3]

(vi)   death was in pursuance of a suicide pact [Homicide Act 1957 section 4]

MAXIMUM PENALTY: LIFE IMPRISONMENT

MURDER

Common law

The defendant killed the victim, either intending to kill or intending to cause grievous bodily harm.

MAXIMUM PENALTY: LIFE IMPRISONMENT

SEXUAL ABUSE

RAPE

Sexual Offences Act 1956 section 1 [As amended by Criminal Justice and Public Order Act 1994 section 142]

(1) It is an offence for a man to rape a woman or another man.

(2) A man commits rape if:

(a) he has sexual intercourse with a person (whether vaginal or anal) who at the time of the intercourse does not consent to it; and

(b) at the time he knows that the person does not consent to the intercourse or is reckless as to whether that person consents to it.

MAXIMUM PENALTY: LIFE IMPRISONMENT

INTERCOURSE WITH A GIRL UNDER 13

Sexual Offences Act 1956 section 5

It is an offence for a man to have unlawful sexual intercourse with a girl under the age of 13.

MAXIMUM PENALTY: LIFE IMPRISONMENT

INTERCOURSE WITH A GIRL UNDER 16

Sexual Offences Act 1956 section 6

(1) It is an offence subject to the exceptions mentioned in this section, for a man to have unlawful sexual intercourse with a girl under the age of 16.

(2) Where a marriage is invalid under section 2 Marriage Act 1949, or section 1 Age of Marriage Act 1929 (the wife being a girl under the age of 16) the invalidity does not make the husband guilty of an offence under this section because he has sexual intercourse with her, if he believes her to be his wife and has reasonable cause for the belief.

(3) A man is not guilty of an offence under this section because he has unlawful sexual intercourse with a girl under the age of 16, if he is under the age of 24 years and has not previously been charged with a like offence, and he believes her to be of the age of 16 or over and has reasonable cause for the belief.

MAXIMUM PENALTY: 2 YEARS' IMPRISONMENT

INCEST BY A MAN

Sexual Offences Act 1956 section S10

(1) It is an offence for a man to have sexual intercourse with a woman he knows to be his granddaughter, daughter, sister or mother.

(2) In the foregoing subsection 'sister' includes half sister, and for the purposes of that subsection any expression importing a relationship between two people shall be taken to apply notwithstanding that the relationship is not traced through lawful wedlock.

MAXIMUM PENALTY: 7 YEARS' IMPRISONMENT
LIFE IMPRISONMENT IF WITH A GIRL UNDER 13

INCEST BY A WOMAN

Sexual Offences Act 1956 section 11

(1) It is an offence for a woman of the age of 16 or over to permit a man who she knows to be her grandfather, father, brother or son to have sexual intercourse with her by her consent.

(2) In the foregoing subsection 'brother' includes half brother, and for the purposes of that subsection any expression importing a relationship between two people shall be taken to apply notwithstanding that the relationship is not traced through lawful wedlock.

MAXIMUM PENALTY: 7 YEARS' IMPRISONMENT

BUGGERY

Sexual Offences Act 1956 section 12 [As amended by Criminal Justice and Public Order Act 1994 section 143]

(1) It is an offence for a person to commit buggery with another person otherwise than in the circumstances described in section (1A) below or with an animal.

(1A)The circumstances referred to in subsection (1) are that the act of buggery takes place in private and both parties have attained the age of 18.

**MAXIMUM PENALTY: LIFE IMPRISONMENT IF WITH A PERSON UNDER 16 YEARS OR AN ANIMAL:
5 YEARS' IMPRISONMENT IF THE ACCUSED IS OF OR OVER THE AGE OF 21 AND THE OTHER PERSON IS UNDER THE AGE OF 18:
OTHERWISE 2 YEARS' IMPRISONMENT**

ASSAULT WITH INTENT TO COMMIT BUGGERY

Sexual Offences Act 1956 section 16

It is an offence for a person to assault another person with intent to commit buggery.

MAXIMUM PENALTY: 10 YEARS' IMPRISONMENT

GROSS INDECENCY BETWEEN MEN

Sexual Offences Act 1956 section 13

It is an offence for a man to commit an act of gross indecency with another man whether in public or private, or to be a party to the commission by a man of an act of gross indecency with another man, or to procure the commission by a man of an act of gross indecency with another man.

**MAXIMUM PENALTY: 5 YEARS' IMPRISONMENT IF BY A MAN OF, OR OVER, THE AGE OF 21 YEARS AND THE OTHER PERSON IS UNDER THE AGE OF 18 YEARS:
TWO YEARS' IMPRISONMENT IN ALL OTHER SITUATIONS**

INDECENT ASSAULT ON A WOMAN

Sexual Offences Act 1956 section 14

(1) It is an offence, subject to the exception mentioned in subsection (3) of this section, for a person to make an indecent assault on a woman.

(2) A girl under the age of 16 cannot in law give any consent which would prevent an act being an assault for the purposes of this section.

MAXIMUM PENALTY: 10 YEARS' IMPRISONMENT

INDECENT ASSAULT ON A MAN

Sexual Offences Act 1956 section 15

(1) It is an offence for a person to make an indecent assault on a man.

(2) A boy under the age of 16 cannot in law give any consent which would prevent an act being an assault for the purposes of this section.

MAXIMUM PENALTY: 10 YEARS' IMPRISONMENT

INDECENCY WITH CHILDREN

Indecency with Children Act 1960 section 1

Any person who commits an act of gross indecency with or towards a child under the age of 14, or who incites a child under that age to such an act with him or another shall be liable on conviction or indictment to imprisonment for a term not exceeding two years or on summary conviction to imprisonment for a term not exceeding six months, to a fine not exceeding the statutory maximum, or to both.

MAXIMUM PENALTY: 2 YEARS' IMPRISONMENT

INCITING A GIRL UNDER 16 TO HAVE INCESTUOUS SEXUAL INTERCOURSE

Criminal Law Act 1977 section 54

(1) It is an offence for a man to incite to have sexual intercourse with him a girl under the age of 16 whom he knows to be his granddaughter, daughter or sister.

(2) In the preceding subsection 'man' includes boy, 'sister' includes half sister, and for the purposes of that subsection any expression importing a relationship between two people shall be taken to apply notwithstanding that the relationship is not traced through lawful wedlock.

MAXIMUM PENALTY: 2 YEARS' IMPRISONMENT

INDECENT PHOTOGRAPHS OF CHILDREN

I Protection of Children Act 1978 section 1 [As amended by Crimial Justice and Public Order Act 1994 section 84]

(1) It is an offence for a person:

(a) to take or permit to be taken or to make any indecent photographs or pseudo-photographs of a child or

(b) to distribute or show such indecent photographs or pseudo-photographs

(c) to have in his possession such indecent photographs or pseudo-photographs with a view to them being distributed or shown by himself or others; or

(d) to publish or cause to be published any advertisement likely to be understood as conveying that the advertiser distributes or shows such indecent photographs or pseudo-photographs, or intends to do so.

(2) For the purposes of this act, a person is to be regarded as distributing an indecent photograph or pseudo-photograph if he parts with possession of it, or exposes or offers it for acquisition by another person

MAXIMUM PENALTY: 3 YEARS' IMPRISONMENT

II Criminal Justice Act 1988 section 160 [As amended by Crimial Justice and Public Order Act 1994 Section 84]

It is an offence for a person to have any indecent photograph or pseudo-photograph of a child in his possession.

MAXIMUM PENALTY: 6 MONTHS' IMPRISONMENT

[Note: 'Pseudo-photograph' means an image, whether made by computer-graphics or otherwise however, which appears to be a photograph].

INDECENT EXPOSURE

I Vagrancy Act 1824 section 4

Every person committing any of the offences hereinbefore mentioned, after having been convicted as an idle and disorderly person ... Every person who wilfully openly, lewdly and obscenely exposes his person with intent to insult any female ... shall be deemed a rogue and a vagabond within the true intent and meaning of this act.

MAXIMUM PENALTY: 3 MONTHS' IMPRISONMENT

II Town Police Clauses Act 1847 section 28

Every person who in any street, to the obstruction, annoyance or danger of the residents or passengers, commits any of the following offences, shall be liable to a penalty ... Every person who wilfully and indecently exposes his person.

MAXIMUM PENALTY: 14 DAYS' IMPRISONMENT

ATTEMPTS

Criminal Attempts Act 1981

If, with intent to commit (an indictable offence), a person does an act which is more than merely preparatory to the commission of the offence, he is guilty of attempting to commit the offence.

MAXIMUM PENALTY: AS FOR COMPLETED OFFENCE

INDEX